BORN
for our
SALVATION

BORN
for our
SALVATION

the nativity and childhood of Jesus Christ

Martyn McGeown

REFORMED
FREE PUBLISHING
ASSOCIATION
Jenison, Michigan

Reformed Free Publishing Association
1894 Georgetown Center Drive
Jenison, Michigan 49428
616-457-5970
rfpa.org
mail@rfpa.org

Cover design by Erika Kiel
Interior design and typesetting by Katherine Lloyd, the DESK

ISBN 978-1-944555-55-9 (hardcover)
ISBN 978-1-944555-56-6 (ebook)
LCCN 2019952936

To my dear wife, Larisa,
a loving companion and helpmeet in my work.

CONTENTS

INTRODUCTION

The greatest miracle in history is unquestionably the incarnation of the Son of God. Every Christian delights in the beautiful, familiar, and comforting history of the birth of Jesus Christ. Even the world has some idea of the events surrounding Christ's birth that are recorded in the gospels according to Matthew and Luke. Mary and Joseph, the angels, the shepherds, and the wise men with their gifts of gold, frankincense, and myrrh strike a chord with them. Although the Christmas season is associated with rank materialism, covetousness, and even idolatry, the story of the "child of Bethlehem" is familiar.

Of the four evangelists, only Matthew and Luke describe the circumstances of the birth and early childhood of Jesus Christ. Mark ignores Christ's childhood altogether, beginning his account with the ministry of John the Baptist; while John begins with a sublime prologue revealing Jesus as the divine, eternally preexistent word or *logos* of God, who is both with God and is God (John 1:1). Matthew describes the role of Joseph as the spouse of Mary and adoptive father of Jesus, and he records Herod's murderous enmity against the Christ child and the visit of the wise men from the East, while he gives the actual birth only a passing mention. Luke, on the other hand, describes Christ's birth in Bethlehem, the city of David, and introduces us to his mother Mary, to Gabriel the announcing angel, to lowly shepherds and the glorious angelic host, and to Simeon and Anna in the temple. Moreover, only Luke provides the enquiring reader with a snapshot of Jesus' childhood, relating the visit of the twelve-year-old Jesus to Jerusalem when he accompanies his family to the holy city to celebrate the Passover feast.

As exciting as the narrative in Matthew 1–2 and Luke 1–2 is, the main focus of scripture—and therefore of this book—is Jesus Christ. He alone is the Son of God made flesh; he alone is the savior of sinners; and he alone is the redeemer of God's elect. The biblical history is not a sentimental story about the birth of the "little Lord Jesus," but it describes the first step of Christ's humiliation, which is his lowly birth. This is the first step that Jesus took in our salvation and the first step that would lead to his death on the cross. Since Jesus did not come to be ministered unto but to minister, and to give his life a ransom for many (Matt. 20:28), it is fitting that his birth be lowly in Bethlehem's stable.

Chapter 1

GABRIEL'S ANNUNCIATION TO MARY

26. And in the sixth month the angel Gabriel was sent from God unto a city of Galilee, named Nazareth,
27. To a virgin espoused to a man whose name was Joseph, of the house of David; and the virgin's name was Mary.
28. And the angel came in unto her, and said, Hail, thou that art highly favoured, the Lord is with thee: blessed art thou among women.
29. And when she saw him, she was troubled at his saying, and cast in her mind what manner of salutation this should be.
30. And the angel said unto her, Fear not, Mary: for thou hast found favour with God.
31. And, behold, thou shalt conceive in thy womb, and bring forth a son, and shalt call his name JESUS.
32. He shall be great, and shall be called the Son of the Highest: and the Lord God shall give unto him the throne of his father David:
33. And he shall reign over the house of Jacob for ever; and of his kingdom there shall be no end. (Luke 1:26–33)

Six months before the beginning of the events recorded in the nativity story proper is the announcement of the coming of the forerunner of the Messiah. While I do not intend to treat that history in detail in this book, a few words about it are in order before we begin.

At the end of the Old Testament the last prophet, Malachi, reveals God's gracious promise to his people: "Behold, I will send you Elijah the prophet before the coming of the great and dreadful day of the LORD" (Mal. 4:5). After Malachi a gloomy period, the intertestamentary period or the four hundred years of darkness, was ushered in. During that time, no new prophets arose in Israel. Heaven was silent. The nation of Israel was a plaything of the nations, acting as a buffer zone between competing regimes: first Persia; then Greece; then Egypt and Syria; and finally Rome. Dreadful persecution ravaged the people of God especially during the time of Antiochus IV Epiphanes (215–164 BC). The land of Israel was enveloped in thick darkness politically and religiously with the rise of the sects of the Pharisees and Sadducees. At the time of the history recorded in the early chapters of Matthew and Luke, therefore, God's people had almost given up hope that the promised Messiah and his promised salvation would come.

And yet a godly remnant remained who still clung in faith to the promises of God.

God broke the silence when the angel Gabriel suddenly appeared to an elderly priest called Zacharias. The angel informed Zacharias that his barren wife Elizabeth would have a son, who would be the forerunner to the Messiah: "He shall go before him in the spirit and power of Elias, to turn the hearts of the fathers to the children, and the disobedient to the wisdom of the just; to make ready a people prepared for the Lord" (Luke 1:17). The child, of course, was John the Baptist, who prepared the people for the coming of Jesus and pointed to him when he came. John was born some six months before Jesus, just as the angel Gabriel had promised.

With the birth of the forerunner, the one who prepares the way for a great king, the birth of the Messiah himself could not be far away. No wonder that Zacharias, John's father, rejoices so vehemently: "Blessed be the Lord God of Israel; for he hath visited and redeemed his people, and hath raised up an horn of salvation for us in the house of his servant David" (vv. 68–69). The "horn of salvation" is not John but the Messiah, whom we know as Jesus. As Zacharias held baby John in his arms, he saw Jesus coming behind him. And he rejoiced!

Some six months after his announcement to Zacharias, the angel Gabriel was commissioned on another holy errand, this time not to visit an aged priest, but to visit a young virgin in Nazareth. Her name was Mary, and it is to Gabriel's annunciation—or announcement—that we turn as we begin our study of the "nativity story."

THE HUMBLE RECIPIENT

The Bible's nativity story is a tale of contrasts: in this text we see the contrast between Gabriel and Mary. Gabriel is a mighty angel of God, for in verse 19 he had declared to Zacharias, "I am Gabriel, that stand in the presence of God." Gabriel appears in the Bible especially as God's messenger. When God has an important message to relate, especially in the New Testament, he sends Gabriel. Thus Gabriel appears in the temple to announce the birth of John the Baptist. Later, the angel, most likely Gabriel, appears to Joseph to command him to take Mary for his wife. And it is likely Gabriel who appears over Bethlehem's hills to announce Christ's birth to the shepherds.

Gabriel is therefore favored with making the most

wonderful announcement the world has ever heard: the long-awaited Savior is to be born. We can well imagine Gabriel standing in the presence of God—in the presence of the God whom he loved, adored, and worshiped. Long had Gabriel pondered the ways of God, for 1 Peter 1:12 reveals that the angels "desire to look into" the things of salvation. Suddenly, Gabriel receives a commission from the Almighty. First, Gabriel must make an announcement to Zacharias the priest, and then, six months later, Gabriel must make an announcement to Mary.

To whom would you have expected the angel Gabriel to be sent? Perhaps Gabriel will wing his way to a noble-woman; perhaps to a princess; perhaps to a queen; at the very least, to a prominent, rich, Jewish family. Contrary to our expectations, Gabriel is sent to Mary.

About this Mary we learn several things. First, Mary was a "virgin" (Luke 1:27), which means that Mary was a young woman of marriageable age. Mary may even have been a teenager, for women married early in those days. More than that, Mary was an espoused virgin. Espousal is not the same as our custom of engagement. Espousal among the Jews was as legally binding as marriage, for in espousal a man and woman exchanged vows publicly and were considered man and wife. Any unfaithfulness during espousal was therefore viewed as and treated as adultery.

In addition, Mary was also actually a virgin or a virgin indeed, that is, Mary and Joseph had not yet consummated their marriage. She was promised to him, and he was promised to her, but as Matthew 1:18 puts it, they had not yet "come together." The custom was that an espoused woman remained with her parents until her husband came to receive her some weeks or months after the espousals.

Second, Mary was poor. Mary was not a noblewoman, living in luxury in a palace, waited on by servants. We do not know what she was doing when Gabriel arrived, but we can imagine that Mary was engaged in some household chore. Mary's prospects of escaping poverty were not good, for she was not espoused to a prosperous nobleman, but to a man called Joseph, the village carpenter. Any children she and Joseph might have would certainly be loved, but they would not belong to the upper echelons of society.

Besides this, Mary's location was obscure. Gabriel's first assignment had been to Zacharias in the temple in Jerusalem, but now Gabriel is assigned to go to Nazareth, which was an obscure village in Galilee. No grandeur was connected to Nazareth; nothing important had ever happened there; and it was not even mentioned in the Old Testament. Gabriel is not even sent to Bethlehem, never mind Jerusalem. At least Bethlehem had some significance in its connection to David, but, as Nathaniel later expresses it in John 1:46, "Can there any good thing come out of Nazareth?"

This young, poor, obscure virgin was God's chosen vessel, for she was "of the house of David" (Luke 1:27), a house or royal family line that ended in Mary of Nazareth. God had promised that the Messiah would come from David's family. Generations of the sons of David had sat upon the royal throne. From Solomon all the way to Zedekiah God had kept his promise: "I will set up thy seed after thee, which shall proceed out of thy bowels, and I will establish his kingdom" (2 Sam. 7:12). The Babylonian captivity had brought an end to the kingdom of David, but God's promise still stood: "David shall never want [lack] a man to sit upon the throne of the house of Israel" (Jer. 33:17). Even after the captivity, God preserved the royal line of David in the earth, for Zerubbabel, a descendant of David, led the captives home in response to the divinely inspired decree of Cyrus recorded in Ezra 1.

Nevertheless, that royal line had fallen upon hard times, for although the descendants of David survived, they had no throne on which to sit. Both Joseph and Mary were of the house of David, but they could not claim the throne, for on it sat a wicked Edomite king called Herod. And behind Herod stood the mighty Roman emperor, by whose permission Herod ruled over the land of Israel. As we shall see, Herod did not take kindly to perceived rivals or usurpers to his throne.

But God had promised that in the latter days "there [would] come forth a rod out of the stem of Jesse, and a Branch [would] grow out of his roots" (Isa. 11:1) and that the Messiah would grow up "as a tender plant, and as a root out of a dry ground" (53:2). Although Mary, as a pious, believing Jewess, looked forward to the coming of the Messiah, and although she longed for it, little did she imagine that *she* had been chosen to be the mother of the Messiah! Surely God could find a worthier home with more earthly promise and potential than a virgin espoused to Joseph in Nazareth!

Mary's circumstances were humble, and she was humble in her own estimation. We see that in her reaction, for she can hardly imagine that the angel would speak thus to her. "Who am I," we might paraphrase her reaction, "that an angel should come to me?" That is always the reaction of God's people to angels in scripture: amazement at God's condescension mixed with fear at being in the presence of a heavenly messenger. Mary did not boast of her encounter with Gabriel: she probably did not tell anyone at that time, because, after all, who would have believed her? Such humility is the necessary, gracious preparation for anyone to receive the word of God.

God does not bring his word to proud, haughty, self-sufficient souls. When we come to hear the word, we must receive it as Mary did: who am I that God should speak to me the words of the gospel of Christ? That kind of demeanor is impossible for sinners. In Mary, it was a fruit of God's grace, and in us, it must also be a fruit of divine grace.

THE UNEXPECTED SALUTATION

As Gabriel enters the house—we presume that Mary was home, that she was alone, and that he entered through the doorway or appeared miraculously in the room—he greets her. The greeting or salutation of the angel has suffered corruption at the hands of the Roman Catholic Church, for they have transformed a simple salutation into a prayer to Mary called "Hail Mary" or the "Ave Maria." Such a prayer is popularly recited during the rosary.

Contrary to the practice of Rome, we notice that the word "Hail" in Luke 1:28 is not a form of worship, nor even a salutation reserved for royal personages, but that it is a common greeting. Gabriel does not worship, adore, or fall prostrate before Mary, nor does he encourage anyone else to do so. The word "Hail" is simply an expression of wellbeing or even an expression of joy. Judas greets Jesus with "Hail" before he kisses him in Matthew 26:49; Jesus greets certain believing women after his resurrection with "Hail" in Matthew 28:9; James greets the church in James 1:1 with the same expression; and an unbelieving soldier writes to the governor with the same word in Acts 23:26.

Never in scripture is "Hail" used as a prayer, and never

in scripture is prayer addressed to anyone except to God. "The Lord is with thee" (Luke 1:28) is simply an expression of God's favor. God is said to be "with" his people when he blesses them in covenantal fellowship. The Lord could—and does—greet any of his believing people in this way.

The circumstances of Mary's life might have seemed difficult, but the angel assures her that the Lord, Jehovah, in his power and grace, is with her, to bless her, to protect her, and to save her. These words encouraged Mary that the angel had come with a gracious purpose, and how she would have to cling to those words in the months ahead, for the news she was about to receive was nothing short of earth-shattering.

The two other controversial phrases used in the Roman Catholic Church's "Hail Mary" prayer require further explanation. Gabriel says, "Thou that art highly favoured" (v. 28). The Roman Catholic Church, following the Latin Vulgate translation, renders this expression as "full of grace." By "full of grace" Rome means several things: first, Mary is so full of grace that she has no sin. By a singular grace, argues Rome, Mary has been preserved from the stain of original sin; hence she is called "immaculate." Second, Mary is so full of grace that she is a fountain of grace for others. Sinners ought to go to her for grace and mercy in time of need. Third, Mary is uniquely graced, for no one has as much grace as she does. Rome teaches that there is a treasury of grace in heaven made up of the merits of Christ, Mary, and the saints. About Mary, Rome declares, "This treasury includes the prayers and good works of the Blessed Virgin Mary. They are truly immense, unfathomable and even pristine in their value before God."[1]

---

1 *The Catechism of the Catholic Church*, paragraph 1477 (Dublin, Ireland: Veritas, 1994), 332.

Thus Rome builds a superstructure of Mariolatry, the idolatrous veneration of Mary, on one word from the angel Gabriel.

But that is not what the phrase means. A better translation is "O favored one" or "O graciously accepted one." The meaning is simply this: Mary is the recipient of grace. In fact, all Christians are "highly favored" (or graced). Grace, remember, is God's favor, which, when it comes to sinners, is undeserved, unmerited favor. The same verb, albeit in a different grammatical form, is employed in Ephesians 1:6 ("accepted in the beloved"), where the reference is to all saints, elect in Christ Jesus.

Gabriel adds, "Blessed art thou among women" (Luke 1:28). The question is not whether Mary is blessed or not, for she most certainly is. The question is, *in what* is she blessed? Is she blessed by being the mediatrix of all graces, is she blessed by being the queen of heaven, is she blessed by being the immaculate, ever-virgin fountain of salvation, as Rome insists? No, of course not. She is blessed among women because she, in distinction from all other women, and merely out of God's unconditional grace, has been chosen and set apart to be the mother of the Messiah. All Christians are recipients of grace, and all Christians are blessed, but only Mary is the mother of Jesus Christ, a task and a privilege given only to her. Incidentally, when in a burst of enthusiasm a Jewish woman extolled the blessedness of Mary, Jesus reminded her of true blessedness: "It came to pass, as he spake these things, a certain woman of the company lifted up her voice, and said unto him, Blessed is the womb that bare thee, and the paps which thou hast sucked. But he said, Yea rather, blessed are they that hear the word of God, and keep it" (11:27–28).

However, before Gabriel gives the explanation for his peculiar greeting, Mary is troubled. She was not troubled so much at the appearance of the angel, although, of course, that surprised her greatly, but she was troubled at the angel's words. In Luke 1:29, we read, "She was troubled *at his saying*" (emphasis added).

The trouble comes from the sudden shock of these words. One moment, she had been occupied with some mundane task, and now an angel stands before her and pronounces her "blessed." She is troubled at the one bringing the words, for how incongruous and how unexpected that an angel would speak to her and say, "Blessed." How could she be "blessed"? Moreover, she is troubled at the setting of the angel's words. Here, in her humble home, the angel comes with such words—"hail," "highly favored," and "blessed," even "blessed among women."

She responds as mortals usually do when confronted with an angel: she fears. Some people think that to meet an angel would be the "coolest, neatest" thing ever. It is well for us that we do not meet with angels because the experience is terrifying. We should be happy that God has wrapped his word in a less intimidating package. He gives us a minister of flesh and blood, or an earthen vessel (2 Cor. 4:7), to explain the scriptures.

Mary feared because she had no idea what the angel meant, for what *could* he mean? Luke 1:29 describes her state of mind: "She...cast in her mind what manner of salutation this should be." She brought together in her mind different threads of thought and tried to make sense of them all. Her mind was terribly confused, as it well might be, given the circumstances.

She probably thought about her past, about her life,

about her sins, about her future, about God's promises, and she wondered, "How does this fit? How does it fit *with me?*" This deliberation did not continue for very long, because almost immediately Gabriel interrupts her thoughts to bring his wonderful news.

THE ROYAL SON

Gabriel's news is similar to the news he brought to Zacharias, for it concerns a "son" (v. 31). Mary was espoused to Joseph; therefore, the news that she would have a son was not all that surprising. Undoubtedly, Mary and Joseph hoped to have children. When Gabriel says, "Thou shalt conceive in thy womb, and bring forth a son" (v. 31), his tidings were not in themselves unusual. Mary was not in the same position as Elizabeth had been. Unlike her cousin, Mary was not old, barren, and past childbearing. She was a young, espoused virgin. The issue was not that she would have a son, but the issue was the identity of the son.

Gabriel continues: "[Thou] shalt call his name JESUS" (v. 31). That is not unusual either. There were many little boys called Jesus in Israel, because Jesus is simply the Greek equivalent of Joshua. It is unusual—and a sign of some significance—for an *angel* to give the name to a child before his birth. Gabriel will repeat that name to Joseph later and give a further explanation of the name's meaning (Matt. 1:21). The fact that an angel came to announce the conception of her son would make Mary imagine that there is something special about him, but Gabriel has not finished his explanation and message.

Next, Gabriel describes the greatness of Mary's son: "He shall be great" (Luke 1:32). When we think of "great," we imagine a military commander, a general, or an artistic genius (a composer, a sculptor, or an award-winning author). But how could that be, for Jesus would not be born into a great family. He would not have access to the great schools, and he would not mix with the great and the good of society. He would live and grow up in a cultural backwater called Nazareth; therefore, his parents would not be able to promote him to high honors.

But the greatness of Mary's son is spiritual: "He...shall be called the Son of the Highest" (v. 32). "The Highest," of course, refers to God, for God is often called "the Highest" or "the Most High" in scripture, which is a reference to his majesty and transcendent glory. This "Son," then, would not only be the son of Mary, but he would also be (and already was, and always is) the Son of God. Gabriel knew this one, for this one is the eternal, only begotten Son of God, the second person of the holy Trinity, whom all heaven adores.

At this point, Mary's eyes must have been widening with utter amazement and wonder, and Gabriel must have been becoming more and more excited. "I, Mary of Nazareth, am going to give birth to the Son of the Highest?" "My son, whom I will conceive in my womb, will be the Son of Yahweh?" "I, Mary of Nazareth, daughter of poor parents, espoused wife of a poor Nazarene carpenter, of all the women in the world and in the history of God's covenant, have been chosen to bear the Messiah?" It is not likely that Mary immediately understood the import of Gabriel's words, but she would begin to grasp the meaning later.

Yes, Mary—and there is more. In this son, thy son, the Son of the Highest, all the promises to David shall be fulfilled. We must understand that this son—Jesus—is fully human and fully divine. He is fully divine: "He...shall be called Son of the Highest" (v. 32). That means that as Jehovah is eternal, so this Son is eternal, for he has all the same attributes as God. The Son is of the same essence with the Father, and he has the same power and glory as the Father.

Before Gabriel came to Nazareth to announce this news to Mary, Gabriel knew the Son of God, for he served him, he worshiped him, and he adored him. To use the language of Paul, this Jesus is "in the form of God" and "equal with God" (Phil. 2:6), or to use the language of John, this one, "the Word," "was with God" and "was God" (John 1:1). Therefore, for Gabriel too, the news that he brings to Mary is a wonder—a marvel. For this "Son of the Highest" was about to become human: he would be "made flesh, and [dwell] among us" (v. 14); he would be "made of a woman, made under the law" (Gal. 4:4); and he would make "himself of no reputation, and [would take] upon him the form of a servant, and [would be] made in the likeness of men" (Phil. 2:7). The Son of the Highest is fully divine, but he would become also fully human, and as a human he would sit on David's throne: "The Lord God shall give unto him the throne of his father David" (Luke 1:32).

The Son has a father, who is David, that is, his father according to the flesh (Rom. 1:3). But David is not the Highest, for God alone is this Son's eternal Father within the Godhead. Therefore, this Jesus is both the Son of God and the son of David; he is both the Son of God and the son of Mary. But how can a poor virgin of Nazareth fathom the depths of that? No wonder she marveled, and well might we marvel at these words, although they are familiar to us!

To your son, who is God's Son, says Gabriel, God will give the throne of David, on which he will sit forever, ruling over the house of Jacob. This was the Messianic promise of salvation set forth in the Old Testament, and many of those prophecies were familiar to Mary. Consider Isaiah 9:6–7, "For unto us a child is born, unto us a son is given: and the government shall be upon his shoulder: and his name shall be called Wonderful, Counsellor, The mighty God, The everlasting Father, The Prince of Peace." Or consider Daniel 7:13–14:

13. I saw in the night visions, and, behold, one like the Son of man came with the clouds of heaven, and came to the Ancient of days, and they brought him near before him.
14. And there was given him dominion, and glory, and a kingdom, that all people, nations, and languages, should serve him: his dominion is an everlasting dominion, which shall not pass away, and his kingdom that which shall not be destroyed.

This Son, born of Mary, would accomplish what neither David, nor Solomon, nor any of his sons had accomplished—an everlasting kingdom, a kingdom without successors, and a kingdom that would never fall because it is God's kingdom. But where is that kingdom, and what is that throne? Clearly, that kingdom and throne are not on the earth, because Jesus never sat on David's earthly throne in Jerusalem. He died while one of the ungodly Herods, the puppet kings of the Roman Empire, occupied David's earthly throne.

Nor is it the case that Jesus will sit upon that throne sometime in our future. Jesus never came to set up such a kingdom, as he himself explained. Indeed, Peter declares this about Jesus on the day of Pentecost in Acts 2:30–33:

30. Therefore being a prophet, and knowing that God had sworn with an oath to him, that of the fruit of his loins, according to the flesh, he would raise up Christ to sit on his throne;

31. He seeing this before spake of the resurrection of Christ, that his soul was not left in hell, neither his flesh did see corruption.

32. This Jesus hath God raised up, whereof we all are witnesses.

33. Therefore being by the right hand of God exalted, and having received of the Father the promise of the Holy Ghost, he hath shed forth this, which ye now see and hear.

Jesus Christ is on David's throne now: that throne is in heaven. All who belong to him and believe in him are citizens of his heavenly, spiritual, everlasting, blessed kingdom.

But there is one aspect of the truth that Gabriel did not explain to Mary because she would not have understood it and because she was not ready to face it. Later, in Luke 2:35, Simeon will hint at it: "A sword shall pierce through thy own soul also." Mary heard about the greatness, the divinity, and the humanity of her son, but she did not yet know about his suffering and death. But we know, for it is in his suffering and death that our salvation lies. Jesus is born of a young, poor, humble, obscure virgin, so that he can die. It is the first step along a painful path that leads to the cross.

O come let us adore him, Christ Jesus our Lord!

Chapter 2

THE WONDER OF
THE VIRGIN CONCEPTION

34. Then said Mary unto the angel, How shall this be, seeing I know not a man?
35. And the angel answered and said unto her, The Holy Ghost shall come upon thee, and the power of the Highest shall overshadow thee: therefore also that holy thing which shall be born of thee shall be called the Son of God.
36. And, behold, thy cousin Elisabeth, she hath also conceived a son in her old age: and this is the sixth month with her, who was called barren.
37. For with God nothing shall be impossible.
38. And Mary said, Behold the handmaid of the Lord; be it unto me according to thy word. And the angel departed from her. (Luke 1:34–38)

In obscure Nazareth a humble virgin received a heavenly visitor. The angel Gabriel brought good news to Mary. She would conceive in her womb and give birth to a son. Such would be glad tidings to any espoused woman, but the son whom Mary would conceive is a very special child, indeed, a unique child. The son of Mary would be—and is—the Son of God, the long-expected and long-awaited Savior and Messiah of the Jews. That child, explained Gabriel, would be great, and would be called the Son of the Highest, and would sit on David's throne forever.

Nevertheless, although this news is joyous, it is also bewildering, for how shall this be? How shall Mary, a poor, obscure Jewish damsel and virgin, bring forth the Messiah? How can this child be her son and also the Son of God? Mary did not understand. Mary longed to comprehend.

To that sincere question Gabriel gives a wonderful explanation. Mary would conceive the child by the power of the Holy Spirit.

GABRIEL'S EXPLANATION

In Luke 1:35 is the fullest description or explanation of the virgin conception of Jesus in holy scripture. Fittingly, the words come from the angel Gabriel, who stands in the very presence of God. Gabriel explains the truth to Mary in beautiful, poetic, but mysterious language. When we study this language, we stand on holy ground, for we are not dealing with the description that might be found in a biology textbook or with man's scientific explanations of the workings of the universe. No human mind can comprehend this. Gabriel speaks in the language of wonder, and we must stand in awe of this word of God.

The agent or the worker of this wonder is the Holy Spirit, called the Holy Ghost in verse 35. It is striking that Gabriel assumes knowledge of the Holy Spirit in Mary, for as a pious Jewess, Mary knew who the Holy Spirit is. She knew that God works his wonders, whether his work of creation, providence, or salvation, by the Holy Spirit. A passage such as Genesis 1:2 would come to mind, where the Spirit is the agent of creation: "The Spirit of God moved upon the face of the waters." Mary might have thought of Psalm 104:30, where the Spirit's work of providence is set forth: "Thou sendest forth thy spirit, they are created: and thou renewest the face of the earth." Or Mary might cast her mind to passages where the Spirit's relationship to the Messiah is set forth: "The spirit of the LORD shall rest upon him, the spirit of wisdom and understanding, the spirit of counsel and might, the spirit of knowledge and of the fear of the Lord" (Isa. 11:2).

Gabriel therefore takes no time to identify the Holy Spirit.

In scripture the Holy Spirit is the power of God, for by him God exercises his mighty works. Thus Gabriel explains, "The Holy Ghost shall come upon thee," and then as a parallel statement he adds, "The power of the Highest shall overshadow thee" (Luke 1:35). The Holy Spirit *is* the power of the Highest. Of course, he is more than that, for he is not a mere power, but the third person of the blessed Trinity. The Belgic Confession says of the Holy Spirit that he "is the eternal power and might, proceeding from the Father and the Son," and that he is "of one and the same essence, majesty, and glory with the Father and the Son; and therefore is the true and eternal God, as the Holy Scriptures teach us."[1]

Here, then, is Gabriel's explanation. Something wonderful will happen *to* Mary and *in* Mary, something that has never happened to any other or in any other human being. The Holy Spirit will operate on and in Mary in a mysterious and powerful way. But Mary must not be afraid, for Gabriel

---

1 Belgic Confession 8, 11, in *The Confessions and the Church Order of the Protestant Reformed Churches* (Grandville, MI: Protestant Reformed Churches in America, 2005), 29, 33.

explains the manner of the Holy Spirit's working. First, "the Holy Ghost shall come upon thee" (v. 35). This emphasizes the heavenly source of the Holy Spirit: he shall *come upon* Mary from heaven. Second, "the power of the Highest shall overshadow thee" (v. 35). To overshadow means to envelop in shadow, which emphasizes the mystery of the Spirit's work, for his activity is hidden. God draws a veil over it, as it were. No one witnesses what the Spirit does: only scripture reveals the secret to us. Moreover, to overshadow is to cover in order to protect and shield. The Holy Spirit will protect Mary during this great work.

That is the only explanation that Gabriel gives. Beyond that we cannot go, for this is a wonder, a wonder of grace. God does not present it for our analysis, but for our adoration. Let us therefore worship the wonderworker of it, who is the Holy Spirit.

The result of this operation is the conception of Jesus. In verse 31, Gabriel promised, "Behold, thou shalt conceive in thy womb," and now in verse 35 the angel explains how: "The Holy Ghost shall come upon thee, and the power of the Highest shall overshadow thee." Therefore, adds the angel, "that holy thing which shall be born of thee shall be called the Son of God" (v. 35).

In the womb of Mary, a virgin, or a woman who has not yet known a man sexually, a wonder takes place. The Holy Spirit forms an embryo, consisting of body and soul, that is, the human nature of Mary's son Jesus Christ. Like other human embryos, this embryo undergoes development for nine months in the womb, and it is fully biologically and genetically human from the moment of conception. Every time a child is conceived a wonder takes place, but this conception is uniquely wonderful and miraculous, for the conception of Jesus is not the conception of a mere human embryo.

First, this one conceived in Mary's womb is called the Son of God. In verse 32 he is called "the Son of the Highest," and in verse 35 he is called "the Son of God." This means that the Holy Spirit did more than form a human nature of body and soul. He united that body and soul to the person of the eternal Son of God, the second person of the holy Trinity. Jesus is God, for he is co-eternal and co-essential or consubstantial with the Father and the Holy Spirit. Jesus is God even as he is a human embryo in the womb of Mary. Jesus did not *become* God sometime later, at his baptism or at his resurrection perhaps, but Jesus is eternally, unchangeably God.

Second, the one formed by the Holy Spirit is formed of the substance of Mary. The angel does not say that the child shall be "born *in* thee" but "born *of* thee." That little preposition "of" is a reference to the source, for the source of the human nature of Jesus is not heaven, but it is Mary. The Spirit formed it, but he used the substance of Mary. If he had not done this, Jesus would not be biologically related to Mary, and in her to David, and to the human race, with the result that Jesus would not be truly human. Therefore, it is essential that Jesus be born "of" Mary. Some of the Anabaptists at the time of the Reformation denied this. Therefore, the creeds emphasize it.

What is the meaning of these words—"He was conceived by the Holy Ghost, born of the Virgin Mary"?

That God's eternal Son, who is and continueth true and eternal God, took upon him the very nature of man, of the flesh and blood of the Virgin Mary, by the operation of the Holy Ghost; that he might also be the true seed of David, like unto his brethren in all things, sin excepted.[2]

We confess (in opposition to the heresy of the Anabaptists, who deny that Christ assumed human flesh of his mother) that Christ is become a partaker of the flesh and blood of the children; that he is a fruit of the loins of David after the flesh.[3]

Third, the result of this sublime operation of the Spirit is that Jesus, also with respect to his human nature, is holy: "that holy thing" (v. 35). Jesus as an undeveloped embryo is holy, for he is perfectly consecrated to God and separated from all defilement. As he grows in Mary's womb, he remains holy. When he is born, he is holy. Throughout his life, he is holy. In death, he is holy. In the resurrection, he is holy. As the ascended and exalted Lord, he is forever holy. He is holy in his body, his soul, his mind, his will, and in his divine person.

At this point the Roman Catholic Church makes a serious error, for they call Mary "the Mother of God." It might surprise the reader to know that the term "Mother of God" appears in one of the ecumenical creeds, the Creed of Chalcedon (AD 451). However, "Mother of God" is an unfortunate and inaccurate translation of the Greek term *theotokos*. The term was the occasion of much controversy in the years leading up to the Council of Chalcedon, for a certain heretic named Nestorius (AD 386–451) refused to use that term in

---

2 Heidelberg Catechism Q&A 35, in *Confessions and Church Order*, 97–98.
3 Belgic Confession 18, in *Confessions and Church Order*, 44.

connection with Mary because of his false view of the person of Christ. Nestorius would not confess that Jesus, even in the womb of the virgin Mary, was God; that is, he refused to confess that Jesus is the incarnate deity from the very moment of his conception.

Theotokos would better be rendered "God-bearer," not "Mother of God." The point that *theotokos* seeks to express is that the one whom Mary bore in her womb is *God*. He did not become God when he was born or at some later date, but he is eternally God. Therefore, the creed calls Mary *theotokos* or "God-bearer" not in order to exalt Mary, for she is not the mother of the divine essence, but to exalt Jesus, who is the incarnate second person of the divine Trinity.

Chalcedon carefully defines the relationships between God the Father, God the Son, and Mary, his earthly mother: "Begotten before all ages of the Father according to the Godhead, and in these latter days, for us and for our salvation, born of the Virgin Mary, the mother of God [*theotokos* or 'God-bearer'], *according to the manhood*."[4] Since the divine person or divine nature of the Son of God is eternal, infinite, and unchangeable, Mary cannot be the mother *of God*. She was the mother of the Son of God *according to his human nature*, or she was the mother of one who as to his person is God. It is therefore a grave, idolatrous error to worship Mary as the "Mother of God."

This raises another important question: how is it that Jesus is holy? Why does the angel say, "Therefore also that holy thing" (v. 35)? First, Christ's person, the eternal Son of God, is holy, and he cannot be anything but holy. Unholiness

---

4   Creed of Chalcedon, in *Confessions and Church Order*, 17 emphasis
    added.

can no more be attributed to the Son than to the Father or to the Spirit. Second, Jesus Christ did not stand under the headship of Adam, for Adam did not represent Christ in the garden of Eden in eating the forbidden fruit. Therefore, the original guilt of Adam's first transgression does not extend to Jesus Christ. Instead, as Christ stands as the head of his elect people, he is the head—or the legal representative and source of life—of Adam also (see Rom. 5). Third, since original guilt did not extend to Jesus, original pollution does not extend to him either. God did not punish Jesus by stripping him of the image of God and by imparting to him a totally depraved nature. Fourth, the Holy Spirit shielded Jesus from the pollution of Mary's flesh.

Mary was not herself immaculately conceived, nor was that necessary. Rome argues that Mary must have been immaculate in order to be a pure vessel for the conception of the Son of God, but that does not follow. Then Mary's mother, traditionally believed to be St. Anne, would also need to have been immaculate in order to be a pure vessel for the conception of Mary. Where would such a succession of immaculate persons end?

Understand that Mary has nothing to do with Jesus' holiness. She could not make him holy or shield his holiness, nor did God permit her to defile him, but the Spirit guarantees Jesus' holiness. The result of the Holy Spirit's work in and upon Mary was to prevent any defilement of Mary from contaminating Jesus, both in his conception and throughout the nine months of Mary's pregnancy: "Therefore also that holy thing which shall be born of thee shall be called the Son of God" (Luke 1:35).

Do you believe that? Unbelief scoffs at it. By faith we receive it, and we adore the worker of it.

MARY'S CONFUSION

Verse 35 is Gabriel's response to Mary's question in verse 34, "How shall this be, seeing I know not a man?" This is not a question of unbelief; rather this is a sincere desire to know and to understand. When Gabriel promises her a son in verse 31, Mary's thoughts naturally turn to a man. She knows that a man is required for the conception of a child: "I know not a man," she exclaims.

How can we explain Mary's question?

Mary is a virgin. Verse 27 calls her a virgin. A virgin is a young woman (in this case) who has not known a man in the intimacy of sexual intercourse. Often the Bible speaks of the sexual intercourse of married persons as "knowledge." The idea is that in the marriage bed, which is undefiled (Heb. 13:4), married persons express love to one another and enjoy the intimacy of their relationship, even becoming one flesh. Often the fruit of such intercourse is the conception of children. But that is not the full explanation of Mary's question.

Rome argues that Mary took a vow of perpetual virginity. But Mary does not say, "I will never know a man," but "I know not [present tense] a man" (Luke 1:34). Jewish women did not take vows of perpetual virginity, especially if they were espoused. To do so would be to defraud Joseph of due benevolence (see 1 Cor. 7:5).

Modern versions obscure the meaning. The NIV renders the text, "Since I am a virgin." That is an interpretation but not a literal translation, for literally the text says, "How shall be this since man I do not know?" The word virgin, *parthenos*, appears in verse 27 but not in verse 34.

The emphasis is on the absence of a man.

On the face of it, Mary's virginity is not an obstacle. She is young, she is espoused, and she and Joseph will soon be together. Then, surely, she could have a son. All things considered, it is very likely that she will have a son without the need for a miraculous angelic announcement and without the need of the Spirit's work. Why then does she ask this question?

The issue is this: "How shall this be, since I do not know a man *capable of doing what the angel has said?*" Mary knows a man, but she does not know a man whose son will be great. Mary does not know a man whose son could conceivably be called the Son of the Highest. Mary does not know a man to whose son God could give the throne of David. Even if Mary did know Joseph in the full biblical sense, she knows that Joseph is *not that man*. If Joseph is not that man, who could that man possibly be? Is the angel suggesting that she find another man, a more suitable man to be the father of the promised child? Which man? "I know not a man."

Now you understand Mary's mistake, and you understand the angel's answer. Mary was looking for a man, but Gabriel attributes the coming of this promised son to the Holy Spirit. Mary was right to say that she did not know a man, but Mary must forget about a man, for man is excluded: this is entirely the work of God. Not a man, but the Holy Spirit, will perform this marvelous work. In other words, the son of Mary (who is also the Son of God) will not have a human father. Moreover, Mary herself will be passive, for the Holy Spirit will operate in her and upon her, while Mary is an instrument or a vessel through whom God will work.

This gives us valuable instruction about salvation: our salvation is not the work of man, but only the work of God.

The Jews could not produce the Savior. They longed for him; they prayed for him; they waited for him; but when he came, God produced him. That is true of every part of our salvation: regeneration, calling, justification, the gift of saving faith, sanctification, preservation, and glorification are entirely the work of God alone. Man is excluded. Salvation is a gift. Every part of salvation is a gracious gift not to be earned, but to be gladly received.

To encourage and help Mary's faith, the angel refers to another work of God: the conception of John the Baptist. "Behold, thy cousin Elisabeth, she hath also conceived a son in her old age: and this is the sixth month with her, who was called barren. For with God nothing shall be impossible" (vv. 36–37). Elizabeth was old and well past childbearing years. Elizabeth was called "barren," for her womb was (literally) stiff and unable to receive children. But she has conceived a son, which is a miracle of God. Gabriel's conclusion is simple: "For with God nothing shall be impossible" (v. 37).

God can give conception to an aged, barren woman, and God can work the even greater wonder of the virgin conception. Do not seek to limit the power of God!

MARY'S RESPONSE

Mary's response to the angel is a beautiful example of faith. She lodges no objections. She does not protest that the virgin conception is absurd or impossible. She does not complain that this news will turn her world upside down. She does not object that the angel's tidings will put a strain on her relationship with Joseph, for how will she explain this to him? She does not protest that this miracle of God will put a blot on her reputation, for how will the villagers of Nazareth, her own parents, and Joseph's parents react to this? She leaves all those issues with God, confident that he will deal with them at the appointed time.

Mary simply confesses herself to be the Lord's servant: "Behold the handmaid of the Lord" (v. 38). Mary would have agreed with the Heidelberg Catechism: "I with body and soul, both in life and death, am not my own, but belong unto my faithful Savior."[5] Mary belonged to God, and so she reasoned that the Almighty could do with her as it pleased him. His it was to decree and to command; hers it was to obey.

There is no reluctance in Mary's words: "Be it unto me according to thy word" (v. 38). Mary expresses her response in the optative mood, a rare Greek construction used in strong wishes and desires. We see it most often in its negative form: "God forbid." Here it is in its positive form: "May it be." We could paraphrase Mary's response, "I eagerly desire to happen to me what God has said."

Again the Roman Catholic Church corrupts the truth. Rome's view is that Mary *consented* to the salvation proposed by God, as if God's eternal plan of redemption depended on the freewill choice of Mary, a creature. The Catechism of the Catholic Church states:

> Thus, giving her consent to God's word, Mary becomes the mother of Jesus. Espousing the divine will for salvation wholeheartedly, without a single sin to restrain her, she gave herself entirely to the person and to the work of her Son; she did so in order to serve the mystery of redemption with him and dependent on him, by God's grace.

---

5 Heidelberg Catechism A 1, in *Confessions and Church Order*, 83.

The Roman Catholic Catechism even quotes one of the church fathers: "The knot of Eve's disobedience was untied by Mary's obedience: what the virgin Eve bound through her disbelief, Mary loosened by her faith."[6]

In the Second Vatican Council Rome wrote, "The Fathers see Mary not merely as passively engaged by God, but as freely cooperating in the work of man's salvation through faith and obedience." Later Rome writes,

> She conceived, brought forth, and nourished Christ, she presented him to the Father in the temple, shared her Son's sufferings as he died on the cross. Thus, in a wholly singular way she cooperated by her obedience, faith, hope, and burning charity in the work of the Savior in restoring supernatural life to souls. For this reason she is a mother to us in the order of grace.[7]

Although it is true that God did not force himself upon Mary against her will, yet the plan of salvation did not depend on Mary's cooperation or consent. The work of salvation was entirely God's. Mary did not contribute to the incarnation or conception of the Son of God in her womb. She was entirely passive in that miracle and was powerless to bring it about. It simply happened *in* her. In a similar way God did not seek consent from Abraham when he declared, "I will establish my covenant between me and thee" (Gen. 17:7), nor did Abraham or Sarah in any way contribute to the birth of their wonder child, Isaac. Nor did God seek

---

6 *The Catechism of the Catholic Church*, paragraph 494, 110–11.
7 "Dogmatic Constitution on the Church" (Lumen Gentium, November 21, 1964; Chapter 8: "Our Lady") in *The Conciliar and Post Conciliar Documents of the Second Vatican Council* [Austin Flannery, O.P., gen. ed.], (Clonskeagh, Dublin, Ireland: Talbot Press, 1975), 416, 418.

consent from Saul of Tarsus on the Damascus road when he called him to preach the gospel to the Gentiles; instead, Paul was a chosen vessel (Acts 9:15), whom God had ordained to preach the gospel to the Gentiles. God created the response of faith in the heart of Abraham, Paul, and Mary, so that they became willing in the day of his power (Ps. 110:3). As the Canons of Dordt express it, "He who works in man both to will and to do, and indeed all things in all, produces both the will to believe and the act of believing also."[8]

Nevertheless, Mary is a beautiful example for us. When the word comes to us, our response must be, "I am the handmaid—or the manservant—of the Lord; be it unto me according to thy word." For the child of God, God's word is law, and the child of God delights to walk according to God's law. The will of God is always more important than our will. Is it God's will that we perform some duty? We do it gladly, seeking from God the grace to do it. Is it God's will that we suffer some affliction? We suffer it patiently, seeking from God the grace to endure it. When God speaks, "no" is not an option.

We obey by the power of the incarnate, crucified, and resurrected Christ.

Is that your response to God's word? May his word be fulfilled in our lives also!

---

8 Canons of Dordt 3–4.14, in *Confessions and Church Order*, 169.

Chapter 3

THE EFFECT OF MARY'S SALUTATION

39. And Mary arose in those days, and went into the hill country with haste, into a city of Juda;
40. And entered into the house of Zacharias, and saluted Elisabeth.
41. And it came to pass, that, when Elisabeth heard the salutation of Mary, the babe leaped in her womb; and Elisabeth was filled with the Holy Ghost:
42. And she spake out with a loud voice, and said, Blessed art thou among women, and blessed is the fruit of thy womb.
43. And whence is this to me, that the mother of my Lord should come to me?
44. For, lo, as soon as the voice of thy salutation sounded in mine ears, the babe leaped in my womb for joy.
45. And blessed is she that believed: for there shall be a performance of those things which were told her from the Lord. (Luke 1:39–45)

*S*hortly after Gabriel's visit, Mary sets out from Nazareth to visit Elizabeth. Very likely Mary told no one about the angel's appearance. She did not tell her parents, or the villagers of Nazareth, or even her betrothed, Joseph. Luke 1:39 says, "Mary arose...and went...with haste" (she was in a hurry and keen to get away). Elizabeth was the only one in whom she could confide at this point.

The idea to visit Elizabeth was suggested to her by Gabriel himself. The angel encouraged her in verse 36 with the example of Elizabeth. If anyone could understand, surely it would be Elizabeth, who had also experienced a miracle.

Zacharias, Elizabeth's husband, is not mentioned in this passage, most likely because he was dumb (the angel had struck him dumb for his unbelief in verse 20). Some even suggest that Zacharias was deaf (see verse 62, where "they made signs" to him). He therefore could not participate in the joy described in the text.

At this point, Elizabeth was six months or about twenty-five weeks pregnant with John the Baptist. By the time Mary reached Elizabeth's home, over ninety-three miles away, she was pregnant also. Gabriel spoke in the future tense—"thou *shalt* conceive in thy womb" (v. 31, emphasis added), and "the Holy Ghost *shall* come upon thee" (v. 35, emphasis added). But Elizabeth refers to "the fruit of [Mary's] womb" (v. 42) and the fact that Mary is already "the mother of [Elizabeth's] Lord" (v. 43). Therefore, the miracle of the virgin conception must have occurred between the departure of Gabriel from Mary's home and the arrival of Mary at the home of Elizabeth. What we have in Luke 1, therefore, is the meeting of two pregnant mothers: one is Elizabeth, who is six months pregnant, and the other is Mary, probably less than two weeks pregnant.

But more important than the mothers are the sons: the son of Elizabeth is John the Baptist, the forerunner to the Messiah; and the son of Mary is Jesus, the Messiah and the savior of the world. This is a meeting neither woman will ever forget, and it all begins with a simple greeting or salutation.

THE SALUTATION ITSELF

It is natural when two people meet that they greet one another. Striking in the text is the effect of Mary's greeting or salutation. The text lays emphasis on Mary's salutation, which is mentioned three times in these verses. In verse 40 we read, "[Mary] saluted Elisabeth." In verse 41 Luke relates, "Elisabeth heard the salutation of Mary." And in verse 44 Elizabeth exclaims, "Lo, as soon as the voice of thy salutation sounded in mine ears." Despite the importance of the salutation, the words that Mary used are not recorded. Therefore, the content is not so important as the fact.

Most likely, the first words out of Mary's mouth as she crossed the threshold of the house of Zacharias and Elizabeth were "Hail, Elizabeth" or something similar. "Hail," as we saw in verse 28, was the common greeting of the day. Where we might say "hello" or "hi," Mary or Elizabeth would say, "Hail." Alternatively, Mary may have said "Shalom," a very common Hebrew greeting, which means peace, wholeness, wellness, or wellbeing. Perhaps Mary's words were accompanied with a smile, a warm embrace, a wave of the hand, or a kiss on Elizabeth's cheek. The issue, however, is not the words as such or the content of Mary's greeting, but the fact of Mary's greeting, and the fact that Mary was the one who gave this salutation. The significance is further the state or condition of Mary when she uttered the greeting: she was pregnant with Jesus, the Son of God.

Who is Mary? Mary is Elizabeth's cousin. The word in verse 36 indicates a female relative: the best translation is "kinswoman." But more than that, Mary was the mother of Jesus, the woman chosen by God to bring forth the promised Messiah and Savior from her womb.

And who is Elizabeth? Elizabeth is a close friend and relative of Mary, someone in whom she can confide, and someone who will understand her joys and fears. What Mary had come to tell Elizabeth would (Mary expected) be a great surprise, even a shock. More than that, Elizabeth was the mother of John the Baptist, who was the direct forerunner to the promised Messiah and Savior. Therefore, Elizabeth is surely expecting that the Messiah will soon come, but little did she expect that Mary, her cousin or kinswoman, would be the mother of the promised Christ.

It is unlikely that Mary had told Elizabeth in advance that she was coming and why she was coming, for there was no time, nor was there the possibility of sending a communication (these were the days before email, texting, or even an official postal service). Besides that, such news as she intended to bring to Elizabeth could only be related face to face. In this meeting and in its salutation scripture records the first meeting between these two pregnant women: the mothers of John the Baptist and Jesus. It is also the only recorded meeting between the unborn John and Jesus. The two women are very different, and yet both of them experience a miracle.

The two women are very different with respect to age and social standing. Elizabeth is married to a priest, Zacharias; and she is an old woman. Since Elizabeth is well past childbearing years, we could estimate her age at about eighty years old or older. She is old enough to be a grandmother or a great-grandmother, not a mother. Mary is a young, espoused virgin: we might estimate her age at the late teens. Mary is espoused to a poor village carpenter.

The two women are also very different with respect to the miracles that they have experienced. Elizabeth is pregnant because she had intercourse with her husband, Zacharias. Apart from the age of Elizabeth and Zacharias, her conception of a child is natural. Mary is pregnant because, although she has not "known" Joseph and although she is still a virgin, the Holy Spirit has come upon her, overshadowed her, and formed in her womb a human nature to which the person of the Son of God has united himself in the wonder of the incarnation. Elizabeth's miracle is similar to that of Abraham and Sarah in the Old Testament (they were also too old to have children), but Mary's miracle is altogether unique.

The babies in their respective wombs are different also. John, the unborn baby in Elizabeth's womb, is older, six months or twenty-five weeks in prenatal development. It is not unusual at the sixth month of pregnancy for the baby to "kick" inside the womb, and it is not unusual for the mother to feel such a movement. Perhaps, as Mary and Elizabeth embraced, the unborn John the Baptist kicked, and both Elizabeth and Mary felt it. However, be that as it may, the "leap" of John in the womb was not an ordinary kick: it was a miracle of grace, as we shall see.

Jesus, the unborn baby in Mary's womb, is much younger. My estimate puts Mary's pregnancy at between week one and week three for reasons that I have explained. If that is true, the child in Mary's womb was smaller than a grain of rice. A baby in its earliest stages of development can only be detected on a pregnancy test at around week four. If Mary had taken such a test, which, of course, was impossible, for such medical tests had not yet been developed, her pregnancy would not yet have registered. Mary would not yet have evidenced the symptoms of pregnancy (fatigue, nausea, and so on), which usually begin at week five.

Application must be made to the evil of abortion at this point. If these two pregnancies had occurred in our day, Mary and Elizabeth could both have walked into an abortion clinic and ended the lives of their babies. Mary could have taken an abortion pill to induce a miscarriage, while Elizabeth could have opted for a surgical procedure to remove John from her womb. It makes us shudder to imagine it. Medical science today has progressed so far that an unborn child can receive lifesaving surgery in the womb, but at the same time man uses the good tools of medical science to murder children in the womb. Ungodly legislators argue today that children in the womb have no human rights. The passage from the word of God in Luke 1 proclaims loudly the *unborn humanity* of both John the Baptist and Jesus Christ.

But I return to the narrative. There is no earthly possibility that Mary or Elizabeth could have known that Mary is already pregnant. She was not far enough along in her pregnancy for that information to be available. But Mary had the word of the angel, which she accepted by faith, and Elizabeth, as we shall see, had the inspiration of the Holy Spirit to inform her of this marvelous fact.

The Effect upon Elizabeth

The effect of Mary's salutation upon Elizabeth was that she "was filled with the Holy Ghost" (v. 41). The text speaks of a sudden act of the Holy Spirit to fill Elizabeth or to control her. We know this because before Mary's salutation, Elizabeth was a spiritual person. This act of the Spirit was not to regenerate Elizabeth, for she was already spiritually alive. In verse 6 we learn that she and her husband were "righteous before God." Therefore, we know that she and her husband were believers (justified by faith alone), and they were, to use Christian terminology, "born again" of the Spirit, for regeneration occurs before justification in the order of salvation. Scripture shows her faith: in verse 45 Elizabeth commends Mary's faith and shows by it that she too believes.

Elizabeth had the Holy Spirit prior to this, but now she was suddenly filled with the Holy Spirit. The purpose of this sudden filling by the Spirit was to make Elizabeth prophesy. The Spirit took hold of Elizabeth when she heard Mary's salutation and put the words of God into her mouth, so that she "spake out with a loud voice" (v. 42). This is a common occurrence in the book of Acts: before someone prophesies, he or she is suddenly filled with the Holy Spirit. We therefore do not expect people to experience this today, because there is no special class of prophets in the church. All believers are prophets, priests, and kings (1 Pet. 2:9).[1]

Elizabeth's prophecy confirms what Gabriel had said and serves to encourage Mary further and to strengthen her faith in God's word. This is remarkable because Mary and Elizabeth had not exchanged notes. Mary had just arrived and had simply greeted Elizabeth, when Elizabeth begins to prophesy. Immediately, by the Spirit, Elizabeth knows everything that Mary had intended to tell Elizabeth. Mary does not need to explain anything, which in itself must have been a great relief to Mary, for how could she explain? Elizabeth knows that Mary has heard a word from God ("those things which were told her from the Lord," Luke 1:45), that Mary is pregnant ("the fruit of thy womb," v. 42), and the identity of the fruit of Mary's womb ("my Lord," v. 43).

---

1 Heidelberg Catechism Q&A 32, in *Confessions and Church Order*, 96.

Compare what Gabriel told Mary with what Elizabeth prophesies here. Both Gabriel and Elizabeth call Mary "blessed...among women" (vv. 28, 42). Elizabeth adds, "Blessed is the fruit of thy womb" (v. 42), because now Mary is pregnant, whereas before this Mary's pregnancy was prophesied but not yet a reality. Both Gabriel and Elizabeth speak of the divinity of Mary's child ("the Son of the Highest," v. 32, and "the Son of God," v. 35, and "my Lord," v. 43). Both Gabriel and Elizabeth encourage Mary in her faith. Gabriel points to the omnipotence of God, as does Elizabeth (vv. 37, 45), and Elizabeth especially reminds Mary of the blessedness of the believer (v. 45).

We notice two additional things about Elizabeth's prophecy: insight and humility. Elizabeth has insight into what exactly Mary's blessedness *is*. Both the angel and Elizabeth confess that Mary is blessed, but we must understand in what Mary's blessedness consists. Mary's blessedness is not independent of the blessedness of Christ. Rather, Mary is blessed *because* the fruit of her womb is blessed. The word "blessed" in verse 42 comes from the verb "to bless," which verb means to speak well of or concerning someone or something. God himself has spoken his word of blessing upon Jesus, and therefore he has also spoken his blessing upon Mary, who bears Jesus in her womb.

Moreover, Elizabeth confesses that Mary is blessed *through faith*. In verse 45, she expresses it, "Blessed [or happy] is she that believed." Mary has believed, and Elizabeth encourages her to continue in that faith, for she shall see the fulfillment of the promises of God.

Our blessing is the same as Mary's. Yes, she has a unique position in the history of redemption, but we are saved in the same way as Mary. We are saved by faith—faith unites us to Jesus Christ; faith enables us to believe whatever the scriptures teach and to have assurance in God's salvation; and faith makes us partakers of Christ's benefits.[2]

In her prophecy, Elizabeth also displays beautiful humility. Notice her demeanor in the presence of Mary, who is her inferior in many respects. Elizabeth was older and socially better off, but she humbly receives Mary. Listen to her exclamation in verse 43: "Whence is this to me, that the mother of my Lord should come to me?"

Elizabeth's words are not designed to exalt Mary, but to exalt Jesus. Even as a two-week-old fetus in Mary's womb, Jesus is Elizabeth's lord, and she recognizes him as such. The emphasis is not on "mother," but on "Lord." Elizabeth confesses the divinity, omnipotence, and absolute sovereignty of Mary's son: he is lord, the owner, ruler, and master of all, especially of his people, especially of Elizabeth; and he is the redeemer and savior of his people, even, mind you, as a two-week-old undeveloped human fetus!

There is no envy—no jealousy, and no rivalry—in the words of Elizabeth. Elizabeth is a recipient of a wonder of grace, for the forerunner to the Messiah is growing in her womb, which means that the Messiah cannot be far away. Now she receives a second blessing, for the mother of the Messiah visits her, and she brings the very Messiah in her womb. So close is Elizabeth to the Messiah that her own child leaps for joy in her womb at his presence. Elizabeth has a lesser task because she is merely the mother of the forerunner, but she is happy to fulfill her role, while she rejoices that her younger cousin has been graciously chosen for the greater role of the mother of the Messiah.

---

2 Heidelberg Catechism A 21, in *Confessions and Church Order*, 90–91.

THE EFFECT UPON ELIZABETH'S CHILD

Even more remarkable is the effect of Mary's salutation on the baby in Elizabeth's womb. In verse 41 Luke writes, "The babe leaped in her womb." The word "leap" means to jump or to skip. Pregnant mothers are familiar with this feeling, for at a certain time in the pregnancy, the baby starts to kick, and the mother can feel the baby's movements. However, this leap of John in the womb was not merely natural. That is not how Elizabeth, under the inspiration of the Holy Spirit, interprets it. The baby leaped in Elizabeth's womb because of the work of the Holy Spirit.

Certainly, Elizabeth was filled with the Holy Spirit and prophesied, and it is fitting, therefore, that her unborn child was filled with the Holy Spirit also. Indeed, Gabriel had promised this to Zacharias, Elizabeth's husband and John's father: "He shall be filled with the Holy Ghost, even from his mother's womb" (v. 15). Likely, then, both Elizabeth and John were filled with the Holy Spirit simultaneously.

Elizabeth gives the inspired interpretation of this leap by her unborn child: joy. In verse 44, Elizabeth exclaims, "For, lo, as soon as the voice of thy salutation sounded in mine ears, the babe leaped in my womb for joy." Joy is a deep gladness of the heart created by the Holy Spirit. Indeed, one of the aspects of the fruit of the Spirit is joy (Gal. 5:22), and one of the blessings of the kingdom is "joy in the Holy Ghost" (Rom. 14:17). If joy is of the Spirit, and if John was filled with the Spirit, John was regenerated already *before he was born.* John was born again *before* his physical birth! The baby expresses joy the only way he can, for he leaps in the womb. John could have smiled, but Elizabeth had no ultrasound to see that. So John kicks, leaps, and skips in the womb, as a sign to Elizabeth that he rejoices with an abundant, exceeding, jubilant joy in the presence of his lord.

You have seen children: they do not walk; they skip; they leap; they dance for joy. Listen to the word of God: "Rejoice ye in that day, and leap for joy" (Luke 6:23). "Ye rejoice with joy unspeakable and full of glory" (1 Pet. 1:8). Why did John rejoice? Why did he leap for joy, so that his mother felt it? The answer is that he too heard the voice of Mary's salutation. That is Elizabeth's answer in Luke 1:44: "For, lo, as soon as the voice of thy salutation sounded in mine ears, the babe leaped in my womb for joy." The unborn John did not know Mary, for this was the first time that Mary had been to Elizabeth's home since Elizabeth's pregnancy. But John did not rejoice because of Mary; he rejoiced because of Mary's identity as the mother of Jesus. If Mary had not been pregnant with Jesus, John would not have rejoiced.

Instead, John rejoiced because the voice of Mary meant the nearness of Jesus, because John, by the power of the Spirit, sensed the nearness of Jesus, the savior. There is something beautiful and deeply mysterious about this, which can only be explained by the work of the Holy Spirit. It is not possible to explain this naturally, for a six-month-old preborn baby cannot recognize the presence of a two-week-old preborn baby inside another woman, nor can one baby identify the other baby. However, the Holy Spirit was able to reveal this to John, so that he leapt in response. Similarly, the Holy Spirit is able to work in unborn children today, using external stimuli (such as music, the mother's voice, and other sounds) to influence children in the womb. Great are the works of God!

Thus we see that John, even before he was born, points to Jesus the Messiah. John did not hear the voice of Jesus, but what he heard was Mary's voice. But if we can hear the voice of Jesus through the preaching of the gospel without deifying the preacher, why could John not hear the voice of Jesus through the salutation of Mary without deifying Mary? John 3:29 applies here: "He that hath the bride is the bridegroom: but the friend of the bridegroom, which standeth and heareth him, rejoiceth greatly because of the bridegroom's voice: this my joy therefore is fulfilled."

That is the only appropriate response to the presence of Jesus for a child of God—joy. Is that your response, dear reader? John rejoiced because he sensed the presence of Jesus. We rejoice because Jesus has fulfilled what God has promised. We rejoice because we have access to Jesus, and through Jesus to God. We rejoice because we have the Holy Spirit in a richer and deeper way than Elizabeth or John did. What John, Mary, and Elizabeth longed for has now been accomplished: salvation in the Messiah. Christ has been born; he has lived his thirty-three years in perfect obedience; he has suffered and died on the cross for our sins; and he is risen from the dead.

Let us rejoice in him and in the salvation that he gives us—in the forgiveness of our sins; in everlasting righteousness; and in eternal life.

Chapter 4

MARY'S MAGNIFICAT OF JOY

46. And Mary said, My soul doth magnify the Lord,
47. And my spirit hath rejoiced in God my Saviour.
48. For he hath regarded the low estate of his handmaiden: for, behold, from henceforth all generations shall call me blessed.
49. For he that is mighty hath done to me great things; and holy is his name.
50. And his mercy is on them that fear him from generation to generation.
51. He hath shewed strength with his arm; he hath scattered the proud in the imagination of their hearts.
52. He hath put down the mighty from their seats, and exalted them of low degree.
53. He hath filled the hungry with good things; and the rich he hath sent empty away.
54. He hath helped his servant Israel, in remembrance of his mercy;
55. As he spake to our fathers, to Abraham, and to his seed for ever.
56. And Mary abode with her about three months, and returned to her own house. (Luke 1:46–56)

So far in the narrative, Mary has not expressed her feelings. Great and overwhelming things have happened to her. An angel has appeared to her, and the word of God has been fulfilled in her. We know from Luke 1:29 that she was troubled at the angel's salutation. We know from verse 34 that she had a question about how God's promise would be accomplished. And we know from verse 38 that her response was one of humble submission to the word of God.

We have also heard how the news has affected other people. Elizabeth is amazed that "the mother of [her] Lord should come to [her]" (v. 43); and Elizabeth's son leaps for joy in the womb at the presence of the unborn Son of God (v. 44). All of this must have filled Mary with wonder. The angel's message, Elizabeth's prophecy, and even John the Baptist's leap for joy were occasions for amazement.

Mary's response is to sing.

Although verse 46 says, "Mary said," many interpret these words as a song. Certainly, the structure is songlike: the words are arranged according to the typical poetical style of Hebrew parallelisms, so I will take it as a song. The song is commonly called the "Magnificat." The word "Magnificat" is simply the translation of the first word into Latin: "magnifies." In these words, which are her response to everything that she has experienced thus far, Mary magnifies the Lord.

In these words, then, we have Mary's interpretation of what has happened to her, and since these words are inspired words, her interpretation is accurate. In these words, we learn something about our salvation and about how we are to praise God for the great things that he has done for us. Jesus was born not only for Mary's benefit and salvation, but also for ours.

REJOICING IN GOD'S SALVATION

Mary's joy is in salvation or in the God of her salvation. Mary describes her salvation in terms of three metaphors.

First, salvation is her personal exaltation. Until this point in her life, Mary was in a "low estate" (v. 48), or in a humble and humbled position. But God has regarded her in that low position, for he has condescended to look upon her as she sat, as it were, in the dust. Now, exclaims Mary, "He hath regarded the low estate of his handmaiden" (v. 48); "He hath...exalted them of low degree" (v. 52). Or to echo Hannah's song in 1 Samuel 2:8, "He raiseth up the poor out of the dust, and lifteth up the beggar from the dunghill."

Second, salvation is to be the beneficiary of the mighty acts of God: "He that is mighty hath done to me great things" (Luke 1:49). These great things include the miracle that the Holy Spirit has performed. The Holy Spirit has come upon her, and the power of the Highest has overshadowed her, and that holy thing conceived in her womb is the Son of God. Mary recognizes God's hand in this; indeed, in verse 51 Mary extols God's "arm." In the Bible, God's arm is a symbol of his strength, for God stretches forth his arm to deliver his people. Mary is conscious that God's arm has operated on her behalf and even upon her. In fact, so great are the works of God toward her that Mary exclaims, "Behold, from henceforth all generations shall call me blessed" (v. 48). The angel Gabriel called Mary "blessed," Elizabeth called Mary "blessed," and every generation of believing Jews and Gentiles will acknowledge Mary's great blessedness, for she was chosen to be the mother of the Messiah. That is her unique blessedness.

Third, salvation is to be filled with good things: "He hath filled the hungry with good things" (v. 53). Mary sees herself as empty and as hungry, for of herself she has nothing. God in his marvelous mercy has filled her mouth so that she is satisfied with the riches of his goodness: peace, joy, and eternal life. Here, Mary echoes Psalm 103:5, "Who satisfieth thy mouth with good things." These three metaphors (God's exaltation of his people, God's mighty acts, and God's satisfying his people), which Mary finds in the Old Testament scriptures, are indicative of spiritual salvation.

In the Bible, true salvation is never merely physical, material, or earthly. God delivered his people from Egypt, by stretching out his arm to destroy the Egyptians, by opening the Red Sea, and by bringing Israel into the Promised Land, but that was a picture of the true deliverance, which is deliverance from sin and death. God took his people Israel, who were miserable slaves, and he made them priests and kings, but that was a picture of true, spiritual fellowship with God. God filled his people's mouths with manna and many other good things, but that was a picture of the true bread, which is Jesus Christ. Therefore, in the Magnificat, Mary rejoices in salvation from sin and death.

Mary calls the Lord "God my Saviour" (Luke 1:47), exactly because she knows that she is a sinner, worthy of death, guilty and depraved, and hopelessly lost. Never does Mary imagine in the Magnificat that she is immaculate or without the stain of original sin. Such a thought never crossed her mind. If she had thought that, she would not have called God "[her] Saviour." She would have said, "I am the one who brings the Savior to others, but I myself do not actually need a savior, because I have no sin of my own."

Mary knows that what has happened to her in the virgin conception of the Son of God is her salvation, and she knows that her son is her savior. In verse 43, Elizabeth has called Mary's unborn son "[her] Lord." In response, Mary rejoices in her lord, and she calls her lord "God my Saviour." Although her lord and her God is a tiny unborn baby, she rejoices in him, because she knows that he will bring to her and all God's people salvation.

Mary probably does not know exactly how her son will save her, but for her it is enough to know that he shall save her, and she leaves the details to the Almighty. We know that her son will save Mary—and us—by his perfect, lifelong obedience, by his sufferings and death, and by his resurrection. Mary's response to this salvation is joy: John leaped for joy, the shepherds will rejoice, the wise men will rejoice, the angels will rejoice, and Mary rejoices. What a joyous story is the nativity for all true believers!

Joy, as we know, is a deep, spiritual gladness of the heart. The word Mary uses is the deepest kind of joy, an exulting or a jubilating joy. The reason for her joy is not her circumstances. Joy is a gladness that does not depend on circumstances. Certainly, Mary's circumstances are joyous. She is pregnant with a child who is the Son of God and who will be the savior of God's people. Yet she has sorrows too, and more sorrows will afflict her in the future. But the object of Mary's joy is the Lord: "My spirit hath rejoiced *in God my Saviour*" (v. 47, emphasis added). "My soul doth magnify *the Lord*" (v. 46, emphasis added). Because she has a spiritual joy in God, she will still rejoice when her circumstances are difficult (when she goes into labor; when her midwife is her husband; when she gives birth in a stable; and when she and her family must flee to Egypt). Although sorrow will pierce her heart and tears will flow, her joy will not be taken from her, for Jesus remains.

Mary does what Paul later urges the Philippians to do: "Rejoice in the Lord alway; and again I say, Rejoice" (Phil. 4:4). Mary rejoices in who God is: she rejoices in his power ("He that is mighty," Luke 1:49; "He hath shewed strength with his arm," v. 51), she rejoices in his holiness ("Holy is his name," v. 49), and she rejoices in his mercy ("His mercy is on them," v. 50; "in remembrance of his mercy," v. 54). When we rejoice in God's perfections as Mary does here, we rejoice in something and someone unchangeable. Our circumstances might change, but God's power, holiness, and mercy do not change. Mary rejoices in this latest manifestation of the unchangeable power, holiness, and mercy, which is the virgin conception of the Son of God in her womb!

Mary's rejoicing in the power, holiness, and mercy of God (and in the salvation of God) leads her to praise God. She begins with the beautiful word "magnify"—literally, "Magnifies my soul the Lord." We know what it is to magnify something: the print on a page seems small to our eyes and we place a magnifying glass on it, so that it seems larger. Or we take a telescope and we look at a distant star, and it seems larger to us. But neither the print on the page nor the star in the sky has increased in size by our magnifying of it; the object has simply become larger to us in our estimation. When we magnify God, we make him more glorious in our own eyes and in the eyes of others. We lift him up in our estimation and in the estimation of others. We exalt him so that he is praised, worshiped, and adored. But God has remained as glorious as he ever was; we did not add to his glory by magnifying him.

This magnifying of the Lord comes from Mary's heart, for it is not a halfhearted, feigned, manufactured, hypocritical praising of God, but one that wells up deep within Mary's soul and now bursts forth in these beautiful words. She speaks of her soul: "*My soul* doth magnify the Lord" (v. 46, emphasis added). She speaks of her spirit: "*My spirit* hath rejoiced in God my Savior" (v. 47, emphasis added). These are parallel statements.

What she means is that the whole of her being is taken up with praising God. Again, we see echoes of Psalm 103:1, "Bless the LORD, O my soul: and all that is within me, bless his holy name." Have you ever felt that way? Have you ever been so overwhelmed at the depth of your sins and at the wonder of your salvation that you have been bursting to praise God? That is the idea of Mary's Magnificat. May we make that our practice!

REJOICING IN GOD'S JUDGMENTS

Mary, as a believing child of God saturated in the scriptures, knows that God's salvation is particular, and she knows that God saves his people by judging his enemies. That comes out especially in the middle section of the Magnificat. God's people are described as those who "fear him" (Luke 1:50), those of "low degree" (v. 52), and those who are "hungry" (v. 53). These are not the conditions of salvation, but they are the spiritual characteristics of those who are saved.

Listen, for example, to Isaiah 66:2: "But to this man will I look, even to him that is poor and of a contrite spirit, and trembleth at my word." Or consider chapter 55:1, "Ho, every one that thirsteth, come ye to the waters, and he that hath no money; come ye, buy, and eat; yea, come, buy wine and milk without money and without price."

Those are the spiritual characteristics of Mary herself.

She calls herself "his handmaiden" or the bond slave of the Lord of glory (Luke 1:48). What he commands, she will do; and it will be her great privilege to serve him. She fears God with a deep reverence, as a daughter fears her father, not because she fears a beating, but because she honors her father and loves him. Is that you? Are you humble, God-fearing, and empty, waiting to be filled with good things that come from your heavenly Father and gracious Savior?

But not all men are like that—indeed, by nature, no one is like that. Mary describes the characteristics of the wicked enemies of God and the fierce foes of his people.

First, they are "proud in the imagination of their hearts" (v. 51). The word means haughty. This is the kind of person who is filled with a sense of his own importance and who looks down in contempt upon others. Our world is filled with such people, from politicians to university professors, from clergymen to business leaders. Perhaps Mary had the religious leaders of Israel in mind, the scribes, the Pharisees, and the Sadducees. How they despised the ordinary people of God!

Second, they are "mighty" (v. 52). The mighty have their seats; literally the word is "thrones." From their seats/ thrones the mighty wield power, and they use that power selfishly, even tyrannically. Consider a man like King Herod, who at this time was sitting on Israel's throne. We will meet him later in this book. Or consider a man like the Roman emperor, who was revered as divine by the Roman citizens.

Third, they are rich (v. 53). The rich are filled with the good things of this earth, and from their exalted and powerful positions they feast on the dainties of this world.

Mary was not proud, she was not mighty, and she was not rich. Instead, she was poor and she was powerless. She was in a "low estate," or of a "low degree."

Mary knew her history: it was the haughty, the mighty, and the rich who crushed and oppressed the lowly, the powerless, and the poor. Think of haughty Pharaoh, or powerful Nebuchadnezzar, or self-righteous Caiaphas. It is the haughty, the mighty, and the rich who even today oppress God's church.

While God exalts the lowly, performs mighty acts for the powerless, and fills the mouths of the hungry with the good things of salvation, he judges the haughty, the mighty, and the rich. God's arm has a double function—with it he saves his people, and with it he scatters and destroys the wicked.

How does God destroy his enemies and thus save his people?

First, "he hath scattered the proud" (v. 51). The proud dream in the imagination of their hearts that they are immovable. But God stretches out his mighty arm and disperses them to the four winds. What a terrible judgment—with one arm, God gathers his people to himself to care for and to protect them; and with the other, he drives the wicked away. He smashes them to pieces, so that they are beaten like the chaff: "The ungodly," says the psalmist, "are like the chaff which the wind driveth away" (Ps. 1:4).

Second, "he hath put down the mighty" (Luke 1:52). The wicked sit on their exalted thrones, ruling over, oppressing, and tyrannizing the people, but God brings them down low to the ground. Such was the fate of Pharaoh, of Nebuchadnezzar, and of King Herod, of the ungodly Roman emperors, and of the chief priests of the Jews, and such is the fate of ungodly rulers in church and state in every age. Death cuts down the wicked: when they appear in judgment, they perish. The power that they exercised in this life will be of no help to them when they appear before the Almighty to render an account of their deeds.

Third, "the rich he hath sent empty away" (v. 53). When God gives the blessings of salvation, he gives nothing to the rich, self-satisfied, and smug. (Even the good things of this life are a curse to them.) They did not hunger and thirst after righteousness, for they had no interest in eternal life, in the forgiveness of sins, or in God's salvation. What a terrible judgment, to be sent away, empty, naked, and guilty, from God's gracious presence. "Depart from me, ye cursed, into everlasting fire, prepared for the devil and his angels" (Matt. 25:41).

All this, mind you, is the work of Jesus Christ. About this Mary sings, and in this Mary rejoices, and for this Mary magnifies the Lord.

We must understand this for our comfort too: it is not God's purpose, intention, or desire to save everyone. It was not God's purpose, intention, and desire to save Israel *and* Egypt. It was not God's purpose, intention, and desire to save Israel *and* Babylon. Instead, it is God's purpose, intention, and desire to save Israel *through* the destruction of Egypt and Babylon; and it is God's purpose, intention, and desire to save his church *through* the destruction of the world. God saves the lowly, weak, and hungry through the destruction of the proud, mighty, and rich.

That too is part of the Savior's work, for Jesus is the savior and the judge. When Jesus died on the cross, he did so to save us from our sins. But at the same time, Jesus' death is, as he himself says, "the judgment of this world" (John 12:31). If the death of Christ on the cross does not save you, it will destroy you. Either you will believe or you will be hardened. The preaching will be a "savour of death unto death" or a "savour of life unto life" unto you (2 Cor. 2:16). Mary understood something of that reality. Later, Simeon will echo this sentiment: "This child is set for the fall and rising again of many in Israel; and for a sign which shall be spoken against" (Luke 2:34).

Rejoicing in God's Faithfulness

Some have identified three stanzas in Mary's song: the first concerns her personal salvation (Luke 1:46–49); the second concerns God's dealings with men more generally (vv. 50–53); and the third concerns the fulfillment of God's covenant (vv. 54–55). If this is true, the third stanza is especially praise for God's fulfillment of his promises.

In other words, Mary's song is not individualistic. We often make that mistake, for we imagine that God saves individuals, but God saves a people or a church. He saves individuals as part of a greater body, which church consists of many generations. In verse 50 Mary exclaims, "His mercy is on them that fear him from generation to generation." In verse 55 she goes on to say, "As he spake to our fathers, to Abraham, and to his seed forever." Every generation from Abraham onward (really from Adam onward) has hoped in the promise of God.

Adam and Eve hoped in the coming of the Seed of the woman (Gen. 3:15), and what they hoped for, says Mary, has now been fulfilled. Seth to Noah hoped in the coming of the Seed of the woman, and what they hoped for, says Mary, has been fulfilled in the miracle in my womb. Abraham, Isaac, Jacob, and the twelve patriarchs hoped in the coming of the Seed of Abraham, and what they hoped for, says Mary, is now here. David hoped for the coming of his Seed, and what David hoped for, and what every generation after David hoped for, says Mary, is now fulfilled. What the angel Gabriel announced and what the Holy Spirit has performed is "in remembrance of his mercy" (Luke 1:54).

Notice that word "remembrance." It is as if, from God's people's perspective, God forgot. We know, of course, that

God never forgets, but the point is that God made his people wait for a long time.

God promised to Abraham that in him "all families of the earth [would] be blessed" (Gen. 12:3), but Jesus was not born until many years, many centuries, after Abraham's death. Abraham himself never saw the promise fulfilled. The same is true for many other generations of God's people: Isaac, Jacob, the patriarchs, Moses, Joshua, David, and even the last prophet of the Old Testament, Malachi, lived and died without seeing the promise. In fact, God ordained that Israel would be miserable, in the dust, and hopelessly oppressed before he sent his Son.

God waited until the royal line of David was almost extinguished in the earth, when only a poor carpenter and a virgin were left. God waited until Israel was under the rule of cruel king Herod and the wicked, pagan Roman Empire. Israel's miserable circumstances at the time of Christ's birth were part of God's counsel, decreed by him, and therefore accomplished in God's providence. Is this not characteristic of God? He remembers his mercy when we are most miserable, for he wants us to experience and appreciate our salvation.

Notice too that beautiful expression in Luke 1:54: "He hath holpen his servant Israel." Israel is God's servant, where the word "servant" means a child. This is covenantal language. Of course it is, for Mary's thoughts turn to the covenant of God. Mary sees God as the father of Israel, for God loves and cares for Israel. Mary sees everything that God does in terms of God's relationship of friendship, which he establishes with Abraham's seed. In fact, "servant" is translated "child" in Acts 4:27: "thy holy child Jesus."

The verb "holpen" means "helped." Jehovah has helped his servant Israel. The idea of the verb is "to lay hold of someone in order to succor him." Think of how a father lays hold of the hand of his son in order to rescue him from some danger and to bring him safely home. That is the idea of "holpen."

In choosing Mary, and in causing his Son to be conceived in her womb, God has holpen Israel, taken him by the hand to rescue him and to bring him to safety. He has done that by sending his Son to die on the cross for our sins.

With that, Mary finishes her song. We do not know what Mary did for the three months during which she stayed with Elizabeth. Undoubtedly, the two women had much to talk about as they related to one another what the Lord had done in their lives. It must have been a great comfort to Mary that she could confide in Elizabeth, and it must have been a great comfort to Elizabeth that she could confide in Mary (especially since her husband was unable to speak during that time).

But after three months, Mary returned to Nazareth.

It seems she left just before the birth of John. Likely, she did not want to be in Elizabeth's house when the house was filled with neighbors and friends. Besides, she had something more that she had to do: she had to break the news to Joseph.

But would he understand? How would he react to her news?

Graciously, God brings comfort to Joseph.

Chapter 5

AN ANGELIC DISPELLING OF JOSEPH'S FEARS

18. Now the birth of Jesus Christ was on this wise: When as his mother Mary was espoused to Joseph, before they came together, she was found with child of the Holy Ghost.

19. Then Joseph her husband, being a just man, and not willing to make her a public example, was minded to put her away privily.

20. But while he thought on these things, behold, the angel of the LORD appeared unto him in a dream, saying, Joseph, thou son of David, fear not to take unto thee Mary thy wife: for that which is conceived in her is of the Holy Ghost.

21. And she shall bring forth a son, and thou shalt call his name Jesus: for he shall save his people from their sins.

22. Now all this was done, that it might be fulfilled which was spoken of the Lord by the prophet, saying,

23. Behold, a virgin shall be with child, and shall bring forth a son, and they shall call his name Emmanuel, which being interpreted is, God with us.

24. Then Joseph being raised from sleep did as the angel of the Lord had bidden him, and took unto him his wife:

25. And knew her not till she had brought forth her firstborn son: and he called his name JESUS. (Matthew 1:18–25)

*W*e sometimes get quite sentimental about the nativity narratives. But we must remember that this is real human history, not a romantic fairy tale, and that the men and women involved in this history had their lives turned upside down. Mary's life was thrown into disarray when an angel announced that she would become pregnant by the power of the Holy Spirit. Could you even imagine that? An angel tells you that you will give birth miraculously to a son, and not just any son, but the Son of God in human flesh! Joseph's life was brought into upheaval when he discovered that Mary was pregnant. Could you imagine that? Your espoused wife informs you that she is pregnant, and although you know that the child cannot possibly be yours, she assures you that you must not worry because an angel told her that she had conceived "of the Holy Ghost"! Could any man believe *that*?

The text introduces us to Joseph, the carpenter of Nazareth. He and Mary were a young couple who planned a happy life together when God's messenger intervened. Joseph had chosen Mary to be his wife, and he looked forward to being with her. Mary was honored to be the espoused wife of Joseph, and she looked to him for love, companionship, support, and protection.

But what the angel had announced to Mary threw all their plans into confusion. When Mary returned from her three-month visit with Elizabeth, Joseph was in for a shock. So great was his shock, dismay, and sadness that an angel had to reassure him.

We see here God's care in comforting the fears of his people in order to assure us of our salvation. And we see

God's care for his Son in providing a loving, stable home in which he will be raised.

Joseph's Fears

Joseph's fear can be expressed very simply: Joseph feared that his wife, Mary, had been unfaithful to him. I should first explain the relationship between Mary and Joseph, for Matthew 1:18 says, "Mary was espoused to Joseph."

Modern readers often make the mistake of equating espousal with engagement. Jewish espousal was much more serious than that. Today, a man can give an engagement ring to his sweetheart, but he or she can call off the wedding at any moment up to the wedding day. Such a decision would bring heartache and spoil the hopes and dreams of family and friends, but it would have few, if any, legal repercussions. That was not the case here, however, for espousal was the same as legal marriage; and if a couple were espoused, it meant that they had exchanged vows before witnesses. As far as the villagers of Nazareth and the families of Joseph and Mary were concerned, they were married.

However, verse 18 adds, "before they came together." First, a couple was espoused, and from that moment they were man and wife. However, the husband did not usually take his espoused wife home at that point. Usually, there was a period of time (often several months) between the "espousal" and the "coming together." Great festivities marked the coming together, for the husband (or bridegroom) would meet his bride and bring her to his home, which he had prepared for her. The parable of the wise and foolish virgins in Matthew 25 is based upon these wedding customs of the Jews.

From Joseph's perspective, something terrible had happened between his espousal to Mary and his coming together with her: "She was found with child" (Matt. 1:18).

We do not know how Joseph became aware of Mary's pregnancy. Luke 1:39 indicates that, after the angel left Mary, she traveled "with haste" to visit Elizabeth, her cousin. This seems to suggest that Mary did not consult with Joseph before she left, and that therefore Mary did not tell Joseph what the angel had revealed to her about the child whom she would conceive. But when Mary returned, some three months later, she was very obviously pregnant. Perhaps she tried to hide her condition from family and friends for a while, but Joseph would have to be informed sooner rather than later. Most likely, therefore, when she could hide the fact no longer, she approached Joseph with some trepidation: she tried to explain to him what the angel Gabriel had said, and especially that the child was conceived of the Holy Ghost (Matt. 1:18 says, "She was found with child of the Holy Ghost"). But would he, did he, and could he understand?

Joseph knew that the child in Mary's womb was not his, and it appears that either he did not hear Mary's explanation or he did not believe it. Mary had been absent for three months, and her news shocked him greatly. Obviously, from Joseph's perspective, she must have met another man, become intimate with him, and become pregnant by him. No doubt, such a discovery hurt Joseph deeply. He loved Mary and he trusted her, but after this shocking revelation he could not marry her. We must not be too harsh on Joseph, for would *you* have believed Mary? Would *you* have judged the story of an angelic appearance and conception by the Holy Spirit credible? Remember that Joseph had not yet received a message from an angel to confirm Mary's explanation. And if he had not even heard Mary's explanation, he had even less reason to believe that there could be an innocent explanation for Mary's condition.

Now that Mary's pregnancy had come to his attention, however that may have been, Joseph faced a dilemma. What should he do? According to verse 19, Joseph was "a just man." "Just" means upright or righteous. A just man lives in harmony with God's standard, which is found in the law. As a just man, Joseph was a believer, for the just shall live by faith. He belonged to that believing remnant, which looked for the Savior and Messiah. As a just man, Joseph was also fair minded: he loved his neighbor and sought (within the law) to be kind to his neighbor. We can try to imagine the twists and turns that tormented the conscience of this "just man."

Joseph was not primarily concerned about himself: "How can I best save face; how can I best get out of a potentially embarrassing situation?" In verse 19, we read that Joseph was "minded." The word means careful deliberation, for Joseph was not rash or foolish. He carefully considered his options and weighed them up in his mind, rather than reacting emotionally or responding with a knee-jerk reaction. This is characteristic of a wise man, not of an impetuous fool. Undoubtedly, Joseph searched the scriptures: what does God's word say? And he prayed: perhaps he wrestled in prayer with God for some time before coming to his conclusion.

Joseph had, within the law, two main options. Neither of them was pleasant, especially for Mary. But neither was pleasant for Joseph either, since he loved Mary. Both options meant that he could not marry Mary as he had hoped.

The first option was the harsh option: "make her a public example" (v. 19). To make a public example is to expose to open shame. Joseph could approach the elders of his city and publicly accuse Mary of adultery. Mary would then be branded an adulteress and would be subject to whatever penalties of the law were in force at the time, possibly death by stoning. Such a course of action, although legitimate, would be disastrous for Mary and her child. Mary would be a social pariah, a woman who has played the harlot in Israel, with an illegitimate son. She and her son would lose all protection, and Mary's character would be forever tainted.

But Joseph, verse 19 says, was "not willing" to do that, for he loved her too much to put her through such an ordeal. He planned to "put her away privily." This means that Joseph would give Mary a bill of divorcement in front of two or three witnesses. Joseph only needed to say that he had found some "uncleanness" in her, and he could be free from Mary. This, although better than the harsher option, would still be disastrous for Mary and her child. Mary and Jesus would lack a protector, and Jesus would not have a legal father. (The genealogy of Matthew 1 is designed to show that Joseph is Jesus' legal/adopted father.)

It is very likely that Joseph, having deliberated, planned to divorce Mary the next day. Therefore, the angel of God must urgently intervene.

THE ANGEL'S REASSURANCE

As Joseph slept, God sent to him wonderful reassurance, for in verse 20 "the angel of the Lord appeared to him in a dream." There is a difference between a vision and a dream. In a vision a person is awake. For example, Mary was awake when the angel Gabriel appeared to her, and Paul was awake when Christ appeared to him on the Damascus road. In a dream, however, one is asleep: Joseph, according to verse 24, was asleep. Joseph will receive another such dream, as will the wise men, in Matthew 2. The significance of the dream is that it was revelatory. Our dreams are not revelatory, but in the past, God at various times gave such revelations to his people (Heb. 1:1–2).

In the dream, Joseph saw an angel, "the angel of the Lord" (Matt. 1:20). It is very possible that this was the same angel (Gabriel) that Mary saw. Possibly the angel appeared this way because such an appearance is less frightening. When angels appear in visions, the reaction is often terror. In a dream, the angel slips into someone's subconscious mind. Be that as it may, the angel had a very important and urgent message to bring.

The angel immediately addresses Joseph's concerns: "Fear not to take unto thee Mary thy wife" (v. 20). The angel addresses Joseph as "Joseph, thou son of David" (v. 20). This is a reference to Joseph's family line, for he too is a descendant of King David. Possibly this is also a reference to Joseph's character. Joseph is a true son of David, a man after God's own heart, and a man of faith, like his father David. Such a man can be expected to heed the command of an angel from heaven.

Joseph might imagine that it would be improper for him to marry Mary, since it appears that she has become defiled with another man. But the angel removes Joseph's fears by teaching him about the true conception of the child. Mary has not been unfaithful: the child has not been conceived through fornication. That was what Joseph had mistakenly imagined about his dear wife.

"That which is conceived in her is of the Holy Ghost" (v. 20). This is what the angel Gabriel had announced to Mary;

this is what Mary most likely had related in her explanation to Joseph; and now the angel confirms it. What a relief this must have been to Joseph! The angel does not explain what "conceived of the Holy Ghost" means. The word "of" (or "out of") refers to the source of the child, and the fullest explanation is found in Luke 1:35, as we have seen.

In addition, the angel reminds Joseph of the prophecy of Isaiah. It is difficult to know if the words of Matthew 1:22–23 are the angel's, or if Matthew the narrator added them as an explanation. It does not matter, however, for the truth of the virgin birth is the significant point. Although the virgin birth is exceptional and unique, it was prophesied: "Now all this was done, that it might be fulfilled which was spoken of the Lord by the prophet, saying, Behold, a virgin shall be with child, and shall bring forth a son, and they shall call his name Emmanuel, which being interpreted is, God with us" (vv. 22–23).

A few words about this prophecy are in order at this point.

In the days of Ahaz, king of Judah, God gave Isaiah a prophecy in Isaiah 7:14. Ahaz was a very wicked king, and in his day a confederacy of Syria and Israel came up against Jerusalem to destroy it. God promised to deliver Jerusalem, adding that within sixty-five years the kingdom of Israel would cease to exist. When Ahaz refused to believe God's word, God commanded him to ask for a sign, which Ahaz also refused to do, claiming with a false and hypocritical piety that he did not want to tempt God.

In judgment upon Ahaz, God gave a sign to his people, but a sign that wicked Ahaz, and that unbelieving generation, would not see. "Therefore the Lord himself shall give you a sign" (7:14). Notice that the passage changes from the singular pronoun ("ask *thee* a sign," v. 11, emphasis added) to the plural pronoun ("The Lord himself shall give *you* a sign," v. 14, emphasis added). This indicates that, although Ahaz did not ask for a sign, God will still give his people (but not Ahaz) a sign, which sign would be fulfilled much later. The angel declares or Matthew explains: "Now all this was done, that it might be fulfilled" (Matt. 1:22). "All this" refers to the virgin conception in the womb of Joseph's espoused wife, Mary.

There has been controversy about this prophecy, for some modern Bible versions translate Isaiah 7:14 with the words "young woman" and not the word "virgin." But the issue is quite simple: a young woman having a child is *not* a sign. A sign is something significant and unusual: there is a "behold" in Isaiah 7:14. Moreover, although the Hebrew word in verse 14 is not the specialized word for "virgin," it can mean it in many contexts. More importantly, however, the Greek word in Matthew 1:23 means virgin (*parthenos*, from which the word *parthenogenesis* is derived). Mary is *that* virgin, for she is the only woman in human history who has ever conceived as a virgin. That makes her unique and her experience the sign promised in Isaiah 7:14, a sign that unbelieving Ahaz never witnessed.

The result of the virgin conception and birth is Emmanuel. Emmanuel is not the name of the Messiah—Christ was not called "Jesus Emmanuel of Nazareth," for example, for his name was Jesus. Emmanuel explains who Jesus is, for he is God dwelling among us and with us. The literal translation of Emmanuel is "with us God." The name Emmanuel, then, explains in one simple word the incarnation: Jesus is God in the flesh.

When the virgin conceived, a tremendous miracle occurred. God came to us; God came to dwell with us, by us, among us, and in us. God did not come to dwell with us as he did at Mount Sinai, in a terrible, awe-inspiring, billowing cloud, which struck terror into Israel. God did not come to dwell with us as he did in the tabernacle and in the temple, in the Shekinah glory in the holy of holies, atop the mercy seat. God came to dwell with us and to be our Emmanuel in flesh and blood, in the deity of the Son of God veiled in flesh. The second person of the Trinity assumed our nature, walked among us, taught us, and even permitted men to touch him (1 John 1:1). Finally, our Emmanuel suffered and died for us on the cross. All of that is implied, and begins, in the womb of Mary in the virgin conception.

THE PROMISED SAVIOR

In addition to explaining the origin or source of Mary's pregnancy, the angel informs Joseph of the name, which is the same name that Gabriel mentioned to Mary in Luke 1:31. Jesus is the Greek equivalent of the Jewish name Joshua. The name Joshua or Jesus means "Jehovah salvation" or "Jehovah saves." That is very significant, for the child will be the Savior.

The child is not merely one who shall proclaim or announce salvation (that is the role of John the Baptist, for example), but he will be the Savior: "He shall save" (Matt. 1:21). In Jesus all God's promises of salvation will be fulfilled, which is wonderful news for Joseph, and for us. The angel came to dispel Joseph's fears about his earthly marriage to Mary, but he gave Joseph glad tidings, more than he could ever have imagined.

Salvation is rescue or deliverance. A savior does not offer a helping hand, nor does he offer advice on how to be saved, nor does he provide opportunities for people to save themselves. A savior delivers or rescues his people from danger and brings them into a permanent condition of safety and wellbeing. The Savior, who is Jesus, delivers people from the greatest danger and misery of sin and death and brings them into the greatest blessedness of eternal life, peace, joy, and glory. "Joseph," says the angel, "the son whom Mary shall bear, and whom you shall call Jesus, shall be *that* Savior."

What a wonder this must have been to Joseph. Joseph, a just man, had, with other saints of his day, long awaited the Savior. Long had they pored over the scriptures: the seed of the woman, the seed of Abraham, the seed of David, he shall come to deliver Israel. But little could Joseph have imagined that his wife, Mary, a poor girl, from a poor family, and a virgin, would be chosen to bring him forth. Little could Joseph have imagined that the Savior would come in this way, and at this time. But the words of the angel are unmistakable: "Thou shalt call his name JESUS: for he shall save his people from their sins" (v. 21).

That is a promise of actual, future salvation, a promise from heaven. That is a promise, first of all, to Israel, for Israel was God's people, but that is a promise also to us, because the Savior is for the Gentiles too. By faith we too are engrafted into God's people and are part of that people that Jesus saves (Rom. 11:17).

We too need a Savior who will save us from our sins. We too lie in sin and death, and on us too the light of the gospel of Christ has shined.

The salvation that Jesus will give is not a political salvation. The angel's words destroy the messianic hopes of many of Joseph's fellow Jews. It was commonly believed that the

Messiah would be a political figure. The Jews expected a Messiah who would arrive with great power, glory, and majesty and who would sweep away the Roman oppressors. The Messiah coveted by many Jews would make Israel great again: politically Jerusalem would become the center of the world. The Messiah would subjugate all Gentiles, enforce Jehovah's laws, and bring earthly peace, prosperity, and fruitfulness.

If Joseph entertained such mistaken notions, they were banished from his mind by the angel's message: "Thou shalt call his name JESUS: for he shall save his people *from their sins*" (Matt. 1:21, emphasis added). He shall not save his people from the Romans, from the Pharisees and Sadducees, from hunger, famine, or poverty, or from any other earthly ill, but from their sins. He shall save his people from sin, death, hell, and the devil; he shall deliver his people from the guilt, pollution, power, and presence of sin. He shall reconcile his sinful people to the holy God of heaven. He shall justify and sanctify his people, and he shall give to his people eternal life. That is the Savior that we need, and the Savior that God graciously gives in his Son. Any other would-be savior, even if he pretends to be Jesus, is *not* the Jesus of the Bible.

Here is the irony: while the great men of Israel were looking for a mighty king, God was quietly preparing to send his Son, the savior. While the scribes and Pharisees fixed their eyes on Jerusalem and in the palace of a great king, God was preparing salvation in obscure and lowly Nazareth. None of the wise men of that day were looking for a poor virgin from Nazareth, married to a poor village carpenter. And none of them would be looking to Bethlehem, in a stable, and in a manger, as we shall see in our next chapter.

Truly, God's ways are not our ways, and his thoughts are not our thoughts!

The same is true today: while men look for deliverance through politicians, world leaders, scientists, and scholars, God is quietly saving his people through the preaching of the gospel of Jesus Christ. While much of the church world is busying itself with changing the world, God is using the foolishness of preaching to save from their sins those who believe in Jesus Christ (1 Cor. 1:21). Those who do not understand who Jesus is, and what salvation is, stumble at God's way of salvation.

The angel did not explain the details: "He shall save his people from their sins" (Matt. 1:21). He did not explain *how* Jesus would do that. Did Joseph understand? Probably not, but it was enough for Joseph to know that Jesus is the savior. Who could have imagined that God would choose this way: the incarnation of his Son, the suffering of his Son, and the death of his Son on a cross? But that is God's way of salvation, for we cannot be saved from our sins unless satisfaction is made for our sins. That is what Jesus came to do. Yes, a great king is coming, but first he must endure the cross, before he receives the everlasting and heavenly crown.

Joseph had his part to play, for although he is excluded from the conception of this child, Joseph was chosen to be the adopted or legal father of Jesus and to be the husband and protector of Mary his mother. Mary would rely upon Joseph in the days, months, and years ahead, as even more upheaval entered their lives, but for now Joseph's fears are dispelled.

After the dream, Joseph awoke and obeyed the angel's instruction. Now there was no delay, for he took Mary to be his wife. How joyful he must have been! Mary was innocent of the sin of which he had suspected her. He could now take her as his wife and Mary would bear a son, who would be the Savior of the world!

Chapter 6

THE LOWLY BIRTH
OF THE SON OF GOD

1. And it came to pass in those days, that there went out a decree from Caesar Augustus that all the world should be taxed.
2. (And this taxing was first made when Cyrenius was governor of Syria.)
3. And all went to be taxed, every one into his own city.
4. And Joseph also went up from Galilee, out of the city of Nazareth, into Judaea, unto the city of David, which is called Bethlehem; (because he was of the house and lineage of David:)
5. To be taxed with Mary his espoused wife, being great with child.
6. And so it was, that, while they were there, the days were accomplished that she should be delivered.
7. And she brought forth her firstborn son, and wrapped him in swaddling clothes, and laid him in a manger; because there was no room for them in the inn. (Luke 2:1–7)

*H*ad you, like Theophilus (to whom the book of Luke is addressed), read these words for the first time, something would have struck you. It all seems so anticlimactic. Luke 1 has given us expectations of something incomparably great. We expect someone "great" (v. 32), "the Son of the

Highest" (v. 32), and "the Son of God" (v. 35). Elizabeth has called the child, even before his birth, "my Lord" (v. 43), and Mary has rejoiced in God her savior (v. 47). Joseph expects "Emmanuel" (Matt. 1:23). Even old Zacharias has sung of a "horn of salvation" (Luke 1:69).

Surely the birth of this great one will take place in greatness! But the birth of this great one is not at all what Theophilus would have expected. Could this really be the way in which the Son of God was born into this world?

Providentially Ordered

On the face of it, God is absent in the text. Instead, we read about human rulers: "It came to pass in those days, that there went out a decree" (Luke 2:1). But the decree was not the decree of God, at least not on the face of it, but the decree of Caesar Augustus.

Caesar Augustus, who ruled from 27 BC to AD 14, was born Gaius Octavius, and he was emperor of Rome. His granduncle was Julius Caesar, who named him as his successor and heir. In honor of Julius Caesar, Gaius Octavius took the name Caesar Gaius Julius Augustus. The title "Augustus" means "Majesty" or "Revered One" and was a title adopted by subsequent Roman emperors.

The decree of Augustus concerned tax, for all rulers require income, and that income comes from the people. Augustus determined to impose a tax on his subjects, including the Jews in Palestine. The word rendered "tax" or "taxing" in verses 1–3 is not taxation as such: it means to be registered or enrolled for the purpose of taxation. We might call it a census. This meant hardship for the Jews, because the emperor would now confiscate some of their money and property, making them even poorer. This was also galling for the Jews because Rome was a foreign power. In fact, the Jews were generally opposed to both censuses and taxation: God had punished David for numbering the people, which the Jews viewed as a warning against repeating David's folly; and the Jews preferred to pay their taxes to God (in the temple tax) and not to the Romans, who were unclean Gentiles in the Jews' estimation.

Augustus himself, of course, did not organize the taxation or enrollment: that was the task of local governors and kings who were answerable to the emperor in Rome. We know that Herod (called "The Great") was king in Judea at this time. We will meet Herod in the account of the wise men in Matthew 2. Suffice it to mention at this point that Herod was a ruthless man, who would do anything to curry the favor of the emperor in Rome and to maintain his position of power. Therefore, Herod could easily and readily have organized the tax enrollment decreed by Caesar Augustus despite any possible Jewish misgivings.

However, Luke does not mention Herod at this point (he had named him earlier in Luke 1:5). Instead, he gives the name of the governor of Syria, a man called Cyrenius. History knows Cyrenius as Publius Sulpicius Quirinius, governor of Syria from AD 6 to 12. One confusing historical note is that Cyrenius was governor *after* the death of Herod the Great (who died in 4 BC), which has led some unbelieving critics of the scriptures to attack the historical accuracy of Luke 2, for how could the taxation have taken place when Cyrenius was governor of Syria if he was not governor of Syria until later? There are two possibilities: either Cyrenius acted in a governing capacity over the region (he was, for example, a military commander at the time, and so he was in charge of the region, although the day-to-day administration was in the hands of his predecessor, Publius Quinctilius Varus [46 BC to AD 9]), or the enrollment took place in the days of Herod the Great, while the actual payment of the tax took place later, during the days of Cyrenius. Either way, the Bible is historically accurate: God's word judges history; history does not judge it.

But why should Luke—and why should we—be concerned about a taxation decree? The reason is that it was by means of this taxation decree that God executed his decree. Augustus knew nothing about God's decree, of course, but God made that ungodly, heathen emperor serve his decree, which is much more important than the decrees of petty despots. God decreed that Jesus, his Son, should be born in Bethlehem, and God had revealed that important geographical detail of his eternal decree to the prophet Micah, who lived some seven hundred years before the events of Luke 2. The eyes of the Jews therefore should have been fixed on Bethlehem, for the Savior of the world would come from there, and that is fitting, because David, who was Israel's greatest king, was born in Bethlehem.

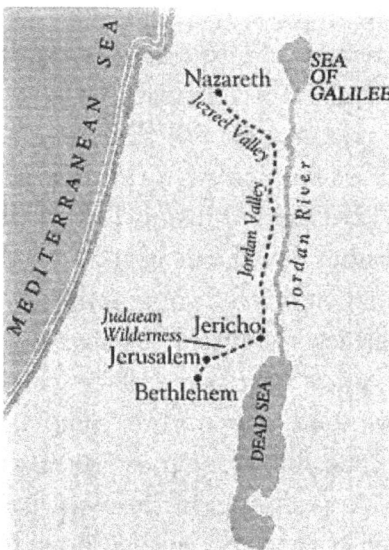

But neither Joseph nor Mary lived in Bethlehem, and there was no earthly reason why they should make a journey there at this time in their lives. The distance from Nazareth, in the northern region of

Galilee, to Bethlehem, in the southern region of Judea, was some ninety miles. Such a journey would take at least three days, maybe even five days, if the going were slow.

Besides, the timing was not right. Perhaps they might have elected to visit Bethlehem if it coincided with a Jewish feast in Jerusalem (Bethlehem and Jerusalem were about six miles apart), but the timing could not have been worse: Mary was pregnant ("great with child," Luke 2:5) and Joseph could not leave her behind alone in Nazareth. The only circumstance that moved Joseph and Mary to travel to Bethlehem at this time was necessity. If they had been permitted to choose, they would have stayed in Nazareth, and God's word would have been unfulfilled. Instead, they were forced to take whatever meager belongings they could carry and make the journey to Bethlehem.

Let the mothers who read this take note: if you were in your final weeks of pregnancy, and your husband informed you that you must take a three- to five-day journey, most likely on the back of a donkey, some ninety miles away, how would you feel? The fulfillment of God's word, however, is more important than our convenience. If God has to turn our lives upside down to achieve his purposes, he will. When he does so, although we might be tempted to complain, he does so in order to serve our salvation.

Not only was the location of Christ's birth eternally decreed and providentially ordered, so was the timing of Christ's birth. It would have been disastrous if Mary had gone into labor before she reached Bethlehem, for the child must be born at the time and in the place of God's choosing.

Joseph had to report to Bethlehem because he was required to register for the taxation in his ancestral city, for he belonged to the "house and lineage of David" (v. 4). In

Bethlehem his genealogies were preserved, along with all those who belonged to that family. Mary too was of the house of David and would be registered with her husband.

God arranged the circumstances of the lives of Mary and Joseph so that "while they were there, the days were accomplished" (v. 6). That word "accomplished" is significant: it means "filled up." The idea is that God has a certain timetable, and as time progresses, time is filled up, until finally a fullness is reached. The fullness of time was not only Mary's due date, but it was also the very moment that God had decreed for his Son to be born into this world. We read in verse 6, "The days were accomplished that she should be delivered" (or should give birth). Galatians 4:4–5 is also instructive here: "But when the fulness of the time was come, God sent forth his Son, made of a woman, made under the law, to redeem them that were under the law, that we might receive the adoption of sons."

It was not Augustus' time and it was not Herod's time; it was not even Mary's or Joseph's time; but it was God's time. From Mary's perspective, the time was wrong, but from God's perspective, it was the perfect time. The moments of time decreed by God were filled up; now was the moment for the birth of the Son of God into this world.

IN LOWLY CIRCUMSTANCES

The journey from Nazareth to Bethlehem must have been difficult, and when Mary and Joseph arrived, accommodation was scarce. Luke does not provide the many details that we now associate with the story but gives only two pertinent facts: "there was no room for them in the inn," and "[she] laid him in a manger" (Luke 2:7). From these two details, elaborate stories, nativity scenes, and plays have been developed, but we should not go beyond what is written.

We can well imagine that Joseph was keen to find a dry, warm, safe place for his wife, especially as she was very soon to give birth. But, alas, the town of Bethlehem was full—full of Roman officials who oversaw the census, and full of Jews who had come to register for the tax. Luke speaks of the inn (singular), but we are probably inaccurate when we imagine a modern guesthouse, bed and breakfast, or hotel. Most people in that day relied upon the hospitality of family, friends, or even strangers, and the Jews took hospitality very seriously. An inn in those days was a simple makeshift shelter, built on the side of a house or erected in the courtyard. Guests in such inns brought their own bedding such as a pillow or a blanket, or they wrapped their own robes around themselves to keep warm. Food was not provided, and most likely there was a place to tether their animals (perhaps a donkey or an ox).

But there was no room in Bethlehem: there was no room with friends or family, and there was no room in the inn. Therefore, Joseph and Mary had no choice but to take shelter with the animals. We know that from the word "manger" in verse 7: the reason Mary laid Jesus in the manger was "because there was no room for them in the inn." The word "manger" comes from the French verb *manger*, to eat. A manger is a feeding trough for animals. It may have been made of wood, or a kind of sack hanging on the wall. It is because of the word "manger" that the story persists that Jesus was born in a stable. Some imagine a structure for the keeping of animals or perhaps a cave. What exactly it was we do not know, for Luke does not tell us.

However, we can envisage something of the scene, and the mothers among my readers can compare this to how they gave birth to their children. Mary gave birth amidst filth and squalor. No doubt, Joseph did what he could to tidy up or perhaps to make a clean spot in the corner. Mary was not in a sanitized hospital with a team of doctors, nurses, and midwives to assist her. Her midwife—if we could call him that—was Joseph, who was there by her side as she went into labor. No cradle was prepared; no nursery was decorated; no toys were laid out; no soothing music played; no beautiful clothes were made ready for the baby to be dressed. Instead, there were animals, dung, and vermin to greet the newborn.

If Mary had imagined anything for the birth of her baby, *this* was not it. But notice how simply and reverently Luke relates the circumstances of Jesus' birth. In our curiosity, we want to pry into all the details, but Luke says very little. Listen to the simplicity of the narrative: "So it was, that, while they were there, the days were accomplished that she should be delivered. And she brought forth her firstborn son..." (vv. 6–7). It sounds like the birth of just any ordinary baby: "she brought forth." Mary started to experience the contractions and birth pangs that signal the end of pregnancy and the beginning of childbirth. Mary's water broke. And the child, after a number of hours, entered the world covered in amniotic fluid, mucus, and blood. The child's umbilical cord was cut; Joseph likely washed and cleansed him with salt (if available); and then he handed the newborn to his mother.

Notice too that everything here is told from the perspective of Mary. Joseph is not mentioned in verses 6–7, and the child is not even named. Listen again: "She brought forth her firstborn son" (v. 7). "[She] wrapped him in swaddling clothes" (v. 7). Swaddling clothes are strips of cloth, wrapped tightly around a newborn to restrict its movements. "[She] laid him in a manger" (v. 7). Perhaps she lay his head on straw, which the donkeys and oxen were accustomed to eat. In everything, the child is passive, helpless, and dependent on Mary and Joseph. And you can be sure that, contrary to sentimental hymns, he cried. How else would he indicate that he was hungry or dirty?

It all sounds so ordinary and so normal—and it is—but, dear reader, the baby born in verse 7 is the Son of God. This, dear reader, is the birth of the Son of God into the world. In this way, he chose to come, as a tiny, helpless baby, just as all of us are born. The mystery of the incarnation had occurred some nine months prior to this date, at which point, the person of the Son of God united himself by the power of the Holy Spirit to the substance of the virgin Mary, forming the human nature of Christ. In his human nature he underwent normal prenatal human development in the womb until finally, nine months later, the child was ready to be born. The result is "the mystery of godliness: God was manifest in the flesh" (1 Tim. 3:16).

What must that have been like for the Son of God? He opened his tiny infant eyes, noises assailed his tiny infant ears, and foul smells assaulted his tiny infant nose. Heaven observed in hushed silence as the Son of God was born!

If you had gone there, you would not have noticed the Son of God. You would simply have seen a tiny newborn baby. As Isaiah said, "He hath no form nor comeliness; and when we shall see him, there is no beauty that we should desire him" (Isa. 53:2). You would not have seen a child with a halo encircling his head; you would not have seen angels hovering over the spot; you would have passed him by, as others did, as unimportant, unworthy of your attention. If Mary had told you, "This, my child, is the Son of God. The angel told me that he will be great, and that God will give him the throne of David, and he will be called the Son of the Highest," you would have laughed and scoffed. "This one is the Son of God? This one is the heir of David's throne? Never!" If Joseph had chipped in: "The angel told me that he shall save God's people from their sins, and that he is Immanuel, God with us," you would have turned away in disgust, and you would have shaken your head in disbelief. "How shall this one save us?" And if Mary had repeated the words of Elizabeth that this child is "the Lord," you would have refused to believe it. Surely, such a thing is impossible!

FOR OUR SALVATION

But we ask the question—Why? Why was the Son of God born, and why was he born in this way? The Son of God was born *for us and for our salvation.* Listen to the sublime words of the Nicene Creed: "Who, for us men and for our salvation, came down from heaven, and was incarnate by the Holy Ghost of the Virgin Mary."[1] The Son of God, who is in the bosom of the Father, one with the Father and the Spirit, took upon himself our flesh and blood to be our Savior. Remember the words of the angel: "Thou shalt call his name JESUS: for he shall save his people from their sins" (Matt. 1:21).

That is why the nativity story must never be a sentimental story for us. Many see in the baby Jesus something sentimental, but the baby Jesus grew up to be the crucified Jesus, and men hate that Jesus. Do you see the manger with baby Jesus? The message of that manger is this: so sinful are we that it took the extreme measure of the Son of God becoming a human being to save us. Nothing else could

---

1 Nicene Creed, in *Confessions and Church Order*, 11.

accomplish our salvation. The circumstances of his birth were lowly as a sign of the humility of our Savior.

The Son of God could easily have arranged better circumstances for himself. God could have decreed that Jesus would be born in Jerusalem in Herod's palace or in the palace of the high priest. At the very least, God could have arranged that Mary and Joseph had a proper bed with suitable attendants at his Son's birth into this world. God could even have arranged for silk cushions, a sanitized environment, a welcoming party of well-wishers, and a procession of worshipers.

But remember what Jesus himself said: "The Son of man came not to be ministered unto, but to minister, and to give his life a ransom for many" (Matt. 20:28). Remember what the apostle Paul wrote: "For ye know the grace of our Lord Jesus Christ, that, though he was rich, yet for your sakes he became poor, that ye through his poverty might be rich" (2 Cor. 8:9). "Let this mind be in you, which was also in Christ Jesus: who, being in the form of God, thought it not robbery to be equal with God: but made himself of no reputation, and took upon him the form of a servant, and was made in the likeness of men" (Phil. 2:5–7).

The fact that there was no room for him is indicative of his entire life. It indicates that he came to be a savior through suffering. There was no room for Jesus in Bethlehem, so that he was squeezed into an obscure corner. The people of David's city were not ready or willing to receive him. There was no room for the baby Jesus. No grand announcement was made of his birth. No herald appeared to the inhabitants of Bethlehem. No trumpet was blown! No fanfare was made! When he was born, no one saw it except Mary and Joseph, and few visitors came to see him except lowly shepherds and, later, visitors from the east.

When he grew up, there was even less room for the man Jesus of Nazareth. For a while, the people tolerated him, until they understood his teaching, and then they rejected him. He was not the Messiah whom they sought; he was not the savior that they wanted; and for many today and in every age of human history (even those who become sentimental about nativity scenes and the story of the baby Jesus) he is not the savior that they want. So they drove him out of the world—not only into a stable in the corner of Bethlehem, but also on to a cross outside of Jerusalem, where he died. But God raised him from the dead and exalted him to his right hand in glory.

That was God's purpose all along, for the Christ must suffer and die. Since we are sinners, Jesus saves us only by making atonement for our sins. The baby Jesus cannot save us except by becoming the crucified and risen Jesus. The lowly birth of Jesus was the first step along a life of suffering by which he would redeem us from sin and death. There is, dear reader, in our lives, by nature, no room for the Son of God. You may have heard a sermon like this at the Christmas season: "There was no room in the inn. Won't you make room in your heart for Jesus?" Such a statement is nonsense: we do not and we cannot make room. But thank God, Jesus makes room for himself. By the power of his Spirit, he opens our closed hearts and he dwells in them (Acts 16:14), for salvation is "not of him that willeth [or accepts Jesus into his heart], nor of him that runneth [or performs works of righteousness], but of God that sheweth mercy" (Rom. 9:16).

Let us adore the mystery of the birth of the Son of God. But let us not dwell too long on the manger. Instead, let us lift our eyes to the cross, for it is not in the manger, but in the cross and in the empty tomb of the resurrected Lord, where our salvation is found.

Chapter 7

CHRIST'S BIRTH ANNOUNCED TO SHEPHERDS

8. And there were in the same country shepherds abiding in the field, keeping watch over their flock by night.

9. And, lo, the angel of the Lord came upon them, and the glory of the Lord shone round about them: and they were sore afraid.

10. And the angel said unto them, Fear not: for, behold, I bring you good tidings of great joy, which shall be to all people.

11. For unto you is born this day in the city of David a Saviour, which is Christ the Lord.

12. And this shall be a sign unto you; Ye shall find the babe wrapped in swaddling clothes, lying in a manger. (Luke 2:8–12)

In Luke 2:6, "the days were accomplished" when Mary gave birth. Mary had been pregnant with this child for some nine months, but, more importantly, the day fixed in God's eternal decree had come. The child, who is the Son of God made flesh, was born in Bethlehem. This is the most significant birth in human history, and yet how ordinary it seems. Luke does not wax lyrical in his description of it.

It appears that Jesus was born at night because the shepherds, whom we meet in this text, were "keeping watch over their flock by night" (v. 8). All was still in Bethlehem, and nobody seems to have noticed Jesus' birth. Certainly, the scene of his birth was not marked by excitement and joy, except, of course, from his very thankful parents, Mary, his biological mother, and Joseph, his adopted father and legal guardian.

But such news could not now be kept a secret—someone must be told. But who and how? God could have sent a prophet, a holy man moved by the Spirit, to announce the coming of Jesus. Instead, God sent an angel, and then a host of angels to announce the birth. To whom did these angels bring the message? The angel and angels did not announce the birth to all the inhabitants of Bethlehem. The angels did not go to Jerusalem or to Rome. Instead, God had prepared his message, and his recipients: shepherds on a nearby hill or in a nearby field would hear the angelic message.

THE HUMBLE RECIPIENTS

"There were in the same country shepherds" (v. 8). About these shepherds we know very little; in fact, we know next to nothing. We do not know their names or even their number. Were there a few shepherds or perhaps a large number of shepherds? Were these men older, mature men, or were they perhaps young men, teenagers or young boys? We remember that it was the task of the youngest son to be the shepherd in the family; David is a case in point. Certainly, these shepherds were not important men in the eyes of the world. They were unlearned or uneducated; it is even possible that they were illiterate. They did not belong to the high and mighty, or to the rich and famous. Recall Mary's Magnificat: they were not counted among the "proud," "mighty," or "rich," but they belonged to "them of low degree," "the hungry," and the poor (Luke 1:51–53). These shepherds were manual workers, and their occupation involved their living outside (the word "abiding" in chapter 2:8 means someone who dwells in the fields under the open sky); and their job was difficult and often dangerous (see Gen. 31:40; 1 Sam. 17:34–35).

However, it is clear from the narrative that these shepherds were believers. They belonged to that elect, believing remnant of Israel who waited for the Messiah. The hope of Israel was in their hearts, and as they looked at the state of the world and of Israel in particular, they must often have wondered: "When will God's promises be fulfilled? Can the situation get any darker than now? Will God make his people wait for deliverance for much longer?" Perhaps they discussed this when they watched their sheep in the lonely watches of the night. Perhaps they recalled what they had learned in the synagogue schools. Surely they mulled over specific texts of promise. Did they remember that Bethlehem would be the birthplace of the Messiah?

We know that they were believers from a couple of considerations, which come from the text. First, and most obviously, it was to these shepherds that an angel is sent. Ordinarily in scripture, angels appear to believers, and rarely, if ever, to unbelievers. Mary, Joseph, and Zacharias were believers, as were these shepherds. Second, the shepherds respond to the angel with faith, and they would not have done so if they had not already believed. The angel comes to confirm and even to reward their faith.

All is very striking and unusual: everything surrounding

the birth of Jesus is unusual and unexpected. It is unusual that God announced the birth of his Son this way. Some time ago (May 2015), the British Royal Family announced the birth of a new princess, Princess Charlotte. That announcement proceeded according to royal protocol. First, the immediate royal family and the royal staff were informed; and then it was announced to the waiting press for general release. Nothing of the kind happened when Jesus was born, and his birth is the most significant birth in human history. There was no crowd of excited fans waiting in hushed expectation. There was no press release; in fact, there was no general announcement at all. And the immediate release of information was made to lowly, obscure shepherds on the lonely hills near to Bethlehem.

Moreover, notice the timing of the announcement, for it was in middle of the night, so that no one for whom it was not intended was able to overhear it. Bethlehem was fast asleep, and they never knew or dreamt what had happened. The angel makes no delay, for he rushes immediately to tell the shepherds: "Unto you is born this day" (Luke 2:11), indicating that Jesus had just been born.

No one else heard, only a handful of shepherds. This unique privilege, to be the first to hear of and see the new-born Savior, belonged to them. If people counted it a privilege to catch a glimpse of the newborn Princess Charlotte, how much more significant to see and meet the Son of God made flesh!

Notice too whom God passed by in this announcement: the high, the mighty, and the rich heard nothing, for this was not good news for them. The mighty Caesar, who boasted the title Augustus (majestic or revered one), knew nothing of the birth of the Son of God. The wicked king Herod, who slept in his palace in Jerusalem, did not hear a peep about the birth of the King of the Jews. When he would hear some months later, he would respond in murderous rage, as we shall see. The Jewish high priest, the Sanhedrin, the scribes and Pharisees, and the Sadducees were left in the dark physically and spiritually. All their searching of the scriptures did not lead them to the birthplace of the Messiah.

But this is the way in which God operates, for as Mary sang, "He hath filled the hungry with good things; and the rich he hath sent empty away" (1:53). Jesus thanked his Father for this: "I thank thee, O Father, Lord of heaven and earth, that thou hast hid these things from the wise and prudent, and hast revealed them unto babes: even so, Father; for so it seemed good in thy sight" (10:21).

This is the great wisdom of God: God did not choose to reveal the birth of his Son to Caesar Augustus, Herod, and the religious leaders of the day. They hated Jesus, and their hatred would become obvious soon enough. Jesus was a threat to them, and as he grew up, he exposed their corruption, he threatened their power, and they killed him by nailing him to a cross.

It was to lowly shepherds, whom the Spirit had prepared by working faith in their hearts, that the angel came. It is to us and to our children that the good news comes today.

THE HEAVENLY MESSENGER

As the shepherds did what they did every night (they watched their sheep and took turns during the four watches of the night), an angel suddenly appeared to them. Angels are the messengers of God, and they do his bidding. We do not even know the angel's name (it was probably Gabriel), but that is not important because the message he brings is more important than the name of the messenger.

God sent this angel on a mission. God has various missions for his angels. Sometimes an angel is sent in judgment. For example, in the Old Testament, in the days of Hezekiah, an angel slew 175,000 Assyrians. Or in Acts 12 the angel of the Lord smote and killed wicked king Herod. But this angel was sent with the announcement of salvation.

The text emphasizes the sudden appearance of the angel and the brightness of his glory. It must have been an awesome, awe-inspiring sight. Luke 2:9 begins with, "And, lo," where "lo" is another word for "behold." The angel "came upon them," where the word means that the angel stood above them, hovering in the night sky in front of them, invading the quiet of the night. Certainly, the angel gave no warning of his imminent coming. He simply appeared like a bolt of lightning out of the night sky.

The effect of the angel's appearance was that "the glory of the Lord shone round about them" (v. 9). Bright, blinding, awesome light encircled and enveloped them. The light of the angel was no ordinary light. It was not the light of the sun or the stars; it was the glory of the Lord, the glory of Jehovah, the God of Israel. This does not mean that the angel was God, of course. It simply means that the angel, having come from the presence of the Lord, reflected God's glory.

We do not often think about the angels, but they stand in the presence of God. Psalm 103:20–22 urges the angels to worship him: "Bless the LORD, ye his angels, that excel in strength." Psalm 104:4 describes the heavenly messenger with these words: "Who maketh his angels spirits; his ministers a flaming fire." If one angel is so glorious with its own created glory and with the reflected glory of God, how much more glorious is the glory of God! How will you or I stand in the presence of the holiness of Almighty God? How will we, who are but dust and ashes, and sinful besides, endure the brightness of the Almighty when the angels themselves must cover their faces in God's presence? How thankful we must be for Christ, who gives us access to the Father!

Sometimes we are tempted to be envious of these men, but we should notice their reaction and learn from it: "They were sore afraid" (v. 9). If you want the living daylights scared out of you, by all means, desire an angelic visit. God will not grant your request, but you should at least understand what it would mean. Literally, "They feared a mega fear." This is similar to the reactions of others: of Zacharias we read, "He was troubled, and fear fell upon him" (1:12); Mary was "troubled at [the angel's] saying" (v. 29). Joseph was spared the terror, because an angel came to him in a less dramatic fashion in a dream. Perhaps Daniel has the most dramatic angelic encounter—read Daniel 10 ("a great quaking," "no strength in me," "I retained no strength," "I [was] in a deep sleep on my face, and my face toward the ground," "I stood trembling," "I became dumb," "there remained no strength in me, neither is there breath left in me"). That is the effect an angel has on a person. Angels are not cute, cuddly, sentimental creatures, sitting on fluffy clouds, but they are terrifying, powerful, spiritual, heavenly beings.

We do not know how this fear manifested itself here, but it was "great" fear. Perhaps they trembled greatly at the presence of the heavenly herald. Perhaps they fell on their faces, or terror filled their souls, visible in their eyes, as they looked at one another. Would they be struck dead? Had God come to judge them? This is the only fitting reaction of sinners in the presence of God's messenger.

Certainly the recipients of the message were lowly, but the messenger was suitably glorious. It was wholly appropriate that an angel should appear on this occasion, for the greatest event in human history had just occurred. He may not have brought a trumpet, but his presence was beyond description and his appearance literally "out of this world." Soon, as we shall see, he will be accompanied by a host of angels. But, for now, one angel was enough—the shepherds could hardly handle that.

We ought to be deeply thankful that God does not send angels to make announcements today. Instead, God proclaims the same news, which the angel proclaimed, by means of weak, sinful men called "pastors." A pastor is a shepherd, for he is called to look after the sheep of Jesus Christ. A pastor brings the word of God, and we must not despise it because it comes in a less glorious manner. Wherever the word of God is preached, God speaks. If you will not receive the word from a faithful pastor, do not expect to hear it from angels. The next time unbelievers will see angels will be to separate them from God's people and bring them to the judgment (Matt. 13:49–50).

THE GLAD TIDINGS

Immediately, the angel moves to still the shepherds' fears: "Fear not" (Luke 2:10). The reason the shepherds must not fear is that the angel brings *good news*. Literally, the angel proclaims, "Behold, I evangelize you mega joy" (Luke 2:10). To evangelize is to proclaim the evangel, which is the good news of salvation. The evangel or the gospel is not something that man does: it is an announcement of what God has done. The angel does not say, "Behold, I bring you good tidings: you must do good works, or you must repent, or you must accept Jesus." Instead, the angel says, "The good news is that the Savior has been born." This was surely welcome news to these lowly shepherds, for this is the news for which they had been waiting and longing. This is the news for which their parents, grandparents, and great-grandparents had been waiting and longing.

In fact, this is the good news for which every believing generation since Adam and Eve had been waiting and longing. Abraham had longed to see this day, as had David, as had countless others. "This day," says the angel, is the day, for "unto you is born this day in the city of David a Saviour, which is Christ the Lord" (v. 11). If Mary had given birth that day and it was still dark, then the child of whom the angel spoke was only a few hours old.

Let us examine a little more closely the content of this news in verse 11. First, the news concerns a savior: "unto you is born…a Saviour" (v. 11). We have seen this term *savior* before: Mary rejoiced in God her savior (1:47), the angel commanded Joseph to "call his name JESUS: for he shall save his people from their sins" (Matt. 1:21), and Zacharias called him "an horn of salvation" (Luke 1:69). A savior, as we know, is a rescuer or a deliverer: the one born in Bethlehem will save these shepherds and us. How will he do that? He will save them and us from our sins by suffering and dying on the cross to atone for our sins and by rising from the dead to give us eternal life. Notice how the angel particularizes the news: "Unto you [not to everyone, but to you] is born this day in the city of David a Saviour" (2:11).

Second, the Savior is identified: he is "Christ the Lord" (v. 11). The savior is not a new emperor or a new Herod. The savior is not a philosopher or a theologian. The Savior is Christ, the Messiah, the anointed of God. The Savior is eternally ordained of God and anointed with God's Holy Spirit to be the prophet, priest, and king of God's people.[1] As the Savior and Messiah (Christ) he is the Lord: he has supreme power and authority, for he owns his people and purchases them with his own blood. To him are owed allegiance, obedience, and worship.

Third, the location of the newborn Savior, Christ, and Lord is important: "Unto you is born this day in the city of David a Saviour, which is Christ the Lord" (v. 11). The angel does not say "Bethlehem" because he expects the shepherds, as believing Israelites, will know what "the city of David" means. David was born in Bethlehem, and the Savior, Messiah, and Lord is born there also. This is not only fitting, but it was prophesied in Micah 5:2. This is good news because the shepherds were "in the same country," that is, in the same local area or region. The Savior was therefore within reach of them.

The effect of this news, says the angel, is "great joy, which shall be to all people" (Luke 2:10). Joy is spiritual gladness of heart. The joy is great, that is, "mega joy." It will bring great joy to these lowly shepherds. Long had been their misery, the misery of Israel as a nation and their own personal misery as sinners. That the Savior has now come means the end of misery and the beginning of joy: if deliverance from sin, death, hell, and the devil does not bring a man joy, then nothing can bring a man joy.

It will bring great joy, "which shall be to all people" (v. 10). Literally, declares the angel, "which shall be to all the

---

1   Heidelberg Catechism Q&A 31, in *Confessions and Church Order*, 95–96.

people." The immediate reference is to the people of Israel, for Christ is first and foremost *their* savior. Jesus says to the Samaritan woman, "Salvation is of the Jews" (John 4:22). This does not mean that all who belong to the earthly nation are saved, were saved, or shall be saved, for "they are not all Israel, which are of Israel" (Rom. 9:6). Indeed, many Israelites did not receive Jesus with joy, but they met him with indifference and even rejected him in hostility.

But the joy includes the Gentiles also—we receive great joy, for all who are the children of Abraham by faith, whether Jew or Gentile, receive this salvation (Gal. 3:29). Rejoice therefore, believing reader, for unto you a savior is born, which is Christ the Lord. He was born over two thousand years ago, but we still rejoice, and we will rejoice forever, because he gives us an everlasting salvation.

The angel ends on a very important note, a note that clarifies for the shepherds and for us exactly the kind of savior, Messiah, and lord whom we should seek. The angel gives the shepherds a "sign," where a sign is an earthly phenomenon that points to a heavenly reality: "And this shall be a sign unto you; Ye shall find the babe wrapped in swaddling clothes, lying in a manger" (Luke 2:12). That was the identifying feature of the child. Do not look in the houses or in the inns of Bethlehem. Do not expect a halo over the child's head or a choir of angels singing over the location. Look for a manger!

We learned in the previous chapter that Mary laid Jesus in a manger because there was no room for them in the inn. A manger bespeaks poverty and squalor. The sign of a child wrapped in swaddling clothes and lying in a manger was an indication to these shepherds of what kind of child this would be, and therefore of what kind of savior, Messiah, and lord he would be. This child has this sign, badge, or identifying mark: he is lowly, and he lives in humiliation, in poverty, and in suffering. He is so poor that his mother has only a few rags in which to dress him and only a manger in which to place him.

But lowly shepherds, you must not stumble at that. Do not be offended at the lowliness of the Savior. Do not say, "How could such a child be the Savior? We expected something grander and more impressive." Instead, ponder the truth of the manger, for it points to Christ's suffering to come. The manger is a sign of the Savior's suffering, of his rejection by men, and ultimately of the cross on which he would die for our sins. "For unto you is born this day in the city of David a Saviour, which is Christ the Lord" (v. 11).

A Savior in a manger.

And a Savior on a cross.

Chapter 8

THE PRAISE OF
THE HEAVENLY HOST

13. And suddenly there was with the angel a multitude
     of the heavenly host praising God, and saying,
14. Glory to God in the highest, and on earth peace,
     good will toward men. (Luke 2:13–14)

*T*he shepherds' peaceful night had been interrupted.
Suddenly, the glory of God shone around them and the
angel spoke. The angel brought good news, the gospel of salvation. The Savior has been born in Bethlehem. The sign by
which they will recognize him is his poverty, for he is "wrapped
in swaddling clothes, lying in a manger" (Luke 2:12).

As the shepherds were beginning to process the news, a
second wonder occurred. Not one angel, but many angels
now filled the sky. We do not know how many, but we do
know that heaven has thousands, tens of thousands, even
hundreds of thousands of angels. The text calls it "a multitude of the heavenly host" (v. 13). This host (or army) has
not come to destroy the shepherds, but to praise God.

Most commentators presume that the angels sang the
words of verse 14. There is nothing in the text that would
forbid such an interpretation, and much to commend it. For
one thing, the words of verse 14 are poetic and therefore
fitting words for a song. The shepherds must have listened

in wonder as the angels praised God. Certainly, it was for them—and for us—a foretaste of the praise of heaven.

Let us pay attention to the angels' song, for it concerns our salvation.

A SONG OF GOD'S GLORY

It is fitting that at this point in the history of salvation angels should praise God. Of course, this is the constant occupation of the angels in heaven. Therefore, how appropriate that they should praise God also on earth. This choir of angels is representative of the hosts of angels. The Bible calls angels God's "hosts." A host in scripture is an army, for literally verse 13 says, "a multitude of heavenly bands [military units]." Consider, for example, Psalm 103:21, "Bless ye the LORD, all ye his hosts; ye ministers of his, that do his pleasure"; and Psalm 148:2, "Praise ye him, all his angels: praise ye him, all his hosts." In addition, one of God's most common names in the Old Testament is "The LORD of hosts," for he has the whole creation, whether of heaven or earth, at his command.

Shortly after the birth of his Son, God issued the command: "Go forth, my hosts: and worship my Son, who has been born in Bethlehem." We know this from Hebrews 1:6, "Again, when he bringeth in the first begotten into the world, he saith, And let all the angels of God worship him."

The angels did not go to the stable, hover above the manger, and at that location worship him. Instead, they worshiped him in the presence of these shepherds. If they worship him, shall not the shepherds also worship him? Shall not we worship him also?

How fitting this is! These angels constantly and uninterruptedly worship the triune God in heaven. Shall they not also worship the second person made flesh? It was no drudgery for the angels to worship the incarnate Son at the Father's command, for this was their pleasure and delight. There is joy in the angels' song, joy for us, but the angels also express joy. The angels are deeply occupied in all the works of God and especially fascinated by the work of redemption.

Although angels are mysterious creatures, the Bible does teach us about them. Like us the angels are creatures and therefore dependent upon God. The creation account of Genesis 1–2 does not mention them, however. Many conclude that the angels were created on the first day of the creation week because they witnessed the creation: "When the morning stars sang together, and all the sons of God shouted for joy" (Job 38:7).

The angels also observed the fall of man into sin, undoubtedly an act that horrified and appalled them, that God's creatures should rebel against their beneficent Creator. They had also witnessed the earlier rebellion of Lucifer, who became Satan. With grief they saw some of their fellow angels, maybe as much as a third of their number, join Lucifer's apostasy and become demons.

Throughout the Old Testament the angels were witnesses to God's mighty acts, of both judgment and salvation or redemption. For example, they were present at Mount Sinai at the giving of the law. Peter tells us that angels "desire to look into" the things pertaining to the salvation of God's people (1 Pet. 1:12).

Now that Jesus has been born, the angels are understandably thrilled. They see in the incarnation of the Son of God the greatest of God's wonders. This is all the more striking because the Son of God did not become incarnate for the benefit of angels, but for us. If *they* sing for joy, how much more shall not *we*? The angels did not fall into sin, and God did not prepare a way of salvation for the angels who did. The fallen angels became, and remain forever, demons, while the elect angels are, and remain forever, holy and faithful to God. The Son of God therefore did not come to die on the cross for angels. The angels are not adopted as God's children. The angels are not united to Christ through faith. And the angels do not receive Christ's benefits. Hebrews 2:16 teaches, "For verily he took not on him the nature of angels; but he took on him the seed of Abraham."

And yet it is the angels who sing!

We see from the angels' song what is important to angels and what should be important to us. Their first words are "Glory to God in the highest" (Luke 2:14). Something, declare the angels in song, has happened in Bethlehem that reveals and displays the glory of God, and we have come to sing about it. And you should sing about it too!

God's glory is the display, the radiance, or the effulgence of God's perfections. The most common figure that the Bible uses for glory is bright light. God is glorious: he is a majestic being with many wonderful attributes. God's glory is the display of his wonderful attributes so that he is seen to be glorious. Something has just happened in Bethlehem that displays the full range of God's perfections or attributes, so much so that the angels of heaven are compelled to sing about it.

This is heaven's perspective (the only true perspective) on what has happened in Bethlehem. It is not merely the birth of a child or even the birth of a child in humiliating, degrading circumstances. That is a superficial, earthly view of the matter. Man does not see God's glory because he is blind to what is true glory, and these shepherds need the angels to interpret the event for them (and us).

Consider only a few of the perfections or attributes of God on display here. In my analysis I am only scratching the surface. Much more could be said about the glory of God and its revelation in the birth of Jesus in Bethlehem.

The events in Bethlehem reveal the power of God. We know that God is powerful: he demonstrated that in creation, in his many miracles, in providence, and even in his destruction of the wicked. But the birth of the Son of God requires even more power and is a greater manifestation of power than all of those other examples. By the power of the Holy Spirit, God has formed a human nature of the flesh and blood of the virgin Mary and has united the person of the Son to that human nature.

The events in Bethlehem reveal the wisdom of God. God's wisdom is his ability to adapt his infinite knowledge in order to accomplish the greatest good, namely, his own glory. God's wisdom is on display in the creation and in all of his mighty works of providence by which in history he delivered his people. But the greatest display of God's wisdom took place when his Son was born in Bethlehem, for God defeated the devil and moved heaven and earth to accomplish that great goal.

The events in Bethlehem reveal the justice of God. Terrifying have been the displays of God's justice in the history of the world: think of the flood, or the ten plagues, or the giving of the law, or the many examples of divine punishment upon transgressors. The angels had witnessed those examples of God's justice, and the angels are aware of a place called hell, where God's just wrath is executed. But the child in Bethlehem came to satisfy God's justice, for that is why he was born in lowly circumstances, and that is why he was destined to suffer, and that is why he must end his life on the cross, to show and satisfy the justice of God, and thus to glorify God's justice.

The events in Bethlehem reveal the goodness of God. God is not only good in that he is ethically perfect, but God is also good in that he is benevolent, kind, or beneficent to his creatures. The angels knew the goodness of God, because God preserved them in their first estate and permitted them to dwell with him in heaven. But the events in Bethlehem are the most astounding display of God's goodness to sinful humans. God loves his people, he has mercy on his people, and he is gracious to his people, exactly in this: he sends his Son to be born in Bethlehem; he sends a savior, who is Christ, the Lord (v. 11).

In short, the events in Bethlehem reveal God's glory and not man's glory. Man was entirely excluded. Man fell into sin and had no way to return to God—even if he wanted to, and he did not. Therefore, the plan of salvation is entirely God's. Moreover, the execution of the plan of salvation is entirely God's: "Unto you is born this day in the city of David a Saviour, which is Christ the Lord" (v. 11). It was God who sent the Son of God into the world; it was God who formed the human nature of Jesus in the womb of the virgin Mary (excluding any activity of Joseph); it was God who brought Mary and Joseph to Bethlehem at the appointed time; and it is God who will preserve Jesus all the way to the cross and will raise him from the dead. Man did nothing.

Indeed, the events in Bethlehem are a powerful testimony to man's depravity. It is man's depravity that necessitated the birth of the Son of God, and that in lowly, humiliating circumstances. It is man's depravity that is on display when no room can be found for Jesus and when Jesus is not welcomed, and it is man's depravity that is on display when

Herod tries to kill Jesus, and man's depravity and Satan's malice shall come to the greatest expression when the Son of God is nailed to a cross.

Glory to God in the highest, and shame upon man here below! And shame upon us if we seek our own glory and do not extol God's glory!

A Song of God's Goodwill

The third line of the song, which I consider before the second, is the most difficult, for what do the angels mean by "goodwill toward men"? We think of "goodwill" as benevolence or a favorable disposition. A popular view is that the reference is to "goodwill among men to one another." But that would be altogether unfitting in a song of praise to God. Why would the angels begin singing God's praises and then extol man's goodwill toward his fellow men? Besides, there is no such thing as goodwill toward men, for here is how Paul describes men: "For we ourselves also were sometimes foolish, disobedient, deceived, serving divers lusts and pleasures, living in malice and envy, hateful, and hating one another" (Titus 3:3). That did not change with the coming of Christ: mankind was not improved when the Son of God became incarnate.

Nor does the expression mean "men of goodwill," that is, men who have goodwill toward God. The idea would be that there are certain men and women who are naturally inclined toward God, and that they will receive Jesus. But the Bible knows nothing of such men and women, for all men and women are at enmity with God: they hate him, they rebel against him, and they refuse to honor him (Rom. 8:7–8). If men and women are to believe in God, God does not seek out from among them the "good-natured" ones, but works faith in his own people so that they embrace the Savior with a believing heart. If there were such men in the world, they would boast of their own goodwill, their free will, or their tendency to seek God, and then the first stanza of this beautiful song would be destroyed: glory not to God in the highest, but glory to men of goodwill in the earth! God forbid!

The other interpretation is that God has a general benevolence or goodwill toward all men. Goodwill toward men is said to be God's general goodwill toward men. Then in this song the angels would be announcing, "Good news! God has a general, favorable disposition toward all men by which he desires to bless and save all men." This is a very popular view among Arminians and evangelicals, and even some Calvinists, because they are committed to the notion that God loves all men, blesses all men, and is gracious toward all men in the birth of Jesus. But such a "well-meant offer,"—a general disposition of God toward all men—does not save all men; in fact, most people are lost. How would such an ineffectual display of general kindness bring glory to God?

Besides that, the context of Luke 2:14 forbids such a foolish interpretation. If God wanted to announce his general goodwill toward men in the birth of his Son, why did he send a multitude of angels to only a handful of shepherds on an isolated hill outside a small Judean village? Surely he could have sent angels to many men, in many parts of the world, to make such an announcement, if that really were his intention! Clearly, God's goodwill is particular: that is why he sends a particular message about a particular Savior to a particular people!

However, those interpretations rest on a mistranslation. In almost all places in the New Testament, and in all places where the reference is to God, the word is translated not as "goodwill," but as "good pleasure" or "purpose." Remember that this song is God centered. The angels sing of God's purpose. The word that the angels use is God's good pleasure. God's good pleasure is simply that which God is pleased to do. Because God's good pleasure is that which God is pleased to do, it is something in which God delights. Because it is something in which God delights, it is something in which we his creatures—and especially now his angels—must delight.

That word "good pleasure" refers especially in scripture to God's good pleasure in election. Paul in Ephesians 1:5 finds the source of our salvation in God's decree: "Having predestinated us unto the adoption of children by Jesus Christ to himself, according to the good pleasure of his will." In Matthew 11:25–26 Jesus praises the decreeing God: "I thank thee, O Father, Lord of heaven and earth, because thou hast hid these things from the wise and prudent, and hast revealed them unto babes. Even so, Father, for so it seemed good in thy sight." (Or, so it was according to thy good pleasure.) God's good pleasure is especially revealed in this, the sending of his Son into this world to be the savior: "For it pleased the Father that in him should all fulness dwell" (Col. 1:19).

If goodwill refers to God's good pleasure, and that goodwill is "toward men," the angels mean the following: "God takes pleasure and delight in his people. His good pleasure is toward you for whom he has sent his Son to be the savior." "God takes pleasure in you, O shepherds, to bless you and to save you. God does not take pleasure in you, O shepherds, because of who you are." The shepherds know that there is nothing in them that is pleasing to God in which God could take pleasure. In fact, in them is everything displeasing to God because they are sinners. But God delights in these shepherds—and in all his people—in Christ. Lest the shepherds should doubt that, here is the proof: the Savior has been born in Bethlehem. God delights in these humble shepherds, and in us, and out of his mere, gracious, good pleasure, he has sent his Son, who is born in Bethlehem. What a wonder of grace! What glad tidings! What great joy!

Out of that goodwill directed toward his people in Christ God gives us peace, which is the final chord of the angels' song.

A Song of God's Peace

"Peace on earth": this is the song of heaven's army. Peace is something that exists in heaven, for there is peace in the being of God, peace between the Father, Son, and Holy Spirit, and there is peace among the angels. Peace is harmony, wellness, or wholeness. To be at peace means to be in a harmonious relationship with God. The angels enjoy peace with God, for they have never sinned.

Man enjoyed peace with God before the fall, but he forfeited it by his sins. Now because of man's sin, God is at war with man, and man is at war with God. Man hates God and fights against him, and peace is lost. As long as man is a sinner, peace with God is impossible. Peace must remain in heaven, but it cannot come to earth. That explains the history of this world, a history of man's inhumanity to man and a history of war, violence, bloodshed, and murder. That explains God's dealings with mankind, a history of terrible judgments because man has rebelled against his Creator.

But God made a promise to his people that he would send peace to men. That peace is brought about because of the coming of Jesus the savior. God creates peace between heaven and earth by coming to earth. The incarnation of the Son of God is the greatest announcement of peace that has ever been heard. In that great act, God says, "I am at peace with you. I am sending my Son to be the Prince of Peace."

Moreover, that coming is not only an announcement, but it also actually accomplishes peace. It accomplishes peace by uniting in one person the divine and the human. Jesus is the second person of the holy Trinity; therefore, he is fully God. The man Jesus is the true son of the virgin Mary, of her flesh and of her blood; therefore, he is fully man. The incarnation brings these two together, the divine and the human. Therefore, Jesus comes as close to us as it is possible for him to come. He becomes one of us, our Immanuel, God with us. That is crucial to establish peace, for the divine Savior suffers for our sins in the human nature.

God will not simply forgive sin, for his justice must be satisfied. But we cannot satisfy God's justice. One who is truly God and truly man does that. Since we can find no such person, God sends his own Son. That is the only way of peace, and all who reject this peace perish as God's enemies. But all who by faith embrace this peace live forever as God's friends.

What a wonder of grace: the Savior is born, to the glory of God, according to God's good pleasure, and as proof of God's goodwill, to bring us peace.

Chapter 9

SHEPHERDS VISIT
THE NEWBORN SAVIOR

15. And it came to pass, as the angels were gone away from them into heaven, the shepherds said one to another, Let us now go even unto Bethlehem, and see this thing which is come to pass, which the Lord hath made known unto us.
16. And they came with haste, and found Mary, and Joseph, and the babe lying in a manger.
17. And when they had seen it, they made known abroad the saying which was told them concerning this child.
18. And all they that heard it wondered at those things which were told them by the shepherds.
19. But Mary kept all these things, and pondered them in her heart.
20. And the shepherds returned, glorifying and praising God for all the things that they had heard and seen, as it was told unto them. (Luke 2:15–20)

It had been an eventful night for the shepherds. All had begun as normal. They were in the fields, as they usually were, keeping watch over their sheep. Suddenly, the stillness of the night was interrupted, for an angel appeared. The angel was the most glorious being they had ever seen. He shone with the very glory of God, with the light of heaven. Terror struck the shepherds: they were "sore afraid" (Luke 2:9). The news that the angel brought was incredible and wonderful. That very day the Savior whom they had hoped and longed for had been born. The angel had been sent to tell them, even them: "Unto you is born this day in the city of David a Saviour, which is Christ the Lord" (v. 11). In confirmation of the word of the first angel, a multitude of angels appeared. What a beautiful sight, and what a heavenly sound! For a few short moments they seemed to have been caught up into paradise.

But then it was quiet again—the angels had departed. The nocturnal silence resumed.

Now what?

WHAT THEY DID

As soon as the angels had departed, the shepherds resolved to go to Bethlehem. There was no delay in their decision to go. Notice verse 15, "Let us *now* go even unto Bethlehem, and see" (emphasis added). The Greek sentence contains a little word that we do not have in English—we call it a "particle of urgency." The KJV translates it with the word "now": "Let us now go." "Quickly, let's go. Up! Let's not lose any time. Let's get on the road now." They encourage one another— "Let us now go." "Let all of us now go." (If any of them was reluctant to go, the others stirred him up: "Let us now go. Something wonderful has just happened. We need to go now!"). Verse 16 adds, "They came with haste," or they hurried and rushed to go.

We might think that such a thing was relatively easy: a short stroll down to Bethlehem, and home again in time for breakfast. However, that is not the case, for they had to leave their sheep behind. They could not herd their sheep together and bring them to Bethlehem with them. The nativity scenes in which a shepherd brings a lamb are inaccurate. In addition, they had to travel some distance. Although verse 8 states that the shepherds were "in the same country," that simply means that they were in the same general area of Judea. They were not in Galilee, but they were not around the corner either. That comes out in the verb "go" in verse 15: it means to "go through." "Let us pass through even as far as Bethlehem" is a more literal rendering. In other words, they might have to pass through several villages before they reached their destination. Besides that, it was still night, so we should picture the shepherds hurriedly gathering their things together, lighting lamps, and trudging through the night on their journey.

Why did they go? Why did they drop everything and make that journey at that time? The answer is because they had heard the word of God. That is how they interpreted it: "this thing...which the Lord hath made known unto us" (v. 15). When the angel of the Lord had announced to them the birth of Christ, they recognized it as the word of the Lord. When the angels had sung "Glory to God in the highest," they understood it to be a message from the Lord. And when the angel had said, "Ye shall find the babe" (v. 12), they knew that that was a message from God: "Go, seek out the babe. Go see the newborn Savior."

The shepherds understood something about the word of God: it is not given merely for information; it is given so that we might obey it. The shepherds did not hear the word of the angel and the song of the angels and then say, "Ah, that was nice," and go back to what they were doing, as if nothing had happened. Instead, the word of God was a call to action: "Don't just sit there. Get up! Go and seek, and you will find the newborn savior, Jesus Christ."

The same is true today: when we hear the word, we do not say, "Ah, that is nice. Jesus is Lord." That truth affects how we live. We believe in and trust in Jesus Christ. We repent of our sins. We obey what God's word says. We devote our lives to the service of our Lord.

Notice, the shepherds did not make excuses. They did not say, "Ah, but who will look after the sheep? Surely we cannot go now." They did not say, "Ah, but Bethlehem is too far away, and besides, it is dark. And how will we find the baby anyway?"

In this, the shepherds are our examples: they obeyed the word of God even though it was difficult and inconvenient. Today, people will not come to worship Jesus because it is raining, or because the walk or drive is too far! If they will not come to hear, how much less likely is it that they will obey the precepts of the word! One who does not regularly attend to the preaching of God's word in a true church in obedience to the fourth commandment does not keep the other nine commandments either. When we are reluctant to hear, believe, and obey the word of God, let us receive the exhortation of the shepherds: "The shepherds said one to another, Let us now go even unto Bethlehem, and see." (v. 15).

Not only did they go, they also searched. The angel did not give them the address: "142 Main Street, Bethlehem." He gave them instructions, which they followed. They had three pieces of information to help them in their search. First, they knew the location, "the city of David" (v. 11). The shepherds, as believing Israelites, knew that the city of David was Bethlehem: "Let us now go *even unto Bethlehem*" (v. 15, emphasis added). In this, the shepherds had an advantage over the wise men who would come later: the wise men mistakenly went to Jerusalem to Herod's palace. The shepherds did not make that mistake.

Second, they knew the event: "unto you is born this day" (v. 11). The shepherds knew that they must look for a newborn baby boy. He had been born that very day. They did not seek for a mighty king, a grown man on a horse commanding an army. They did not seek for a prophet bringing words of wisdom. They sought for a baby.

Third, the angel gave them a sign: "This shall be a sign unto you; Ye shall find the babe wrapped in swaddling clothes, lying in a manger" (v. 12). This was most mysterious of all: this identified the baby whom they must seek. Look for abject poverty. Look for deprivation. Look for squalor. Do not, in other words, look for a nice house or a rich family.

We can well imagine that it took the shepherds many hours before they found a child matching that description. In fact, verse 16 indicates that their search was quite arduous. The verb used in verse 16 means "they found out by searching." If I "find" a coin lying on the street while I am out walking, I do not use this verb. (I was not looking for the coin. I just came across it). But if I eagerly and diligently look for something and then find it, I use this verb. Picture the shepherds knocking on doors in Bethlehem: "Excuse me. Was a boy born in this house today?" Perhaps they found some newborns in Bethlehem, but they did not match the description. "Excuse me. Do you have a manger here?" Perhaps they found several mangers, but no babies in them. The search may even have been discouraging: perhaps they were tempted to stop looking, but they kept going. They simply had to find the baby. He was here somewhere.

Our search for Jesus is less arduous, but it should be just as earnest. We do not need to look high and low for Jesus: we know where he is, in heaven at the right hand of God. And we know where to find him. We know how he is accessible today. He speaks to us in the scriptures, and especially in the preaching. Indeed, so near is Jesus to us that, by the power of the Spirit, he dwells in us. But do we make the effort to seek him—do we pray, do we read, do we meditate on him, do we seek membership in a faithful church, or are we troubled by cares and earthly concerns?

What They Saw

What the shepherds saw was what the angel promised: "They...found Mary, and Joseph, and the babe lying in a manger" (v. 16). Notice what they did not see. They did not see any outward tokens of glory identifying the child as Lord. Many nativity scenes embellish the scene and really take away from its simplicity and beauty. Besides, nativity scenes are idolatrous: we ought not make any visible representation of Jesus. There were no angels hovering over the place, for the angels had gone away into heaven. There was no heavenly light to fill the stable with a hallowed glow and no halo around the child's head to mark the child as divine. Furthermore, there was no star to direct the shepherds' steps to the stable. It is a mistake, reflected in nativity scenes, to place the wise men with the shepherds. Their visit was at a different time and in different circumstances.

There was nothing here to impress the senses and, in fact, everything here to repel the flesh. There was no beautifully decorated nursery, perhaps in pastels of blue. There was no soothing lullaby playing in the background, and there were no scented candles to make the place smell pleasant. There were no silk cushions or royal robes, and there was no retinue of servants attending to the child. If a child was born in such circumstances today, Social Services might be called, and the child would be taken into care. What the shepherds observed was an ordinary family in extraordinary poverty.

They found Mary and Joseph. Mary was the child's mother, and she was doubtless a joyful mother, although she was still recovering from the rigors of childbirth. She was a new mother, learning how to breastfeed and how to swaddle her baby. Joseph was, as far as they knew, the father of the child: he was the husband of Mary and the adopted, legal guardian of Jesus. He was probably anxiously trying to do the best for Mary and the child with his limited resources. Mary and Joseph were not at home: they were, in fact, far from home; and they did not even have a room in the inn.

Above all they saw the baby: they had not come to see Mary and Joseph, and the angel had not mentioned Mary and Joseph, but they had come to see the baby. "Ye shall find the babe," the angel had said, and so they did. The text emphasizes the manger: in fact, three times in chapter 2, Luke highlights the manger (vv. 7, 12, and 16). A little baby wrapped in rags, lying on straw in an animal's feeding trough! Verse 17 says, "When they had seen it." They did not see, however, only with physical eyes. They saw with the eyes of faith. Without faith, they would have found the whole scene disgraceful and offensive. By faith, they rejoiced in what they saw.

The shepherds believed three things about the child in the manger. First, they believed that he is the Savior—their Savior. The shepherds believed that this child was born in order to deliver them from sin, death, and hell. They did not see merely a helpless newborn; they saw a mighty deliverer, the one who had come to crush the head of Satan. They believed this not because he looked like a savior, but because the angel had told them that he is the Savior.

Second, they believed that he is the Christ, the Messiah of Israel. The shepherds believed that this child was the anointed servant of Jehovah, the prophet, priest, and king of God's people. They believed that all of God's promises were fulfilled in him and that this tiny baby in the manger was the sum of all of Israel's hopes. Again, they believed this because, despite all appearances, the angel said that he is the Christ.

Third, they believed that he is the Lord: the word "Lord" in the Greek New Testament is often the translation of Jehovah in the Old Testament. The shepherds believed that this child is their lord, their master, their sovereign king, and their owner and redeemer. Therefore, they certainly must have worshiped him: they did not merely peer into the manger to get a glimpse of him. They adored and worshiped him. They saw in this tiny baby the God of Abraham, Isaac, and Jacob, the great I AM, the God of the covenant, the Creator of heaven and earth. What a wonder—the Creator become a creature, the Infinite become finite, the Eternal become a tiny day-old baby!

This is the mystery of the incarnation: "Without controversy great is the mystery of godliness: God was manifest in flesh" (1 Tim. 3:16). The shepherds were—after Mary and Joseph—the first humans to see the incarnate Son of God. They could have echoed the words of 1 John 1:1, "That which was from the beginning, which we have heard, which we have seen with our eyes, which we have looked upon, and our hands have handled, of the Word of life." Did they perhaps hold the baby or touch his cheek? Did they perhaps hear him make a gurgling sound or even hear him cry for his mother's milk? What they saw was the Son of God made flesh.

The Son of God, who is eternally and unchangeably God, took upon himself a real, complete, weakened, and sinless human nature. He became a baby and was born as we are. Yet he did not look divine—you can only know his divinity by faith. The shepherds knew his divinity by faith. Listen to the words of the Belgic Confession: "The Godhead did not cease to be in him, any more than it did when he was an infant."[1]

Yet consider this: what the shepherds saw was only the beginning, only a glimpse, or a peek, into the kingdom of God. As far as we know, these shepherds never met Jesus again—if they were fifteen years old at this time, they would have been forty-five years old when Jesus began his public ministry; if they were twenty years old at this time, they would have been fifty years old when Jesus began his public ministry. They probably did not witness the adult Jesus of Nazareth; in that case, they did not see his miracles, hear his preaching, or know about his cross and resurrection. But they did have an opportunity to see this—and they grasped that opportunity—they saw the Savior. They saw their Savior, their Christ, and their Lord.

We should not envy the shepherds, therefore, for what they saw is nothing in comparison to what we see. By faith we see Jesus crucified on a cross for the forgiveness of our sins. The shepherds saw merely the manger, which was the sign of the cross. By faith we see Jesus raised from the dead on the third day, having conquered sin and death.

---

1 Belgic Confession 19, in *Confessions and Church Order*, 46.

The shepherds did not see that. By faith we see Jesus at the right hand of God coming again on the clouds of glory; we have the Spirit; we have the completed scriptures; we have it all, the whole panorama of messianic salvation. The shepherds saw only a flicker of light, but they rejoiced in it and embraced it with believing hearts.

WHAT THEY SAID

Having seen, the shepherds spoke. "When they had seen it, they made known abroad the saying which was told them concerning this child" (Luke 2:17). First, we assume, they told Mary and Joseph. It is inconceivable that strangers and shepherds could have come to visit the newborn without explaining the reason for their visit to Mary and Joseph. They must have told Mary and Joseph about the appearance of the angel of the Lord and about the praise of the multitude of angels. Undoubtedly, they told Mary and Joseph what the angels had said.

We imagine also that, encouraged by the visit, Mary and Joseph told the shepherds what Gabriel had said, about the virgin conception, the Son of the Highest, and the throne of David. Joseph must have related his dream: "Thou shalt call his name JESUS: for he shall save his people from their sins" (Matt. 1:21). "They shall call his name Emmanuel, which being interpreted is, God with us" (v. 23). Thus Mary, Joseph, and the shepherds were strengthened in their mutual faith.

The shepherds did not keep quiet: "They made known abroad" (Luke 2:17). The same verb appears in verses 15 and 17: "which the Lord hath made known unto us" and "they made known abroad the saying." More so than Mary and Joseph, who did not tell anyone, the shepherds became the first witnesses of Jesus Christ. As they passed through the villages on their way home, they told people, "We have just visited a newborn baby, and angels told us that he is the Savior, the Christ, and the Lord." "There is a baby in Bethlehem, lying in a manger, and he is Christ the Lord. Rejoice and be glad, for these are glad tidings."

What of us? Do we make known abroad what the angels, what the prophets, what the apostles, and what the scriptures teach about Jesus Christ? Do we tell our family, our friends, our neighbors, our colleagues, our fellow students, and all whom we meet about Jesus Christ? Do we tell anyone? If we do not think we can tell anyone, do we at least tell people where they can hear about Jesus? Do we offer them literature, do we direct them to our church's website, or do we invite them to lectures or worship services? If the shepherds, who had very little understanding and knowledge of salvation in Christ, could spread it abroad, should not we proclaim the good news, who have the entire gospel of Christ's birth, life, miracles, teachings, sufferings, death, resurrection, ascension, session at God's right hand, and glorious future return at our fingertips?

The reaction to the shepherds' testimony was twofold—faith and unbelief. Mary's reaction is given in verse 19: "But Mary kept all these things, and pondered them in her heart." A mother's heart loves to treasure everything about her children. A mother remembers her child's first smile, first step, and first tooth. But Mary's child was unique: she remembered the angel's words, the testimony of Joseph's dream, the prophecy of Elizabeth, and the visit of the shepherds. Verse 19 says that she "kept" and she "pondered." The idea is that she preserved them all as mementos; she carefully guarded them, keeping them safe, lest they slip out of her mind. She compared them all in her mind, trying to make sense of them. What did they mean? How could these things be true of her son? Why the birth in Bethlehem? Why the manger? Why the angels? What did all of this foreshadow for her son? Mary said little, but she thought much; she was deeply contemplative. Her faith increased as she thought on these things.

The reaction of the people is given in verse 18: "All they that heard it wondered at those things which were told them by the shepherds." The word "wondered" does not mean what we often mean by "wonder." We think of wonder in terms of doubt: "I wonder if that is true." "Wonder" here has the idea of amazement or marveling: "All they that heard it were amazed or marveled." What the shepherds said was amazing: the Christ has been born in Bethlehem. The promised Savior has come. The Lord has visited his people!

Some may have believed, but it appears that the majority marveled in unbelief. They were amazed that some shepherds from the countryside would spread such a story. Certainly, few were impressed enough to act on the news. Few, if any, said, as the shepherds had done, "Let us now go even unto Bethlehem, and see this thing." What they heard was a curiosity for a few days, but it had no lasting effect upon Bethlehem or the surrounding area. If the people had believed the shepherds' testimony, there would have been a queue of well-wishers and a procession of worshipers to see Jesus. Instead, the birth of the Son of God passed relatively unnoticed.

The shepherds went home; they could not stay long in Bethlehem, for that was not their calling. Verse 20 tells us that "the shepherds returned, glorifying and praising God." You can imagine them singing as they went, perhaps using the angels' words, "Glory to God in the highest, and on earth peace, good will toward men." Certainly, their lives were never the same again, for they lived and died in the comfort that the Savior had come, and that they had seen him. It was exactly as the angel had said: "as it was told unto them" (v. 20). Not a word remained unfulfilled: he was in Bethlehem, as the angel had said; and they did find him wrapped in swaddling clothes and lying in a manger.

What is our response? Are we curious, perhaps? Or do we worship him, as the shepherds did, and do we glorify and praise God for him, for our Savior, our Christ, and our Lord, born in poverty, born to die, and the God of our salvation?

Chapter 10

THE INFANT SAVIOR
SUBJECT TO THE LAW

21. And when eight days were accomplished for the circumcising of the child, his name was called JESUS, which was so named of the angel before he was conceived in the womb.
22. And when the days of her purification according to the law of Moses were accomplished, they brought him to Jerusalem, to present him to the Lord;
23. (As it is written in the law of the Lord, Every male that openeth the womb shall be called holy to the Lord;)
24. And to offer a sacrifice according to that which is said in the law of the Lord, A pair of turtledoves, or two young pigeons. (Luke 2:21–24)

After Jesus was born, Mary and Joseph were careful to observe the law of Moses. The events in these verses concern the first forty days of Jesus' life on this earth. They occurred after the visit of the shepherds and before the visit of the wise men. They happened when Jesus was a tiny newborn infant. On the eighth day Jesus was circumcised according to the law of Moses. On the fortieth day Jesus was presented to the Lord according to the law of Moses. Luke 2 emphasizes the law of Moses in verses 22–24, 27, and 39.

This observance of the law was the expression of this godly couple's piety or devotion to God and their love of him. Mary and Joseph were religious Jews. Jesus came from a deeply religious, devout, God-fearing home. Christians keep God's commandments today, and for the same reasons: out of love and thankfulness for the redemption that we have in Christ.

Our text teaches us something very important about Jesus: he was subject to the law. He was not exempt from it. This is true, of course, with respect to Jesus as a human being. As the Son of God, Jesus was not subject to the law. Indeed, as the Son of God, Jesus is the lawgiver. It is his law and he is the judge. Nevertheless, Jesus was (and remains) a true human being, born of a Jewish mother. Therefore, he must keep the same law that every other human being (and especially every other Jew) must keep.

That is vitally important for our salvation, which is why the evangelist makes a point of including these details of Jesus' childhood here in Luke 2. As human beings, we are subject to the law, both to its commands or demands and to its penalties and punishments. As sinners, we are subject to the curse of a broken law, and we are guilty because of our sin. Jesus came into this world to represent us: he came with our guilt already imputed to him, and he came to clear us of that guilt. He did that by becoming subject to the law, by fulfilling the demands of the law, and by bearing the punishment of the law, especially on the cross.

But his law keeping begins with his childhood. Therefore, Mary and Joseph observe the requirements of the law with respect to their infant son.

THE CIRCUMCISION

Jesus' first exposure to the law of God was on the eighth day of his life when he was circumcised. To "circumcise" is to "cut around." Circumcision is the removal of the flesh of the foreskin with a sharp implement, usually a knife, or sometimes a sharp stone (Ex. 4:25). This act involved the shedding of a small amount of blood and therefore some pain or discomfort for the child. The circumcision of a child is much less painful than the circumcision of an adult male, however (Gen. 34:25; Josh. 5:8). In Genesis 17:12 God requires circumcision for Abraham's household: "He that is eight days old shall be circumcised among you, every man child in your generations."

Circumcision was not performed in the temple. A superficial reading of the text might give the impression that everything happened in the temple on the same day, but the events were actually thirty-three days apart. Circumcision was a local affair. It was too early for both the child and the mother to go to the temple, unless they were already in Jerusalem. Therefore, the father of the child usually performed circumcision—Joseph most likely circumcised Jesus. At the same time, the child was named. In Luke 2:21 there is special mention of the naming of the child with the name given by the angel, the name Jesus, which means savior, as we have seen.

Circumcision was the official reception of the child into the people of God. It was the Old Testament covenantal sign, where the covenant is God's relationship of friendship and communion with his people in Jesus Christ in which he says to us, "I will be your God, and ye shall be my people." God declared to Abraham in Genesis 17:11, "Ye shall circumcise the flesh of your foreskin; and it shall be a token [sign] of the covenant betwixt me and you." Jesus was born into the sphere of the covenant in Israel.

Since Jesus is the head of the covenant, and since he came to establish the covenant, it is necessary that he himself should also be circumcised on the eighth day. Indeed, if Jesus had not been circumcised, he could not be the savior, for without circumcision a male would be cut off from the people of God as a covenant-breaker: "The uncircumcised man child whose flesh of his foreskin is not circumcised, that soul shall be cut off from his people; he hath broken my covenant" (v. 14). If Jesus had come to the Jewish people uncircumcised, he would have been accounted as a heathen and as a Gentile, and even as an enemy of God. Therefore, it was necessary for Jesus to be circumcised, and so we read, "When eight days were accomplished for the circumcising of the child, his name was called JESUS" (Luke 2:21).

Circumcision also had several important spiritual meanings.

First, circumcision was a sign and seal of the righteousness of faith. God promised to Abraham, and therefore to all believers, the gift of righteousness. Righteousness is a legal status in which a person is in harmony with God's standard; the theological term is justification. In Genesis 15:6 we read of Abraham, "He believed in the LORD; and he counted it to him for righteousness." When in Genesis 17 God gives Abraham circumcision, Paul explains it in these words: "He received the sign of circumcision, a seal of the righteousness of the faith which he had yet being uncircumcised" (Rom. 4:11). Therefore, the sign of circumcision was designed by God to assure Abraham and every believing Jew of the righteousness in Jesus Christ. When Abraham contemplated his circumcision, he did not trust in the external act of circumcision or seek righteousness in circumcision. Instead, circumcision pointed to what God would do in Jesus Christ. Therefore, it was fitting that the one in whom righteousness itself would be accomplished should himself be circumcised with the sign and seal of the righteousness of faith.

Second, circumcision was a sign of human sinfulness and of the cleansing of sin. God commanded the circumcision of the male reproductive organ shortly after birth. This was a powerful testimony to the truth of original sin. Every child born by natural generation is guilty of Adam's first sin of rebellion and consequently is polluted with the corruption of his nature, which pollution passes from generation to generation. The Canons of Dordt describe this as "the propagation of a vicious nature."[1] The Belgic Confession calls it "a corruption of the whole nature and an hereditary disease, wherewith infants themselves are infected even in their mother's womb, and which produceth in man all sorts of sin, being in him as a root thereof."[2]

Therefore, it is fitting that the foreskin of the male reproductive organ is circumcised shortly after birth. In circumcision the removal of the foreskin is a sign of the removal of sinful flesh. What was God saying to the Israelites when he commanded them to cut away a part of their own flesh and the flesh of the children? He testified that their sin and the sin of their children must be cut away and removed. Paul makes this explicit in Colossians 2:11: "In whom also ye are circumcised with the circumcision made without hands, in putting off the body of the sins of the flesh

---

1   Canons of Dordt 3–4.2, in *Confessions and Church Order*, 166.
2   Belgic Confession 15, in *Confessions and Church Order*, 40.

by the circumcision of Christ." The father's knife could cut away physical flesh, but only the Spirit of God ("without hands") cuts away the sinful flesh of man's depraved nature.

Third, circumcision was a sign of the spiritual circumcision of the heart. In the Bible there were two kinds of circumcision. First, there was physical circumcision: every infant male of eight days was circumcised with physical circumcision, as was every adult male proselyte. Second, there was spiritual circumcision, for not every Israelite was spiritually circumcised. Only God's elect, only believers, received that circumcision. For example, God promises, "The LORD thy God will circumcise thine heart, and the heart of thy seed, to love the LORD thy God" (Deut. 30:6). Yet there are also passages in the Bible where Israel is called uncircumcised in heart and ears (Jer. 9:26; Acts 7:51).

The circumcision of the heart is the Old Testament description of regeneration. When God circumcises someone's heart, he inwardly cleanses it by the Holy Spirit. When God circumcises a heart, he takes away the heart of stone and writes his law on that person's inward being, so that he believes, repents, and obeys. If a person has an uncircumcised heart, it makes no real difference whether he is physically circumcised or not. "For he is not a Jew, which is one outwardly; neither is that circumcision, which is outward in the flesh: but he is a Jew, which is one inwardly; and circumcision is that of the heart, in the spirit, and not in the letter; whose praise is not of men, but of God" (Rom. 2:28–29).

Why, then, was Jesus circumcised? He did not need the righteousness of faith, for he is already righteous; and he did not need to have his sinful flesh cut away, for he has no sinful flesh; and he did not need to have a circumcised heart, for his heart is filled with the Holy Spirit and perfectly consecrated to God.

Christ's circumcision was necessary for at least two reasons. First, Christ must keep the covenant, which includes receiving the sign. Second, Christ must identify with God's people, with us, which includes identification with our sin and guilt. From the moment of his conception in his mother's womb, Jesus was guilty of our sin, although never polluted by it. Because he was guilty of it, he suffered for it. Because he suffered for it, he made satisfaction to God for it. This was signified in his circumcision.

THE PURIFICATION

Circumcision occurred in Bethlehem eight days after Jesus' birth. The next two events occurred thirty-three days later. The first is the purification of Mary. In Luke 2:22 we read, "When the days of her purification according to the law of Moses were accomplished." "Purification" indicates the removal of defilement, but how was Mary defiled? The issue here is not physical dirt or spiritual sin. If someone falls into mud, he needs to wash his clothes and have a shower. If someone breaks a commandment, he becomes guilty and has to be forgiven. But this is a third type of defilement called "ceremonial uncleanness."

Ceremonial uncleanness is an Old Testament concept. In the New Testament there is no ceremonial law and therefore no ceremonial uncleanness. For that reason, the concept of ceremonial uncleanness is utterly foreign to us. However, the Old Testament saints were very familiar with ceremonial uncleanness: it was part of their daily lives. It was exceedingly easy to become ceremonially unclean. To be ceremonially unclean means to be ritually impure so that you are unable to participate in the worship of God, attend the feasts, or have fellowship with God's people. It reminded God's people of the absolute holiness of Jehovah.

One of the ways in which a person became ceremonially unclean was by bodily discharges or, as the KJV puts it, "issues." Perhaps you remember the woman with the "issue of blood" in Luke 8:43. Because of an abnormal blood flow from that poor woman's body, she was unclean. More common is a woman's monthly period (her menstrual cycle): such an issue or discharge of blood made a woman unclean. This did not mean that she was sinful, as if it were sinful for her to have her period, but she was ceremonially unclean.

In that category the law includes the natural process of childbirth, for childbirth itself made a woman unclean, ceremonially unclean. When a woman gives birth, she has bodily discharges: amniotic fluid, blood, and mucus, which make her ceremonially unclean. Leviticus 12 speaks of "the days of the separation for her infirmity" (v. 2), "the blood of her purifying" (v. 4), and "the issue of her blood" (v. 7). This does not mean that the baby is unclean (the mother is unclean), or that the mother is sinful because she had given birth to a baby, or that the act of childbirth is morally repugnant, but it is merely a matter of ceremonial defilement.

Because Mary had recently given birth, she had to be purified before she could be declared ceremonially clean again. That is why she went to the temple in Luke 2. There were various ways to be purified according to the law of Moses, depending on the source of uncleanness and the type of uncleanness. Take, for example, someone who ate food that was not clean. If a Jew ate a piece of meat from an unclean animal or touched the carcass of an unclean animal, he became defiled. That defilement continued until the evening; to be cleansed, he must wash his clothes and bathe in water. Take, as another example, someone who touches a human corpse. Such a person was unclean for seven days, after which time he had to be cleansed with water, and with the sprinkling of blood, and with the sprinkling of the ashes of a red heifer (Num. 19). There is a reference to this in Hebrews 9:13–14:

13. For if the blood of bulls and of goats, and the ashes of an heifer sprinkling the unclean, sanctifieth to the purifying of the flesh:

14. How much more shall the blood of Christ, who through the eternal Spirit offered himself without spot to God, purge your conscience from dead works to serve the living God?

According to the law of Moses, then, a new mother such as Mary was unclean *for a full forty days*. Therefore, Mary, Joseph, and Jesus appeared in the temple on Jesus' fortieth day.

That period of uncleanness for a male child was divided into two parts. First, the new mother was unclean for a period of seven days, after which time, on the eighth day, the child was circumcised (Lev. 12:2–3). After the child's circumcision, the mother remained unclean for a further thirty-three days, which is a total of forty days (v. 4). During that period of forty days, the new mother was not permitted because of her uncleanness to attend the temple services or to worship God there. At the end of the forty days, Mary had to go to the temple for her purification: "When the days of her purification according to the law of Moses were accomplished" (Luke 2:22). The law required two offerings for the new mother, a lamb for a burnt offering and a young pigeon or turtledove for a sin offering (Lev. 12:6–7). If the new mother was too poor to afford a lamb, she could offer a pigeon or dove instead of the lamb. For this reason, Mary offered a pair of turtledoves for her cleansing in Luke 2:24. This confirms to us that Mary and Joseph were poor.

All this teaches us that the birth of Jesus Christ was perfectly normal and emphasizes his true and complete humanity. Jesus was born into this world in the same messy way as all other babies. The same bodily discharges, which made other women unclean, rendered Mary unclean. Although his conception was supernatural (by the Holy Spirit), his birth was normal. It also teaches us that Mary was not exempt from the law of Moses: she could not claim, as the mother of the Messiah, that she did not contract uncleanness from childbirth.

But remember that this had nothing to do with the child. *He* was not unclean. He was not sinful, and he was not ceremonially defiled. In every sense, Jesus was pure.

THE REDEMPTION

The third ceremony performed at the temple is the redemption of the firstborn: "They brought him to Jerusalem, to present him to the Lord" (v. 22). For this reason Mary and Joseph brought Jesus to the temple. His circumcision did not require his presence at the temple: he was circumcised in Bethlehem on the eighth day of his life. Mary did not need to bring her son to her purification ceremony: *he* was not ceremonially unclean; only she was. But they did have to bring Jesus to the temple to be presented to the Lord.

There is an important Old Testament principle here: the "first" of anything belongs to God as a sign that everything

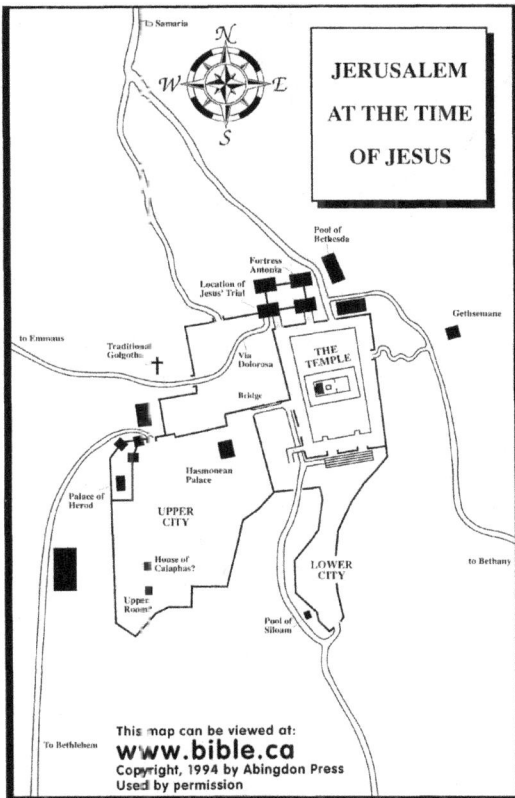

JERUSALEM AT THE TIME OF JESUS

This map can be viewed at:
www.bible.ca
Copyright, 1994 by Abingdon Press
Used by permission

belongs to the Lord. When a farmer grew his crops in Israel, he brought the first sheaf to the Lord as a token of the entire harvest, which feast was the festival of "firstfruits" (Lev. 23:10). When the harvest took place, he brought the first loaf of bread to the Lord as a token that all the bread belonged to the Lord, which feast was the feast of Pentecost (v. 17). Similarly, there was the "law of the firstborn": the firstborn son belonged to the Lord as a sign that the entire people of Israel belonged to the Lord.

This explains why Jesus is called three times in the nativity narratives the "firstborn." Joseph "knew her not till she had brought forth her firstborn son: and he called his name JESUS" (Matt. 1:25). "She brought forth her firstborn son, and wrapped him in swaddling clothes, and laid him in a manger" (Luke 2:7). "Every male that openeth the womb [the firstborn] shall be called holy to the Lord" (v. 23). Jesus was not called the firstborn only because he was born first before his siblings, although that is also true, but he was called the firstborn for deeply spiritual reasons.

At the presentation of the firstborn, he had to be redeemed. Jesus therefore had to be redeemed. The redemption price was five shekels of silver. To redeem means to "buy back"; an Israelite had to "buy back" (redeem) his firstborn son from the Lord. All firstborn sons rightly belonged to the Lord; indeed, all sons and all daughters belonged to the Lord. God made merciful provision in the law for the redemption (the buying back) of the firstborn. He did that for two main reasons, as explained in Exodus and Numbers.

The law of the firstborn is, first, a reminder of the tenth plague in Egypt. God killed the firstborn of the Egyptians, and at the same time, he spared the firstborn of Israel in the Passover. In order to teach Israel that their firstborn deserved to perish as much as the Egyptians' firstborn did, and that their salvation was by grace alone without their merits, God commanded Israel to devote her firstborn *to* him, and then to redeem them *from* him (Ex. 13:2, 12–15).

The law of the firstborn is, second, redemption from service in the priesthood. God could have taken the whole nation of Israel to be priests, but instead he chose the Levites. They were given the task of sacrificing to the Lord. God commanded Israel to remember this by the redemption of the firstborn from the priesthood at a cost of five shekels (Num. 3:12–13; 8:14–18; 18:15–16). Jesus too had to be redeemed from service in the Levitical priesthood, for he served in a different priestly order, that of Melchizedek (Ps. 110; Heb. 7).

But there is a deeper significance to the firstborn. The truth that Jesus is the firstborn is highly significant for our salvation. The firstborn "opens the womb." He does that in order to prepare the way for the other children who follow the firstborn. The firstborn in the Bible is the prominent, preeminent son: "Reuben, thou art my firstborn, my might, and the beginning of my strength, the excellency of dignity, and the excellency of power" (Gen. 49:3). God "smote all the firstborn in Egypt: the chief of their strength in the tabernacles of Ham" (Ps. 78:51). Concerning the Messiah, God promises, "Also I will make him my firstborn, higher than the kings of the earth" (89:27).

The firstborn also occupied a position of privilege, authority, and responsibility for the sake of the younger siblings. Read, for example, the law of Deuteronomy 21:15–17. When the father died, the firstborn son assumed leadership in the household and cared for the family. Jesus is the firstborn; therefore, the law stipulates that he must be redeemed with the price of five shekels.

Moreover, as the eternal Son of God and as the Messiah, Jesus is the firstborn in at least two senses. First, he is, as Paul puts it in Colossians 1:15, "the image of the invisible God, the firstborn of every creature." This does not mean that Jesus is the first one created, for Jesus is *not* created. Instead, it is a reference to his transcendent exaltation as the Creator over all creatures.

Second, he is, as Paul puts it in verse 18, "the head of the body, the church: who is the beginning, the firstborn from the dead; that in all things he might have the preeminence."

We know that Jesus is not the first one resurrected in history, for there are several Old Testament and New Testament resurrections before his. Rather, the reference is to his pre-eminence, for he is the source of life for all others who are resurrected from the dead. Without his resurrection, there is no other resurrection. Paul puts it somewhat differently in 1 Corinthians 15:20: "But now is Christ risen from the dead, and become the firstfruits of them that slept"; and in verse 23, "But every man in his own order: Christ the first-fruits; afterward they that are Christ's at his coming." Christ rises first, then at the end of history Christ will gather all his saints in one mighty harvest.

But above all, Christ, as the firstborn, redeems us, his brethren. We are sinners, guilty, depraved, and polluted in God's sight. We deserve to perish in our sins and to be and remain slaves of the devil. Jesus pays the redemption price, by dying on the cross for our sins. All of that is signified in the redemption of the firstborn. When Mary and Joseph paid the five shekels to redeem their son, little did they know that in less than forty years' time, he would pay his own lifeblood to redeem them from their sins!

What a wonder of grace! God's Son is born subject to the law, the law that we have transgressed: "But when the fulness of the time was come, God sent forth his Son, made of a woman, made under the law, to redeem them that were under the law, that we might receive the adoption of sons" (Gal. 4:4–5).

Before Mary and Joseph leave the temple, they encounter two saints of God. These two saints, one a man and the other a woman, have important messages to tell Mary and Joseph about this infant Savior. It is to them that we turn next.

Chapter 11

SIMEON'S RECEPTION OF THE LORD'S SALVATION

25. And, behold, there was a man in Jerusalem, whose name was Simeon; and the same man was just and devout, waiting for the consolation of Israel: and the Holy Ghost was upon him.

26. And it was revealed unto him by the Holy Ghost, that he should not see death, before he had seen the Lord's Christ.

27. And he came by the Spirit into the temple: and when the parents brought in the child Jesus, to do for him after the custom of the law,

28. Then took he him up in his arms, and blessed God, and said,

29. Lord, now lettest thou thy servant depart in peace, according to thy word:

30. For mine eyes have seen thy salvation,

31. Which thou hast prepared before the face of all people;

32. A light to lighten the Gentiles, and the glory of thy people Israel. (Luke 2:25–32)

*I*n every age, God preserves a remnant. When the vast majority of mankind goes astray and even when much of the visible church apostatizes, God reserves to himself a faithful few. When Elijah lamented under the juniper tree in

1 Kings 19 that he was the only one left, God reminded him that God had reserved unto himself seven thousand who had not bowed the knee to Baal (v. 18). In the days of Isaiah, the prophet declared, "Except the LORD of hosts had left unto us a very small remnant, we should have been as Sodom" (Isa. 1:9). Paul explains in Romans 11:5, "Even so then at this present time also there is a remnant according to the election of grace." The days just before the coming of Jesus Christ into the world were very dark, so dark that an observer might have imagined that there were no true people of God left.

Politically, it was very dark: the scepter had departed from Judah. David's sons no longer sat on the throne in Jerusalem. An ungodly Edomite called Herod sat there. Even that ungodly king was a mere puppet king who took orders from the Roman emperor, Augustus. The people paid taxes to the Roman government and had to endure the presence of Roman soldiers in their streets.

Religiously, it was very dark. The nation was apostate. The religious ceremonies of the temple were largely formalistic. The religious leaders were wicked, covetous, self-righteous, and cruel. The truth of the gospel had been all but lost.

Perhaps worst of all, God seemed to have forgotten about his people. The last prophet whom God had sent was Malachi, some four hundred years prior. Malachi had promised the coming of "the great and dreadful day of the LORD" (Mal. 4:5). But where was that day? There was no sign of such a day approaching. How much longer would God's people languish in their sins without deliverance? Psalm 74:9 seems appropriate: "We see not our signs: there is no more any prophet: neither is there among us any that knoweth how long."

But God does not forget his people. We have seen some of them already: Zacharias and Elizabeth, Joseph and Mary, and the shepherds are examples. Such men and women were waiting for God's salvation, and by God's grace they recognized God's salvation when it finally came.

In the temple in Luke 2 Mary and Joseph met two others who belonged to that remnant according to the election of grace: Simeon and Anna. In the next two chapters we shall consider the unforgettable meeting of Mary and Joseph with Simeon, which meeting is the greatest moment of Simeon's life, for he finally sees and receives the promised and long-awaited Savior.

WAITING FOR THE LORD'S SALVATION

About Simeon the Bible tells us very little. Scripture focuses less on the man than on the salvation that he embraced. Most commentators believe that Simeon was a very old man, although his age is not recorded in scripture. We expect that he was old for at least two reasons. First, he speaks of his departure in verse 29: "Lord, now lettest thou thy servant depart in peace." The imagery is of a servant who has waited for a long time faithfully on his master and who is now ready to die. He expects to die, now that he has seen what he had been waiting for. Many elderly saints speak in such terms: they long to depart, for their pilgrimage has been long. Second, we get the impression that Simeon had been waiting for a very long time (v. 25). That too would indicate that he was well advanced in years.

Apart from that, scripture simply calls him "a man" (v. 25). He was, most likely, an ordinary Israelite: he was not a professional prophet or a priest; he was not a rabbi or a teacher. He was a man, an ordinary believer in Israel. Most likely he was a resident in Jerusalem, for verse 25 declares, "Behold, there was a man *in Jerusalem*" (emphasis added). We would love to know more—about his occupation, his life, and his history, for example—but scripture withholds such details.

The one thing that we must know and that we do know about this man Simeon is that he was "waiting for the consolation of Israel" (v. 25). The idea of waiting here is of someone who eagerly anticipates some great blessing. It carries the idea of longing for something. We do not know how long Simeon had been waiting, but we expect it was for a long time: years, maybe decades, maybe his whole life long. If Simeon's parents had been believers, they would have taught him to wait for the promises of God, and now that Simeon was an old man he was still waiting. He was not the only one waiting, for all of God's people waited. Such a long wait requires hope, which is an assured confidence in a certain, future, promised good; faith, which is a firm trust that God will perform his word; and patience, which is the ability to endure hardship and disappointment while one waits.

The object of Simeon's waiting was "the consolation of Israel" (v. 25). "Consolation" is comfort, and comfort presupposes misery. In Simeon's day, Israel was miserable, wretched, and pitiable, politically and religiously so. Simeon personally was miserable: he knew his sins; he knew his need for a savior; and he longed for that promised salvation. God had promised salvation in the form of "consolation" or comfort. Especially the prophets describe the coming days of comfort and salvation for God's people (Isa. 40:1–2; 49:13; 51:3; 52:9–10). For that consolation Simeon waited. All pious Israelites waited for the consolation of Israel, which would occur when the Messiah would come, but Simeon had a specific promise, unique to him.

God had promised to Simeon that he would see the Lord's Christ.

Specifically, God had promised that "he should not see death, before he had seen the Lord's Christ" (v. 26). That is a remarkable promise: no one else in Israel possessed that promise. Yes, God promised to send Christ, but he did not promise that any specific person would see him. Only Simeon had the guarantee of seeing him. Countless generations had lived and died without seeing Christ, and many of Simeon's contemporaries would die without seeing Christ. Many of them waited for and longed for Christ as much as Simeon did.

This promise was not recorded in scripture. Simeon could not turn to a passage in the Psalms or in Isaiah and read, "Simeon shall see Christ." Instead, God revealed this truth directly to Simeon: "It was revealed unto him *by the Holy Ghost*" (v. 26, emphasis added). What a wonderful assurance Simeon had! Christ shall come in his lifetime, and he, Simeon, shall see him before he dies. What a motivating word of God! How that must have comforted him in the dark days in which he lived! How that must have given him hope! How that must have strengthened his faith! How that must have encouraged his patience!

Every day for years, maybe decades, Simeon had clung to that promise. Perhaps that was the first thought on his mind each morning: "Today could be the day," and at the end of every day, he lay down with this thought: "Perhaps I will see Christ tomorrow." As the years passed, and as Simeon grew older, there may have been times when he was tempted to doubt God's promise, but he knew that Christ would come and that he would see him before he died.

Surely, that promise must also have been a matter of prayer as he searched the scriptures to determine when or how Christ would come. That promise also determined how Simeon lived, for "the same man was just and devout" (v. 25). One living in anticipation of seeing the Messiah, and one waiting for the consolation of Israel, does not live an ungodly life. Promises in scripture are always an incentive to godly living, never an excuse for living in sin. A just man lives in harmony with God's standard revealed in the law. A devout man lives in consecration or dedication to God, as a pious, God-fearing believer. He worships God regularly using the means of grace. He studies the scriptures; he prays to God; he keeps God's commandments. Such a man was Simeon. This is characteristic of all who wait for the coming of the Messiah. Compare Simeon with Zacharias and Elizabeth (Luke 1:6) and with Joseph (Matt. 1:19).

This does not mean, of course, that Simeon was a sinless man, but he was a man who loved God and served him from the heart, albeit imperfectly. In Luke 2:29, Simeon calls God "Lord," a title that refers to God's sovereignty and power; and he designates himself "thy servant," a term that refers to Simeon's loyal, devoted service to God for many years.

For years, decades, Simeon had lovingly, devotedly, patiently served God. One of the reasons Simeon so looked forward to seeing the Messiah was his understanding of his own sins. He needed the Messiah to forgive his sins, for he understood that the great work of the Messiah was to take away Israel's iniquities.

We are like Simeon in this respect, for we also wait for Christ's coming. For us, of course, Christ has already come: we live after the birth, life, death, resurrection, and ascension of the Lord Jesus. We live in the glory days of the New Testament age. The Spirit has been poured out. The church is being gathered. But we are also waiting: we are waiting for Christ's second coming. We do not have the same specific promise that Simeon did, for we have no guarantee that Christ will return in our lifetime, but we eagerly wait for, and live for, the return of our Lord (Rom. 8:24–25; 1 Thess. 1:10; 1 John 3:2–3).

That determines how we live. God's grace teaches us, while we wait for Christ, to live "soberly, righteously, and godly, in this present world" (Titus 2:12). Because we eagerly wait for Christ, we keep ourselves "unspotted from the world" (James 1:27). Since we have such precious promises in Christ, we "cleanse ourselves from all filthiness of the flesh and spirit, perfecting holiness in the fear of God" (2 Cor. 7:1). Because we anticipate the coming of Christ, we watch and keep our garments, lest we walk naked, and they see our shame (Rev. 16:15).

A holy and pious waiting for Christ always has as its fruit a life of good works.

SEEING THE LORD'S SALVATION

Imagine Simeon's excitement when the Spirit moved him to enter the temple: "He came by the Spirit into the temple" (Luke 2:27). The passage indicates that the Spirit worked in a special way in Simeon's life. In verse 25 we read, "The Holy Ghost was upon him." In verse 26 Luke adds, "It was revealed unto him by the Holy Ghost." Now in verse 27 we read, "He came by the Spirit into the temple." A man like Simeon was often in the temple, but this day was different. The Spirit moved Simeon to go to the temple at that exact moment. Perhaps Simeon did not know why the Spirit moved him, but he obeyed his leading.

The Spirit directed Simeon toward one particular couple among the crowds of worshipers in the temple. They were carrying a newborn baby boy, who was now only forty days old. Simeon approached this couple, whose names he did not know, but whom we know as Mary and Joseph. Simeon took their baby, who, unknown to Simeon, was called Jesus, and held him in the curve of the arm in which one cradles a baby.

What a beautiful and moving scene this is! Simeon is an old man, and he holds a tiny baby. Think of the picture of a grandfather holding his newborn grandson or even great-grandson. The baby is just over a month old—tiny and helpless, unaware of what is happening, and Simeon has never seen him before or met his parents before. Mary and Joseph have come to the temple for Mary's purification and for the presentation of the firstborn son to the Lord. This man Simeon is not a relative but a complete stranger. Yet he insists on holding their baby, which they permit him to do.

Simeon speaks the words of verses 29–32, which is often called Simeon's song. For Simeon this is the greatest day of his life, the day for which he had waited, hoped, and prayed. Finally, he sees the Lord's Christ.

The baby did not look like the Lord's Christ, for he had no power, no outward glory, and his family was poor and undistinguished in Israel. If Simeon had looked for some mighty king, perhaps for a majestic ruler riding on a horse or commanding an army against the Romans, he would have been disappointed. But Simeon is not disappointed. He is thrilled. The Lord's Christ was a baby, and when he saw the Lord's Christ, he saw a baby, but by faith he recognized the significance of that little child: "Mine eyes have seen thy salvation" (v. 30).

Notice three things that Simeon says about the Lord's Christ.

First, Simeon sees salvation. Salvation is deliverance or rescue. When God saves us, he delivers us from sin. He pardons the guilt of our sin; he removes the curse of sin; he cancels the penalty of sin; he cleanses us from the defilement of sin; and he delivers us from the power of sin. Those benefits comprise only the negative aspect of salvation: salvation is never merely escape from damnation. Salvation is to be brought into possession of the greatest possible blessedness, eternal life, which is life with God forever. Salvation, then, is deliverance from the greatest evil (sin) into enjoyment of the greatest good (fellowship and life with God). Simeon recognized all that in the little child whom he cradled in his arms.

Salvation is the work of God. Speaking to the Lord, Simeon says, "Mine eyes have seen thy salvation, *which thou hast prepared*" (vv. 30–31, emphasis added). Salvation is never a work of man, or even a cooperative effort between God and man. Simeon had no part to play in his own salvation. Simeon's calling was simply to wait for God's salvation. Simeon could not prepare that salvation, and Simeon could not bring that salvation into being. While Simeon and countless other faithful souls had been waiting, God was preparing salvation: he prepared it before the foundation of the world; he prepared it in the calling of Abraham; he prepared it in the four hundred years of Egyptian bondage; he prepared it in the conquest of Canaan; he prepared it in the raising up of David; and he prepared it during the Babylonian captivity. Despite the folly and sinfulness of Israel and despite the opposition and malice of Satan, God prepared salvation. Now the salvation had arrived and Simeon held it in his arms!

Second, Simeon sees a universal Savior, that is, a Savior for both Jews and Gentiles. Sometimes we get the impression that the Jews in Jesus' day were very bigoted because they viewed the Savior as only for Israel. That is certainly true of some Jews. The view of the Pharisees, for example, was that the Gentiles are only fit to be firewood for hell! The Pharisees despised the Gentiles as dogs. They could never imagine that God would ever save the Gentiles. But Simeon had a different view, for he says of God's salvation that God prepared it "before the face of all people" (literally, "all the peoples," verse 31), and that God's salvation is "a light to lighten the Gentiles" (v. 32).

In fact, Simeon calls Christ "a light to lighten the Gentiles" first *before* he mentions salvation's relationship to Israel. Jesus is the light sent into the world to lighten (or enlighten) the Gentiles. This presupposes that the Gentiles dwell in darkness, and we do. We dwell in thick, spiritual darkness, the darkness of sin and death. Jesus brings light, because he is the light. He brings the knowledge of God to the ignorant and foolish; he brings joy to the miserable; and he brings holiness to the defiled and depraved. Simeon knew the Old Testament scriptures and how they promised salvation for the Gentiles through the Messiah (Isa. 49:6; 60:1–3).

Third, Simeon sees Christ as the glory of Israel. Israel boasted in many things, but Simeon saw the real glory of Israel. Israel boasted in the temple, which stood among them, but Simeon understood that the temple is nothing without the Messiah, who is its glory. Israel boasted in the law of Moses, which distinguished the Jews from other nations, but Simeon understood that the law is nothing without the Messiah, of whom the law speaks and whom the law promises. Israel boasted in physical descent from Abraham, but

Simeon understood that the seed of Abraham, the promised Son of Abraham, is the Messiah (Gal. 3:16). Jesus Christ is the glory of Israel. Jesus explained it this way: "Salvation is of the Jews" (John 4:22).

It was the great glory, privilege, and honor of Israel that Jesus according to the flesh came from the Jewish nation, that he is a true son of Abraham, Isaac, and Jacob and the true seed of David (Rom. 9:4–5). The glory of Israel was always the presence of God, for God dwelled in their midst in the cloud of Shekinah glory. But Israel had become an empty shell, for God's glory had departed from the temple. Now the glory had returned in the person of the Son of God, and Simeon was one of the few to see it with the eyes of faith.

Simeon's faith is remarkable because of what he saw and because of what he did not see. Simeon did not witness one single miracle or hear one single sermon of Jesus Christ. No angel visited Simeon, as Gabriel had visited Mary, Joseph, Zacharias, and the shepherds. Yet Simeon believed with all his heart that this child is the Lord's salvation. Simeon did not witness this child grow up to heal the sick, cleanse the lepers, feed the five thousand, calm the storm, or raise the dead. Simeon did not see the crucifixion of the Son of God, and Simeon was not a witness to Jesus' resurrection. Yet, for all that, he believed!

If Simeon believed by the power of the Holy Spirit after seeing a helpless child, how are the Jews without excuse who rejected Jesus after seeing all his miracles? And how shall we be without excuse, if we reject Jesus after reading his sermons, reading the account of his miracles, and reading of his death and resurrection in scripture? It is remarkable how readily the elect remnant believed on the scantest of evidence.

How did Simeon know that this baby would accomplish his salvation? How did the shepherds believe in Jesus? How did the wise men believe in Jesus?

The answer is really quite simple: Simeon believed, and we believe, not because he or we have evidence (which evidence even the unbeliever has), but because of the power of the Spirit, who works faith in our hearts. Only if Jesus enlightens us will we ever believe. Do you see in Jesus the light that lightens you; do you see in him your salvation; do you see in him glory? If you do, do not boast in your wise choice, but give all glory to God, and like Simeon you will rejoice.

REJOICING IN THE LORD'S SALVATION

If you had been there, you would have seen Simeon's face beaming with joy. Now that Simeon had seen the Lord's salvation, he was ready to go home. Simeon had been like a watchman waiting for the dawn of the new age, and he had seen a glimpse of it in the face of this baby Jesus. Now there was no more reason for him to remain in this world. He had reached the goal of his life, and he asks to be relieved of his duty. What beautiful words he speaks in Luke 2:29: "Lord, now lettest thou thy servant depart in peace." That word "depart" means to loosen, to let go, to release, or to dismiss. Simeon had served the Lord for many years. Now, with the blessing of God, he is resigning his post; he is leaving; he is being released, for his work is done.

Everything that God had said, according to his word, has been fulfilled.

That is a beautiful testimony: to go in peace, or to depart in peace. Simeon has no fear of death: for him to die is to "depart in peace" (v. 29). Simeon faces death, which may have occurred soon after this meeting with the infant Jesus, with calm repose and even with delight. Simeon is ready to depart and to be with his God, whom he has served, whether today, tomorrow, or next week. For Simeon, to live is Jehovah and to die is gain. For Simeon, life is peace with God, and death is a fuller enjoyment of that peace. "Our death," teaches the Heidelberg Catechism of the death of the believer, "is not a satisfaction for our sins, but only an abolishing of sin, and a passage into eternal life."[1]

That is only possible because of God's salvation: Simeon fully believes that all of his sins are forgiven because of the coming of that child. He may not understand all the details, for the redemption of the cross has not yet occurred; he leaves them to God, but he believes.

We have an even greater reason to depart in peace, because, unlike Simeon, we have the full picture. We know not only that Jesus is the Lord's salvation, but we also know *how* he is the Lord's salvation. We know, unlike Simeon, that Jesus died upon the cross to atone for our sins; we know, unlike Simeon, that Jesus rose again from the dead; and we know, unlike Simeon, that Jesus ascended into heaven, sits at God's right hand, and will come again.

If Simeon could rejoice, how much more can we! Let us wait for that day, and as we wait, let us see Jesus as our salvation, and let us serve God, waiting for the day when we too will depart in peace according to his word.

---

1 Heidelberg Catechism A 42, in *Confessions and Church Order*, 100.

Chapter 12

SIMEON'S PROPHECY
OF CHRIST'S REJECTION

33. And Joseph and his mother marvelled at those things which were spoken of him.
34. And Simeon blessed them, and said unto Mary his mother, Behold, this child is set for the fall and rising again of many in Israel; and for a sign which shall be spoken against;
35. (Yea, a sword shall pierce through thy own soul also,) that the thoughts of many hearts may be revealed. (Luke 2:33–35)

When Mary and Joseph brought their newborn to the temple, they did not expect to be the center of attention. But Jesus' birth brought many surprises. Mary was troubled when Gabriel first appeared to her. She must have been astonished when her cousin Elizabeth called her "the mother of [her] Lord" (Luke 1:43). And it must have been a surprise when shepherds turned up to worship her newborn son. We are told in chapter 2:33 that "Joseph and his mother marveled at those things which were spoken of him." What Simeon had said was marvelous or astonishing: "Mine eyes have seen thy salvation, which thou hast prepared before the face of all people; a light to lighten the Gentiles, and the glory of thy people Israel" (vv. 30–32). Certainly, Mary and

151

Joseph had not been expecting such a reception from an old man whom they had never met.

But then Simeon's demeanor changed. Perhaps a shadow passed over his face. He became solemn, because he had another astonishing word to utter. This word is different from all the other words that we have heard concerning this child. Gabriel, Elizabeth, Joseph, the angels, and the shepherds have spoken only good things concerning the future of this child. No one has breathed a word about future suffering. There have been indications, for example in the sign of the manger, but nothing has been spelled out.

It is Simeon who first brings explicit prophecy that this child shall be rejected. The Spirit was on Simeon, and he gives him a glimpse into the future, which Simeon faithfully relays to Mary, who will live to see the fulfillment of that prophecy. This is both an inspiring prophecy and a necessary warning. The way to the throne for Jesus is the way of suffering, the way of the cross.

A Contradicted Sign

"This child is set...for a sign" (v. 34). A sign is something remarkable, unusual, or distinguished. Christ will, when he becomes an adult, attract attention. By his teaching he will be noticed; his behavior will make him stand out; and his miracles will make him notable. In fact, no one in Israel will be able to ignore Jesus of Nazareth. Everyone will have an opinion about him, one way or another. That is because he is, and will claim to be, the Messiah and the Son of God.

But more than that, a sign is something remarkable that points away from itself to something greater. Jesus Christ will be God's sign, a sign from God, a sign directing men's attention to the Almighty. Everything Jesus does will be to glorify God, to point to God, and to make God known. The teachings of Jesus will be about God and the kingdom of God; his miracles will demonstrate the power and grace of God; those who see him will see God. They will not be able to avoid seeing God. Jesus said, "He that hath seen me hath seen the Father" (John 14:9).

That Jesus is a sign is deliberate, for Simeon warns in Luke 2:34, "This child is set." That word "set" means placed, put, or appointed. The Jews did not make Jesus into a sign. The disciples did not promote Jesus as the sign. Jesus did not even make himself a sign. God set him as a sign. God deliberately placed Jesus as a sign in the midst of Israel: he placed him there to testify of God. God vindicated him in the midst of his people, for he confirmed Christ's teaching by authenticating it with miracles (Acts 2:22). By placing Jesus as a sign, God forcefully confronted Israel with his Son: "This is my Son. Hear ye him. What think ye of him?" No one who encountered Jesus could be left in doubt that they had met the Son of God.

The same thing is true today. Jesus is still the sign, which God has set in the midst of the world, a sign that confronts sinful mankind and demands a response. When God raised his Son from the dead, poured out the Spirit, and sent forth the gospel, he placed Jesus as a sign in the midst of the world. As it were, in the gospel, God sets up a beacon of light or unfurls a banner. The whole Bible with every faithful sermon testifies of Christ: This is my Son. I, the Almighty God, command every one of you to believe in him. "In that day there shall be a root of Jesse, which shall stand for an ensign of the people; to it shall the Gentiles seek: and his rest shall be glorious" (Isa. 11:10).

But that sign, says Simeon, "shall be spoken against" (Luke 2:34). God will set (or place or put) a sign right in the middle of Israel, which will clearly and unmistakably glorify him, but the sign shall be contradicted. This is the first word Mary has heard about her Son that indicates that he will not be received, but rejected. Gabriel announced to her the conception of the child in her womb by the power of the Holy Spirit, but he breathed no word about this. Gabriel even promised that God would give David's throne to her son, but now Simeon indicates a difficult path to that throne. None of the others, such as Joseph, Elizabeth, or the shepherds, made mention of the fact that Jesus would be "spoken against" (v. 34).

This word is very solemn and very unexpected. You would imagine that Israel, who claimed to be waiting for the Messiah, would enthusiastically and joyously welcome God's sign. Instead, warns Simeon, "This child is set...for a sign which shall be spoken against" (v. 34). Jesus, warns Simeon, will be contradicted, rejected, and opposed. The word Simeon uses indicates prolonged, continuous contradiction. A possible translation is "for a sign continuously being spoken against."

So it was. Christ was not contradicted once or twice, on a few isolated occasions. People were *always* contradicting him and speaking evil of him. Just think of his life on this earth. His first opponent was King Herod, who tried to kill him. As soon as Jesus appeared in public, the Jews opposed him; his fellow Nazarenes rejected his preaching; the Jewish leaders called him a blasphemer, a winebibber, and a glutton; he was labeled a man with a devil; he was slandered as one in league with the prince of the devils; he was condemned as an alleged law breaker; and he was vilified as a deceiver of the people. The Pharisees, who hated him, even persecuted those who confessed him. The common people rejected him: "He hath a devil, and is mad; why hear ye him?" (John 10:20). "Not this man, but Barabbas" (18:40).

Finally, the opposition to Jesus was so great that they crucified him. At his trial, the Sanhedrin declared him a blasphemer, worthy of death. They accused him before Pontius Pilate: "We found this fellow perverting the nation, and forbidding to give tribute to Caesar, saying that he himself is Christ a King" (Luke 23:2). Finally, they cried out, "Away with him! Crucify him!" and even when he was on the cross, they still spoke against him. Acts 28:22 sums it up: "As concerning this sect, we know that every where it is spoken against."

Nothing has changed. Jesus, the sign of God, is still spoken against, everywhere, and by everybody. There is scarcely a place under heaven where the name "Jesus" is not employed as a curse word. Where the name of Jesus is mentioned, the reaction to that name is irritation, annoyance, anger, and sometimes even violence. The fact that Jesus is—as Simeon prophesied—"a sign which shall be spoken against" (Luke 2:34) explains all the opposition to Jesus and his church in all ages, including today.

THE DIVINE PURPOSE

God has a purpose in setting Christ as a sign in the midst of Israel. Notice that word "set" again in verse 34: "Behold, this child is set for." This is a very difficult word for many people to accept. Most professing Christians will say that some will believe in Jesus and be saved. Some professing Christians will even concede that some will stumble at Jesus and perish.

Most professing evangelicals agree so far. But Simeon is much more emphatic than that, for Simeon indicates divine intention. That word "set" means to place or to put. It also means to appoint. God put Jesus Christ as a sign in the midst of Israel with the deliberate, purposeful intention that many would fall: "This child is set *for* the fall...of many" (v. 34, emphasis added). God put Jesus Christ as a sign in the midst of Israel with the deliberate, purposeful intention that many would be saved and others would be damned: "This child is set for the fall and rising again of many in Israel." Christ is, by God's design, the occasion of the fall of some and the occasion of the salvation (the rising again) of others. Moreover, God determines who falls and who is saved, which is the very point that Simeon is making here.

Negatively, "This child is set for the fall...of many" (v. 34). The word "fall" refers to spiritual ruin, destruction, and ultimately damnation. The same word appears in Matthew 7:27: "The rain descended, and the floods came, and the winds blew, and beat upon that house; and it fell: and great was the fall of it." Many in Israel shall see the sign of Jesus, they shall speak against it, and they shall stumble with a fatal, ruinous, calamitous fall into perdition and hell. That is God's intention, for "this child is *set* for the fall...of many."

How true this was! Many, even the majority of people in Israel, hated Jesus; they were offended at his teachings; they stumbled at his miracles, and they fell. But in doing so, they fulfilled God's purpose—God's sovereign, good, wise, and just purpose—of reprobation. This too was prophesied. Simeon is not the only one to speak of this. Consider Isaiah 8:14–15, 1 Peter 2:6–8, and Matthew 21:42–44.

God's second purpose with Christ, which is really his main and primary purpose, is salvation. We must never forget that reprobation serves election. "This child is set for the...rising again of many in Israel" (v. 34). The phrase "rising again" simply means "resurrection."

The English reads as if the people who fall are the same who then rise again, but that is not the meaning of Simeon's words. The meaning is rather that this child is set for the fall of some and for the resurrection of others. Some stumble at the contradicted sign and perish, according to God's purpose. Others believe in the contradicted sign, and even repent of their earlier blasphemous speech against him, and are saved, again, according to God's purpose. The word "resurrection" is significant, for it means that salvation is a rising from the dead. When a sinner is saved, he is raised from the spiritual death of sin and guilt, and he is delivered from the death of corruption or spiritual slavery.

Again, how true this was! Many in Israel, and beyond Israel, were raised to new life through their encounter with Jesus Christ. Many who lay in the misery of sin, signified by leprosy, or lameness, or blindness, or even physical death, were saved from their misery by the touch or the word of Jesus Christ. To many Jesus spoke the comforting words, "Go in peace. Thy faith hath made thee whole." There were even some who began by railing against him, but who came to repentance later. The thief on the cross is an example of this (compare Matthew 27:44 with Luke 23:39–43), as is the apostle Paul, who persecuted Jesus and was later brought to saving faith. Many in Israel and later among the Gentiles beheld in Jesus the Messiah and the Lord, and they believed in him by the power of the Holy Spirit. Yes, indeed, "this child is set [by God] for the...rising again of many in Israel" (2:34)!

These two things are connected, for God used the fall of many in Israel to accomplish the salvation of many others in Israel and beyond. God brought Jesus to the cross *exactly through* the wicked stumbling at him. Had Judas Iscariot not betrayed him, because Jesus was set for the fall of Judas Iscariot, the events on Calvary's cross would not have occurred. If the Pharisees, Sadducees, and scribes had not hated him, because Jesus was set for the fall of the Pharisees, Sadducees, and scribes, Jesus would never have been crucified (see John 15:25). If Pontius Pilate, Herod, and the people of Israel had not rejected him, because Jesus was set for the fall of Pontius Pilate, Herod, and the people of Israel, Jesus Christ would never have died on the hill of Golgotha. That is a great mystery and wonder. Those wicked men were accountable for their sins, they willingly and willfully rejected Jesus, and yet they performed their wicked deeds because God determined it (Acts 2:23; 4:27–28).

On the cross, Jesus, the contradicted sign, makes atonement for sin, and by doing so, he destroys Satan, abolishes death, removes sin and guilt, and brings in everlasting life and immortality, all according to God's eternal good purpose.

The reprobate in Israel and among the Gentiles stumbled into perdition and perished so that the elect might receive the gift of eternal life purchased on the cross. Jesus became the contradicted sign so that he could bear the wrath of an offended God and bear the curse of a broken law, to procure for us the salvation of a reconciled God and Father. Those great truths are contained in Simeon's significant word, "This child is set for the fall and rising again of many in Israel; and for a sign which shall be spoken against" (Luke 2:34).

With that there is a third purpose, namely, "that the thoughts of many hearts may be revealed" (v. 35). God placed Jesus as a sign, which shall occasion the fall and rising again of many in Israel, to reveal the thoughts of men. Jesus did this through his preaching and miracles and through his explicit claims to be the Son of God. When you set up a sign like a beacon of light in a dark place, you will reveal what is occurring in the dark. This will have a twofold effect, for some will be attracted to the light and come and dwell under it, while others will be scattered and will scurry deeper into the darkness.

19. And this is the condemnation, that light is come into the world, and men loved darkness rather than light, because their deeds were evil.
20. For every one that doeth evil hateth the light, neither cometh to the light, lest his deeds should be reproved.
21. But he that doeth truth cometh to the light, that his deeds may be made manifest, that they are wrought in God (John 3:19–21).

22. If I had not come and spoken unto them, they had not had sin: but now they have no cloak for their sin.
23. He that hateth me hateth my Father also.
24. If I had not done among them the works which none other man did, they had not had sin: but now have they both seen and hated both me and my Father (15:22–24).

This revelation of thoughts was necessary because there were many hypocrites lurking in Israel who had to be exposed. There were many in Israel who professed to be waiting for the Messiah to come, but when God placed the Messiah among them, they showed what was truly in their hearts: unbelief and sin. Observe how the Pharisees, Sadducees, and scribes reacted to Jesus. He exposed their hypocrisy, self-righteousness, and worldliness. It was this especially that caused his enemies to hate him. When they encountered holiness, it exposed their wickedness. Their response was not to repent, but to seek to extinguish the light.

The same thing happens today. Nothing exposes what is in a man's heart more than an encounter with Jesus in the gospel. Men will gladly talk about God in general and in the abstract. They are happy to have a philosophical or theological discussion about the divine. But if you really want to provoke a reaction, talk about Jesus and talk about the cross. There is the real dividing line. Some will be revealed as inveterate haters of Christ, and others will be brought to shame and sorrow, and ultimately to repentance and faith in him.

A Piercing Sorrow

Every mother has high hopes for her son, especially when she holds him in her arms as a tiny baby. Jesus was forty days old when Simeon brought this crushing news. Mary looked forward to Jesus living a long, happy, and fulfilled life. Every mother dreams of such a future for her children, and she thinks about what might become of her son or daughter. But Mary had greater reason to be optimistic: her Son is the Messiah; he will rule; he shall be called the Son of the Highest, even the Son of God. But Simeon had sobering news for Mary, news that must have startled, shocked, and unsettled her. Your Son will bring division, for not all men will welcome him, so do not expect crowds of adoring fans following him. Nevertheless, as crushing as this word is to a mother's heart, it is also a merciful word for Mary, for it is good to have honest, realistic expectations, and thus to be prepared for the future.

Simeon adds the personal application to Mary of Luke 2:35: "Yea, a sword shall pierce through thy own soul also." This division and opposition will bring you great sorrow, Mary. The sword is a symbol of intense pain, anguish, sorrow, and suffering. Simeon refers to a long, sharp sword. Imagine such a sword slowly passing through Mary's soul or heart; as it passes through her soul, she feels intense pain, for the sword tears and lacerates Mary's heart. Thus the rejection of Jesus will deeply affect Mary. She will see the people turning against her son, and it will cause her pain. But the greatest pain that Mary shall experience will be at the cross. She will stand helplessly at the foot of the cross while her beloved son suffers and dies. That is something no mother should ever have to see, but Mary will see it. When she does, a long, sharp sword will slowly pass through her soul.

Although Simeon mercifully forewarned Mary of the coming sorrow, the suffering of Jesus on the cross was unexpected for Mary and for all the disciples and followers of Jesus. The archangel Gabriel had not mentioned this aspect of the Messiah's work, and Simeon had only vaguely referred to it. The general opinion among Jesus' followers—and this includes Mary—was that Jesus was the Messiah and that he would establish some kind of kingdom. What Jesus' followers, including Mary, failed to grasp was that Jesus would establish the kingdom of God by *dying* to pay the penalty for sin. That none understood this is clear because none expected the cross. Mary was not prepared for it, and even less did she expect the resurrection.

We need to understand what Mary failed to grasp, that Jesus' sufferings were both necessary and beneficial. We need to understand that Jesus' sufferings were necessary for our salvation. Had Jesus simply preached the sermon on the mount, healed the multitudes, and then ruled in Jerusalem *without the cross and resurrection*, we could not be saved. Without Jesus' atonement there could be no possibility for our entering into the kingdom of God: Jesus would have a kingdom with no citizens because sinners cannot be citizens unless their sins are forgiven.

Moreover, Mary contributed nothing to salvation because Jesus must suffer *alone*. The Roman Catholic Church tries to make Mary a co-redeemer or co-redemptrix, arguing that Mary actively offered up her son and therefore participated in the redemption of the world. We repudiate such teaching. Mary did not actively offer up her son, for she had no choice in the matter; and if she had been allowed to choose, she would have desired to take Jesus down from the cross to save him from death. It was not until after the resurrection that the followers of Jesus understood the necessity of the death of Christ.

The sorrows of Mary were intense, but they were not redemptive sorrows or sufferings. Mary's sufferings did not pay for the sins of the world. Mary is not qualified in any sense to suffer as a payment for sin. She is a mere woman; she is a sinner; and she is not divine. Only Jesus qualifies as the redeemer, and he has no helpers or co-redeemers in that great work. Mary did not understand it, but later it would be clear to her. She would understand that by his death Jesus had paid for her sins, redeemed her from sin and death, borne her curse, and endured the wrath of God against her sins. We with the completed scriptures understand even more clearly the work of Christ for our salvation.

Mary's anguish—or the sword in Mary's soul—is nothing in comparison to the sword that passes through the soul of Jesus. Jesus will say in the garden of Gethsemane, "My soul is exceeding sorrowful, even unto death" (Matt. 26:38). About him the prophet said, "He is despised and rejected of men; a man of sorrows, and acquainted with grief" (Isa. 53:3). But unlike the helpless anguish of Mary, Jesus' sorrow will accomplish something wonderful. Christ atoned for our sins when God pierced him with the sword of his wrath.

When Mary's son was about thirty-three years old, he would give his life as an atoning sacrifice for the sins of his people. Cruel men would arrest him, but only because he willingly surrendered himself to them. Wicked men would beat him and spit upon him, but only because he suffered it to be so. As a sheep before her shearers is dumb, so Christ did not open his mouth to protest his enemies' cruel treatment of him. He would submit to the cruelties and indignities of his foes because in this way he endured the wrath of God against our sins. Finally, the sword of God's justice would pierce Jesus on the cross, a sword that brought great anguish to the Son of God.

Only through the people's rejection of him could Mary's son—the Son of God and our Savior—accomplish our redemption from sin and death.

All of that is God's purpose with this marvelous child.

Chapter 13

AGED ANNA SPEAKING OF REDEMPTION IN JERUSALEM

36. And there was one Anna, a prophetess, the daughter of Phanuel, of the tribe of Aser: she was of a great age, and had lived with an husband seven years from her virginity;

37. And she was a widow of about fourscore and four years, which departed not from the temple, but served God with fastings and prayers night and day.

38. And she coming in that instant gave thanks likewise unto the Lord, and spake of him to all them that looked for redemption in Jerusalem.

39. And when they had performed all things according to the law of the Lord, they returned into Galilee, to their own city Nazareth. (Luke 2:36–39)

God does not leave himself without a witness. In the most unlikely of places, and in the most unlikely of times, God raises up witnesses. He did so in the temple on that day when Jesus was presented as an infant of forty days to the Lord. He did that by raising in the temple two witnesses to the identity of this child, Jesus Christ. We have already considered Simeon, a man to whom God promised that he would see the Lord's Christ before he died. He both rejoiced in the fulfillment of God's promise and uttered a mysterious, solemn prophecy concerning Christ's future rejection.

There was a second witness in the temple that day, a very old woman called Anna. She too testified to the identity of Jesus Christ. Anna is a mysterious person, one who appears suddenly on the pages of scripture, speaks a short word concerning the Son of God, and then disappears from the record of the Bible. In so doing, she fulfilled God's purpose, and in this chapter, we consider another mysterious and faithful witness to Jesus Christ.

Anna's Long Life

Of the two individuals whom Mary and Joseph met in the temple, Anna has the longest introduction. Two verses are devoted to her life and character, one verse is devoted to what she did that day, and none of her words are recorded.

Who was she?

First, she was a prophetess. A prophet in scripture is one who receives direct communication from God and who makes that word known to God's people. Almost all such individuals in the Bible are men, but there are a few prophetesses or female prophets in scripture. Usually prophetesses appear in times of deep spiritual declension or apostasy. For example, Josiah in 2 Chronicles 34:22 consulted Huldah the prophetess. Prophetesses exercised their prophetic gift in submission to God's will; therefore, the presence of Anna the prophetess does not make women eligible for the offices in the church, for God's will clearly revealed in the New Testament is that only men be pastors, elders, and deacons (1 Tim. 2:11–12; 3:1–13).

Second, she was of the tribe of Asher, which is also very significant. Asher was one of the ten tribes of the northern kingdom, which as a whole apostatized from Jehovah in the days of Jeroboam, and which was destroyed in the Assyrian conquest in the days when Hezekiah was king of Judah and Hoshea was king of Israel. Asher was in northwestern Israel, adjacent to that region of Israel called Galilee. That Anna was from Asher makes her a remnant of a remnant, for she is one of the faithful few whose family line still survived the Assyrian conquest and the Babylonian captivity. We know nothing more about her family, except that her father's name, Phanuel, is the New Testament equivalent of Penuel or Peniel, which means "face of God" (see Gen. 32:30).

Anna's outstanding characteristic, on which Luke places the emphasis, was her great age. She was a very aged woman. In Luke 2:36 we read, "She was of a great age." The phrase is used to describe other old people in the Bible. For example, of Zacharias and Elizabeth we read, "They both were now well stricken in years" (1:7). Zacharias calls his wife "well stricken in years" (v. 18). Anna was much older than Zacharias or Elizabeth, however, for she was "of a great age," or literally, "advanced in many days." Anna had outlived many in her own generation. She was much older than the standard "three score and ten" or even the exceptional "fourscore" years (Ps. 90:10).

Her exact age is somewhat difficult to determine, but Luke appears to divide her life into three phases, from which we can calculate her age.

First, Anna lived from her birth to her virginity. The word "virginity" in Luke 2:36 simply means the age at which a young woman is marriageable. We will take age 16 as a ballpark figure, although Anna, as was customary in that era, probably married younger than age 16. Second, Anna lived with her husband for seven years, at the end of which period her husband died. That would make Anna a widow at age 23.

Third, Anna lived as a widow for eighty-four years. That would make her 107 years old when the events recorded in Luke 2 took place. We do not know how much longer after this she lived, but we suspect it was not much longer. Most historians believe that King Herod died in 4 BC, so if we date this incident in the temple in Luke 2 to about 6 BC, we can make the following assertions about Anna's life.

Anna was born around 113 BC and became a widow at about 90 BC. In 63 BC, when Anna was 50 years old, Judah and Jerusalem fell to the Romans, who made it a vassal state, a dreadful event that she had witnessed and through which she had lived. In 37 BC, when Anna was 76 years old, the Romans placed Herod on the throne in Jerusalem. In 20 BC, when Anna was 93 years old, Herod began his extension of the temple in Jerusalem. The point that I am belaboring is that Anna was a very old woman, who had experienced and witnessed a lot in her long life. If you met a 107-year-old woman today (in 2019), she would have been born in 1912 and would have lived through two world wars. She certainly would have a lot of stories to tell anyone who would be willing to listen!

Anna's life had also been a difficult one. Anna was a widow, which means that she had tasted the bitterness of the loss of, and the bereavement for, her husband. Anna had married young, as soon as she had reached marriageable age (her virginity), but her marriage had been short and, we assume, sweet. We estimate that she became a widow at the tender age of twenty-three, after having lived with her husband for only seven years. Deep must have been her sorrow to lose her husband, and it appears that she never remarried. Her widowhood of eighty-four years was now twelve times as long as her marriage.

Scripture does not mention if Anna had any children. If she did have children, it is very possible that they had also predeceased her. She may have experienced sorrow upon sorrow. Widowhood is miserable in any circumstances: widows and widowers are intensely lonely, and they are lonely with a loneliness that is unlike any other kind of loneliness. Not only do they have no companion, but they have also lost the companion whom they once loved.

Widowhood in the ancient world was much more painful, for a widow was helpless. No welfare state existed to help widows, and while Israel was supposed to care for her widows, she rarely did. God's people faithfully cared for her widows only when they walked in the ways of the Lord. With neither husband nor sons to provide for her, protect her, or support her, widows like Anna were poor and vulnerable and were often victims of oppression.

Add to that the peculiar time in which Anna lived, and we can see that Anna had a long and difficult earthly pilgrimage. Anna lived through Israel's deep, dark, miserable apostasy. Her time was like the days of the judges, or like the days of bondage in Egypt, or like the days under one of the ungodly kings, for Herod was king. The religious leaders from the high priest to the Pharisees, scribes, and Sadducees were proud, self-righteous, carnal, and ungodly. The people, in general, were as carnal or profane as their religious leaders. It must have been a grief of mind to Anna to see the downward spiral of Israel.

She also lived, as we have seen, when Israel came under Roman occupation. She had witnessed and lived through the awful events of 63 BC, in which year the Roman general Pompey had besieged the city, invaded the city, desecrated the temple, and slaughtered thousands of Jerusalem's inhabitants.

The invasion of 63 BC was a precursor to a much worse event in AD 70, when the city of Jerusalem was destroyed with the temple. That would take place about seventy-four years after the events in Luke 2, but of course Anna would be dead by then.

But Anna's greatest burden was sin, which is the same burden that oppresses all of God's saints on earth. With each passing year, Anna's sense of sin grew greater and her longing for redemption grew more intense. Anna was 107 years old, and Israel was still not redeemed. Jerusalem was under Roman occupation, and no Davidic king sat on the throne, and still Israel was not redeemed. When would Christ come to redeem Israel?

That is the same longing of the elderly saint today, and it should be the longing of younger saints also: when will Christ come to deliver me finally and fully from sin? My body and my soul groan for the promised redemption. My soul waits for the Lord, as they that wait for the morning light. Remember Hebrews 9:28: "So Christ was once offered to bear the sins of many; and unto them that look for him shall he appear the second time without sin unto salvation."

ANNA'S CONSTANT DEVOTION

If you had looked for Anna, there is one place where you would have found her: in the temple, for in Luke 2:37 we read, "Which departed not from the temple." The temple was God's house and the place of God's worship, and that was where Anna loved to be. Anna either lived in close proximity to the temple, or she had lodgings in the temple itself, or (what is more likely) she was regular in her attendance at the temple. Every day of the week, from the moment the doors of the temple opened in the morning to the moment the doors closed for the evening, Anna was in the sacred precincts of the Lord's temple. She was there for the morning and evening offerings; she was there for the Sabbath services; and she was there for the great feasts of Jehovah, such as Passover, Pentecost, and the Feast of Tabernacles. Nothing could have kept her from the temple: not inclement weather, not the infirmities of old age, not prior engagements.

She diligently frequented the temple because she loved to be there, near to her God, as near as she could come. Anna must have been something of a curiosity. Doubtless, the priests knew her; the pilgrims who came to Jerusalem must have seen her year after year; and the people of Jerusalem knew her as Anna the prophetess. As a prophetess, she may have spoken to the people who came to the temple. If she did, she spoke to them about the Lord's promised redemption. Every year, she became older and older. The people might have wondered how many more years she might live; but although her body was marked with the infirmity of old age, her spirit was youthful as she anticipated the coming of the Lord Jesus Christ. Perhaps she reminded the people, "Behold, I will send my messenger, and he shall prepare the way before me: and the Lord, whom ye seek, shall suddenly come to his temple, even the messenger of the covenant, whom ye delight in: behold, he shall come, saith the LORD of hosts" (Mal. 3:1).

Anna's devotion to the Lord is remarkable and is a rebuke to many of us today. Anna did not permit the bitter experiences of life to embitter her against God. Anna was not like Naomi, who cried out, "Call me not Naomi, call me Mara: for the Almighty hath dealt very bitterly with me" (Ruth

1:20). Anna's name means "grace," and she did not change it to Mara, which means "bitter." She remained gracious.

Anna did not turn against God and refuse to worship him when he deprived her of a husband after only seven years of marriage, or when he caused her to experience poverty and loneliness for eighty-four years, or when he prolonged her years to one hundred seven years, so that she endured the weaknesses and pains of old age. Anna was not like Jacob, when in a pique of impatient unbelief he cried out, "Me have ye bereaved of my children: Joseph is not, and Simeon is not, and ye will take Benjamin away: all these things are against me" (Gen. 42:36). Anna was like the saints of God in Psalm 92:13–14: "Those that be planted in the house of the LORD shall flourish in the courts of our God. They shall still bring forth fruit in old age; they shall be fat and flourishing." Anna was also not like many professing Christians today who never darken the door of a church building to worship God. Anna was one who "departed not from the temple" (Luke 2:37).

We live in an age in which Christians are known more for their excuses for not attending public worship than for their devotion to the Lord's house. Anna did not make excuses, for she did not want to make excuses. No one had to cajole Anna into coming to the temple. She desired to be there; she desired to be nowhere else. Anna would have been happy to die in the temple.

Worship is a matter of the heart. If a person does not want to be in worship, there is nothing the church can do. Exhortations and even discipline will be ineffective, unless God changes the heart. If a person desires to be in worship, there is nothing the church can do to keep him or her away.

In the temple, Anna served God (v. 37). The verb that Luke uses means religious service, most often used when referring to priestly service; but Anna was not a priest. She did not have an official position. She served the Lord as an ordinary believer and as a prophetess.

Anna served God with "fastings" (v. 37). Fasting is voluntary abstinence from food in order to devote oneself to God. When a person fasts, he or she does not eat breakfast, lunch, and dinner, around which most of our lives revolve. Anna did not fast because she was on a diet or because she was against certain kinds of food, but Anna fasted so that she would be less distracted and would have more time to focus her attention on God. Imagine it this way: Anna did not need to spend time shopping for food in the marketplace, preparing food at home, and eating food: she fasted. The time that she saved by fasting, she devoted to the Lord's service.

For Anna fasting was an act of love. For Anna God was more important and more precious than food. Whatever activity, even necessary activities, hindered her devotional life, she removed or curtailed. This does not mean that Anna starved herself: she did eat, but she ate infrequently and sparingly. She had continued this practice of fasting for many, many years. She was probably a skinny, emaciated old woman by this time.

Besides that, fasting was a sign of her humiliation. In the Bible, people would commonly fast as an act of contrition and sorrow over sin. Anna fasted because she saw herself as a sinner and because she mourned for the nation. And she prayed: "[She] served God with fastings and prayers night and day" (v. 37). She had a lot of time to pray, for she did not have a family to care for; she did not spend a lot of time cooking or looking after a house; and she did not sleep much, for she fasted and prayed night and day.

Sometimes the elderly saints wonder, "What has God got

for me to do in the church? I cannot do much. After many years, my strength has failed. My eyes are dim. My hearing is impaired." The answer is, you can pray! Prayer is not an inferior activity. Without prayer, nothing in the church will accomplish anything. The preaching, the catechism, the mission work, and the godly witness of the members all require prayer. Anna did not think it a waste of her time to pray—she was determined to free up as much time as possible in her life to devote to prayer. What does that say to us with our TVs, laptops, iPhones, and social media accounts?

Anna's prayers were especially petitionary, that is, in her prayers she made requests to God; the word translated "prayers" indicates this. We are not told the nature of her petitions, but she must have prayed for the redemption of Israel. She prayed for the coming of the Lord to his temple, as God had promised in the prophets. That was her one great desire, redemption from sin for herself, and redemption from sin for God's people Israel. For that great blessing she prayed night and day with fasting and petitions, seeking, knocking, and begging at heaven's door. Anna knew God's word in Isaiah 62:7: "Give him no rest, till he establish, and till he make Jerusalem a praise in the earth." For that great blessing she had been praying for over one hundred years. Do you think that God is slow to grant your petitions? Are you tempted to give up praying? Let Anna be your example: she prayed for a century before she received her request.

ANNA'S GREAT BLESSING

Anna's great blessing was the same as Simeon's: she lived to see the Christ. Although Anna did not have a specific promise to see Christ (which Simeon did), it is clear that

God had prolonged Anna's life for this very reason. Anna must have anticipated something because of the interesting occurrences in and around Jerusalem at that time. Apply what we have already studied to Anna's situation. Some fifteen months earlier Zacharias the priest had been ministering in the temple when the angel Gabriel had appeared to him. Because of his unbelief, Zacharias had been struck dumb. Had Anna been present when Zacharias the priest emerged from the holy place unable to speak? Surely, if Anna never departed from the temple, she had been present or at least had heard of it. That would give her pause. Did Anna encounter the shepherds or hear the rumor of what they had said? Since they made known abroad the saying, the likelihood that Anna heard it is high. That too would quicken her hope.

Whatever Anna might have known beforehand, she came into the temple at just the right time at God's appointment: "She coming in that instant" (Luke 2:38). Mary and Joseph had just finished the ceremonies for their forty-day-old child. Simeon had just pronounced a blessing, and she must have overheard him say, "Lord, now lettest thou thy servant depart in peace, according to thy word: for mine eyes have seen thy salvation" (vv. 29–30). If she did not overhear Simeon, she recognized the child herself by the power of the Holy Spirit, for remember that she was a prophetess.

Anna's first response to seeing the Christ child is thanksgiving: "[She] gave thanks likewise unto the Lord" (v. 38). This is the fitting response of one who has waited for one hundred years to see the salvation of God. Before she said anything to Mary, Joseph, or Simeon—and her utterances are not recorded—she lifted her heart and her voice to God.

This was the day of days. All her days, and all her years

of days, a whole century, were worth the wait to see this: to see a tiny baby in whom all her salvation and our salvation lies. I have said it before, and I say it again—this is remarkable. Anna sees only a baby, but her thanksgiving is as if she has seen everything. Anna lived on the edge of the new dispensation, and yet her patience, her devotion, and her joy put us to shame. Are we half as excited to enjoy complete and full salvation as Anna was to see a glimpse of salvation? Out of her joy and thanksgiving, Anna testified: "She…spake of him to all them that looked for redemption in Jerusalem" (v. 38).

Simeon saw the Lord's salvation; Anna speaks of redemption. The two ideas or concepts are related, but redemption is more specific. Redemption is a specific kind of salvation, or salvation in a specific way, for the Bible uses different words to describe different aspects of salvation. Redemption is to deliver from bondage by paying a ransom price. Since Anna saw her chief misery as bondage—bondage to sin—and the chief blessing as redemption, she expected the Lord to pay some kind of price to deliver her and all of God's people from sin. What Anna understood by redemption is not altogether clear. How did she expect this little child to bring redemption? She may not have known all the details, but she knew the fact, and that was enough for her.

Certainly, Anna was not expecting a political redemption. That was the common view among the unbelieving Jews—redemption from Rome. God's people are not interested in political redemption, for their cry is not, "Deliver us from the Romans," but "Deliver us from our sins. Deliver us from the bondage of sin, death, and Satan." Christ did that by paying the ransom price on the cross.

Some thirty years later, Christ would die on the cross

to pay for the sins of Anna and to pay for the sins of all God's elect people. Anna would not live to see it, of course, but she died happy knowing its certainty. Moreover, Anna did not keep this truth to herself, for she "spake of him" (v. 38). There is a beautifully encouraging phrase in verse 38: "all them that looked for redemption in Jerusalem." While it is true there were many who did not look for redemption, there were some who did. Anna and Simeon, Zacharias and Elizabeth, and Mary and Joseph were not the only ones. There were others, a hidden, reserved remnant, who longed for the messianic redemption that Anna and Simeon were privileged to behold.

Anna spoke to the saints in the temple who longed for the coming of the Messiah. Jesus has come! He has suddenly come to his temple—not in the way we expected—but he has come! Rejoice and be glad! Our redemption is surely near!

Jesus was only forty days old, and already he was causing a stir. Angels announce his coming and rejoice in his birth. Shepherds, aged saints, prophets, and prophetesses worship him.

Wise men will seek and find him.

Chapter 14

WISE MEN SEEKING THE NEWBORN KING

1. Now when Jesus was born in Bethlehem of Judaea in the days of Herod the king, behold, there came wise men from the east to Jerusalem,

2. Saying, Where is he that is born King of the Jews? for we have seen his star in the east, and are come to worship him. (Matthew 2:1–2)

The reader may have noticed that in the last chapter I did not deal with Luke 2:39, "And when they had performed all things according to the law of the Lord, they returned into Galilee, to their own city Nazareth." Luke omits the visit of the wise men and the flight of Mary, Joseph, and Jesus into Egypt, which the wise men's visit occasioned. He seems to bring Mary, Joseph, and Jesus *directly* from the temple in Jerusalem to Nazareth. Matthew, on his part, omits the birth of Jesus in Bethlehem (he mentions it only in passing), he omits the manger, he omits the visit of the shepherds, and he omits the events in the temple with Simeon and Anna.

When an evangelist omits an event in Jesus' life, we must not imagine that he was ignorant of it (perhaps he was, but the Holy Spirit was not). This simply means that under the inspiration of the Holy Spirit he chose to emphasize something else in the narrative, or that the Holy Spirit was not pleased to reveal it to the evangelist or to remind him of it. The gospel accounts complement one another, but they do not conflict with or contradict one another. As a case in point, Luke 2:39 does not state that Mary, Joseph, and Jesus went *directly or immediately* from the temple to Nazareth. Even without Matthew's account, that would be very unlikely given the age of the child. One does not make a journey with a forty-day-old infant unless it is absolutely necessary. Luke simply chooses to omit the events that Matthew records elsewhere.

If we compare the two accounts—we do not include Mark or John, as they are silent about the events surrounding the birth of Jesus—we can piece together the following chronology. First, Jesus is born in Bethlehem (Luke 2:6–7); second, that night angels announce his birth to shepherds, who immediately depart to see him (vv. 8–20). Third, on the eighth day Jesus is circumcised in Bethlehem (v. 21). Fourth, Mary remains ceremonially unclean until the fortieth day, after which the events in the temple occur (vv. 22–38). Fifth, after the ceremonies in the temple are completed, Mary, Joseph, and Jesus return to Bethlehem, where Joseph has secured a house in which his family might live (Matt. 2:11). The stable/manger arrangement was temporary because of overcrowding in Bethlehem, and it appears that Joseph had intended to stay in Bethlehem.

Sixth, sometime between the child's fortieth day and the child's second birthday, wise men visit the house in Bethlehem (Matt. 2:1–12). Seventh, shortly thereafter, the family is forced to flee to Egypt, where they remain until the death of Herod, who died in 4 BC when Jesus was probably around two years old (vv. 13–20). Finally, because Herod's son

Archelaus was king of Judea (4 BC to AD 6), Joseph brought his family not to Bethlehem, which was his preference, but to Nazareth, which was safer (vv. 21–23).

Therefore, in the nativity story, we move from Luke 2 to Matthew 2, where again we are in familiar territory, for even little children know about the visit of the wise men. There is a very striking contrast in the nativity story. The King of the Jews is born, but it is wise men—Gentiles from the east—who visit him. These mysterious wise men are the first Gentiles to worship the newborn King.

Already Simeon's words are being fulfilled: Christ is indeed "a light to lighten the Gentiles" (Luke 2:32).

WHO THEY WERE

If the shepherds were mysterious (we do not know their names, ages, or number), even more mysterious are the wise men. Like the shepherds, they appear as witnesses of Jesus Christ, and then they disappear from the pages of scripture.

We begin with the words "wise men." The word is *magos*, of which the plural is *magi*. There is only one other *magos* in the New Testament, the wicked sorcerer Elymas, or Bar-Jesus, in Acts 13. (In Acts 8 the verb "to practice magic" is used in connection with Simon). However, the term is very broad: it designates anything from a priest, to a scientist, to a sorcerer or magician. A *magos* is a person trained or educated in human learning, even one steeped in superstition and paganism, although not necessarily so.

Oriental kings in the ancient world employed magi or wise men to be their advisors. Perhaps the best Old Testament examples of magi are in the book of Daniel. Nebuchadnezzar surrounded himself with magicians, astrologers, sorcerers, and Chaldeans in Daniel 2:2. Daniel himself was a magos or wise man. He was educated in all the learning of Babylon, although he remained pure of the pagan idolatry.

The famous Christmas carol is misleading therefore: "We three kings of orient are." They were not kings. Magi were rich, powerful, and influential, but they were not kings. They were high-ranking officials, but not kings. There may have been three of them—the Roman Catholic Church even names them as Melchior, Caspar, and Balthazar and celebrates them as saints—but the Bible does not reveal their number or their names. The only part of the Christmas carol that is accurate is that the magi or wise men came from the orient or from the east. Scripture expressly states that in Matthew 2:1: "Behold, there came wise men from the east to Jerusalem." We do not know, however, the country in the east from which they had journeyed; our best guess is Persia, or perhaps Babylon or Arabia.

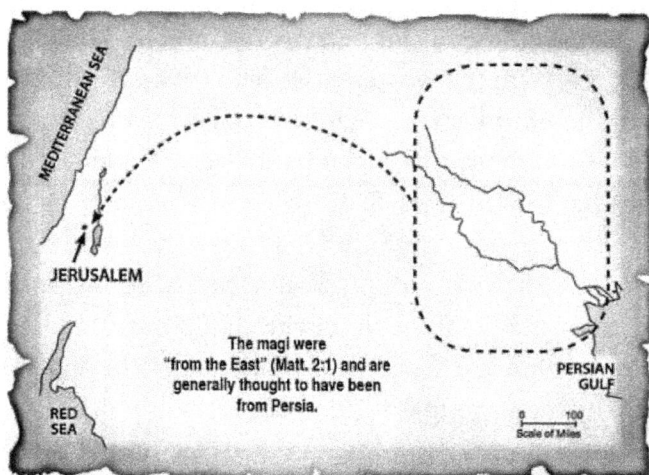

Map credit: answersingenesis.org: "What Was the Christmas Star?"

MEDITERRANEAN SEA

JERUSALEM

RED SEA

The magi were "from the East" (Matt. 2:1) and are generally thought to have been from Persia.

PERSIAN GULF

0   100
Scale of Miles

The Bible deprives us of such details so that it can focus our attention on this: they were Gentiles from a far-off country. Verse 1 wants us to notice that: "*Behold*, magi from the east" (emphasis added). In Matthew 1:21 the angel told Joseph, "She shall bring forth a son, and thou shalt call his name JESUS: for he shall save his people from their sins." You would expect the Jews to welcome him, but in verse 1 of the next chapter, "Now when Jesus was born…behold, there came wise men from the east."

This is curious: what are wise men from the east doing in Jerusalem? The answer is, "We have seen his star in the east" (Matt. 2:2). Magi were often astronomers or astrologers; they studied the stars and superstitiously imagined that stars influence human lives. It is clear from Matthew 2 that these wise men were influenced by the appearance of a star. We do not know to what degree they were influenced by superstition as well.

Sometime earlier, months earlier, maybe over a year earlier, the wise men had noticed an unusual star. In verse 2 they call it "*his* star" (emphasis added). That has the emphasis in the Greek: "For we have seen *of him* the star." These men therefore linked the appearance of the star to the birth of the King of the Jews. Many have attempted to identify this star. Was it a strange conjunction of planets? Was it a supernova? This too is speculation. God, who had eternally decreed this star, caused the star to appear in his providence so that only these wise men noticed it or understood its significance.

Notice a few details about the star.

First, they saw the star in the east. The word for "east" in the Greek is the same as the word for "rising." That is because the sun rises in the east and sets in the west. "We saw his star in the rising." They most likely observed it rising in such a way that it indicated the land of Judea.

Second, the star appeared, and then disappeared, and

then appeared again. The star is a miraculous star. Herod did not see it, for example. It reappeared only after the wise men's audience with Herod.

Third, the wise men did not follow the star from Persia to Jerusalem. The lines of the carol, "We three kings of orient are…following yonder star" are also incorrect. They knew that the star meant that the King of the Jews had been born, but the star did not direct them all the way to Jerusalem. It only directed them after their audience with King Herod.

But the most mysterious aspect of this history is this: how did these Gentiles conclude that the star indicated Christ's birth? The only explanation is that somehow God revealed it to them. It is very possible that these men had some acquaintance with the Jews and with their scriptures. The Jews had a diaspora, which means dispersion. There were Jews in every land where there were magi: in Egypt, in Babylon, in Arabia, and in Persia. The Jews had messianic expectations: a great king would arise to deliver Israel. Perhaps the magi were acquainted with Numbers 24:17: "I shall see him, but not now: I shall behold him, but not nigh: there shall come a Star out of Jacob, and a Sceptre shall rise out of Israel, and shall smite the corners of Moab, and destroy all the children of Sheth."

Clearly, God created the star, God revealed the significance of his star to these men, and they understood. Therefore, we conclude that these men were not superstitious pagans but believers. God made them believers. God made them believers while many in Israel remained unbelievers. They believed God's word, they believed God's sign, and they obeyed God's call, as believers do. God determined that there should be Gentiles to recognize the birth of his Son into the world. Therefore, God prepared these men to be witnesses to Christ from a far country, both to magnify the wonder of his grace, and as a judgment upon unbelieving Israel.

God does not reveal himself to people in the stars today. It is true that the heavens declare God's glory, but heavenly signs are insufficient to reveal the salvation of God in Jesus Christ. God has spoken decisively in the scriptures. It would be folly to cast away the scriptures today in favor of stargazing.

WHAT THEY DID

Shortly after the appearance of the star, as soon as they could get organized, the wise men embarked on a journey. The distance was about one thousand miles, about as far as from Moscow to Berlin or from Denver to San Francisco. That was a long, arduous, difficult, and dangerous journey on camels, unless perhaps they had a chariot. Still, the journey would take months. But they did not hesitate. They did not think that such a journey was a waste of their time. They were absolutely determined and committed to go. God worked a burning desire in their hearts to see Christ.

After some time they arrived. They must have been disappointed. They were sure that the King of the Jews had been born, but where was he? The city of Jerusalem showed no interest, for there was no festival to celebrate the king's birth; there was no parade; people were not dancing and feasting; there was no joy. Jerusalem carried on as usual; the people continued their buying and selling, while they had not heard of, and did not care about, the coming of Christ into the world. Anxiously, the wise men began to ask in Matthew 2:2, "Where is he that is born King of the Jews?" They traversed the city: where is he? We know that his birth has just taken place, but where is he?

What a contrast: Jesus is born on Jerusalem's doorstep, and the Jews do not know or care! These Gentiles with the scantest of knowledge of the scriptures travel one thousand miles to see Jesus and eagerly enquire about his whereabouts, while the Jews who knew the promises of the scriptures are disinterested. This is another sign of Jesus' suffering: in his birth, and in his life, he is rejected, and he will be rejected by being nailed to a cross. That is how he enters into his kingdom! The wisdom of God is foolishness with men!

The same attitude is evident today. These wise men from the east traveled one thousand miles to see the King of the Jews. Today people will not even walk down the street to hear the gospel of Jesus Christ. These wise men will rise up in judgment upon this generation. They saw a star and came; while we possess the completed scriptures—the full gospel of the death and resurrection of Jesus Christ—many do not come! How many live as if Jesus Christ had not come into the world!

WHY THEY CAME

The wise men explain the purpose of their coming in Matthew 2:2: "We...are come to worship him." Some want to dilute the meaning of that word. We are told that they only wanted to pay their respects or to do homage at a royal birth. But why would these men come on such a journey only to do that? No, they had come to offer him divine worship. They understood that the King of the Jews is the title of the Messiah and the title of God himself. These men were high and mighty, sophisticated, educated men. They were not ashamed to confess that they had come to worship the Messiah: "Where is he that is born King of the Jews? for we have seen his star in the east, and are come to worship him" (v. 2). We desire to bow down before him.

The people of Jerusalem were troubled (v. 3). They most likely mocked at this curious spectacle of foreigners coming to worship the King of the Jews. What nonsense! But no one welcomed the news and said, "Let us go with you to worship him!" We will see Jerusalem's reaction next time. But what is our attitude, especially on Sunday? "Where is he that is born King of the Jews, for we have heard his gospel, and are come to worship him!" "Where is he that was crucified for sinners? Where is he that rose again for our justification? Where is he that ascended into heaven? We are come to worship him!"

Paul answers:

6. But the righteousness which is of faith speaketh on this wise, Say not in thine heart, Who shall ascend into heaven? (that is, to bring Christ down from above:)
7. Or, Who shall descend into the deep? (that is, to bring up Christ again from the dead.)
8. But what saith it? The word is nigh thee, even in thy mouth, and in thy heart: that is, the word of faith, which we preach (Rom. 10:6–8).

The people of Jerusalem did not worship Jesus, so God brought worshipers all the way from the east. They confess with all true believers that he is Lord of all.

Chapter 15

HEROD'S ALARM AT
THE WISE MEN'S TIDINGS

3. When Herod the king had heard these things, he was troubled, and all Jerusalem with him.
4. And when he had gathered all the chief priests and scribes of the people together, he demanded of them where Christ should be born.
5. And they said unto him, In Bethlehem of Judaea: for thus it is written by the prophet,
6. And thou Bethlehem, in the land of Juda, art not the least among the princes of Juda: for out of thee shall come a Governor, that shall rule my people Israel.
7. Then Herod, when he had privily called the wise men, enquired of them diligently what time the star appeared.
8. And he sent them to Bethlehem, and said, Go and search diligently for the young child; and when ye have found him, bring me word again, that I may come and worship him also. (Matthew 2:3–8)

In Matthew 2 we meet King Herod. There are several kings called Herod in the Bible, and this is the first. History knows him as "Herod the Great," and he ruled Judea from 37 BC to 4 BC. Herod was not an absolute ruler, however. He ruled only with the permission of the Roman emperor, Caesar Augustus. Upon Herod was conferred the title "the king of the Jews," which gave him the right to rule over the Jews in Judea. However, Herod was not a Jew. His father, Antipater, was an Edomite, which means that he was a descendant of the reprobate Esau. There was longstanding enmity between the Jews and the Edomites, and it is an indication of Israel's miserable state that the scepter had departed from Jacob, and Esau ruled in Jerusalem.

Herod was a very ungodly man. Both the Bible and secular history record his wickedness. The history books describe him as a bloodthirsty tyrant, a man of reckless ambition, and a cruel, greedy despot. Many historians believe that Herod suffered from acute paranoia, in that he suspected everyone around him of plotting to take away his throne. In fact, he put his own wife and several of his sons to death because he viewed them as rivals to his power.

It was this man who sat on the throne when the true King of the Jews was born. Therefore, we are not surprised at his reaction to Christ's birth.

Herod saw in Christ one thing: a threat to his power, a threat that must be eliminated.

HEROD'S GREAT AGITATION

It did not take long for the news of the wise men to reach the palace of King Herod. This was truly a strange message for Herod to hear: foreign magi, possibly from Persia, asking about the recent birth of the "King of the Jews" (v. 2). Herod's reaction is described in verse 3: "He was troubled." The word means agitated, alarmed, shaken, or upset. When Herod heard about the possibility of another "King of the Jews," he was filled with fear and dread.

The idea that there was another rival king of the Jews was intolerable to him. Herod was troubled because he loved one thing above all other things: power. Herod had worked long and hard to obtain the coveted title "King of the Jews." The Roman senate had conferred that title upon him; and he had employed political intrigue and great cunning to obtain that honor from Caesar Augustus. Throughout Herod's life, many had perished because he suspected that they were—or could be—rivals to him or claimants to his throne.

This might appear strange to us, for why would Herod feel threatened by the rumor of the birth of a king? Would he not be long dead before such a king could stake a claim on his throne? That is true, for at this point, Herod was an old man. Indeed, he would die less than two years after the events described in Matthew 2. But Herod cared about his legacy; he cared about his family maintaining the rule in Judea after him.

Besides that, Herod feared an attempted coup, for if the Jews were caught up in messianic fervor, if they believed that the Messiah had come, they might attempt to overthrow him. Therefore, Herod was determined to eliminate this rival, whoever he might be. As long as this newborn pretender to the title "King of the Jews" lived, Herod felt unsafe. All of this tells us something about Herod's and the Jews' misconceptions about the Messiah: they viewed him as a threat, not as a savior. When they did think of salvation, they expected political deliverance. Herod did not want political deliverance: he wanted the *status quo*, his rule and even the rule of his successors.

Make no mistake: Herod knew that "the King of the Jews" was the Messiah. That comes out in his question to the religious scholars in verse 4, "He demanded of them where Christ should be born." Herod knew and expected that a Christ—an Anointed One or a Messiah—would come. But Herod did not welcome him. Herod expected that the Messiah would be an earthly king, but Herod recognized only one earthly king—himself! Herod expected that the Messiah, as an earthly king, would bring earthly peace and prosperity, but that was intolerable to Herod if he, Herod, was not king. Herod expected that the Messiah would overthrow the Romans, but Herod was a friend of the Romans. He was on good terms with the emperor, and he wanted to maintain that relationship.

The same applies to the ungodly religious rulers: "If we let him thus alone, all men will believe on him: and the Romans shall come and take away both our place and nation" (John 11:48). "We have no king but Caesar" (19:15). This also explains Jerusalem's agitation: "He was troubled, and all Jerusalem with him" (Matt. 2:3).

When the people of Jerusalem—and especially Jerusalem's ruling classes—heard what the wise men were saying, they too were thrown into confusion. What could this mean? What will this mean for the nation? What will this mean for our political future? This Messiah is a threat to us too. Besides, all Jerusalem was troubled because Herod was troubled. The people feared what Herod would do, for they were familiar with his cruelty and his rage. Herod was unpredictable in his reactions, and if anyone were even suspected of sympathizing with the rival "King of the Jews," he or she would be at risk.

This troubled reaction of both Herod and Jerusalem has spiritual significance. First, this reaction is a harbinger of Christ's future rejection. You would expect that Jerusalem, when they heard that Christ had been born, would welcome the news of that birth. Jerusalem should have been praising God. At the very least, they should have been carefully inquiring of the wise men: "What did you see? When did you see it? Let us help you find the newborn King. He is the one for whom we also have been waiting and longing." But instead of joy, the reaction is trouble, agitation, and fear.

This shows us that—apart from a remnant according to the election of grace—the people of Judah were not interested in the coming of the Messiah. They were not really looking forward to deliverance, and they certainly were not looking forward to salvation from sin. They did not want their lives to be interrupted or disrupted by the coming of Christ. Christ is an inconvenience. Christ is a threat. Christ, for them, is not a savior.

That also is how they will react when Christ appears in his public ministry—they will be initially curious, but in the end, they will reject and crucify him. This rejection of Christ is necessary for our salvation. That does not make it right or good, for God uses their sin for our salvation. Nevertheless, the cross is necessary, for on that cross Jesus will suffer and die for our sins. It is not God's purpose that Jesus be hailed as an earthly king. Therefore, that cross is already foreshadowed in the rejection of Christ at his birth.

Second, this troubled reaction is indicative of the sinner's reaction to Christ today. When Christ confronts the sinner, the whole soul of man is troubled. The soul of man is at peace, living happily in sin, serving Satan. But when the gospel comes, and Christ is preached, the sinner's soul is troubled. Satan is stirred up to prevent the conversion of the soul at all costs. The soul's response is always the same: "I will not have this man to rule over me. I will not submit to the King of the Jews. I will be my own king."

Sinners are troubled at Christ because they fear Christ. Sinners fear that if they believe in Christ, they will have to give up their sins. Sinners fear that if Christ comes to dwell and rule in their lives, he will turn their lives upside down—and he will! If Christ is to dwell in us by faith, he must overcome our resistance, which he does by irresistible grace: "When a strong man armed keepeth his palace, his goods are in peace: but when a stronger than he shall come upon him, and overcome him, he taketh from him all his armour wherein he trusted, and divideth his spoils" (Luke 11:21–22).

HEROD'S INTERROGATION OF THE RELIGIOUS LEADERS

Herod's next move was to call a counsel of the religious leaders: "when he had gathered all the chief priests and scribes of the people together" (Matt. 2:4). Herod posed one question to these men, the religious elite of the day. That question was, "Where will Christ be born?" It is very likely that Herod knew the answer to that question, because it was common knowledge among the Jews (John 7:40–43). Herod, although he was an Edomite, had been raised in the Jewish religion, and he observed many of the Jewish religious ceremonies. Herod was like many politicians today: he pretended to be religious out of political expediency.

Nevertheless, Herod required official confirmation, so he called the theological experts. The high priest was the religious leader of the people. By this time, the position of high priest was also a political appointment, and former high priests retained the title "high priest," hence the plural, "chief priests." The scribes were the experts in Jewish law.

Therefore, if anyone knew the scriptures, it was the scribes. Their occupation was to study the scriptures and to apply them to the lives of the people. They did that very strictly.

These men answered Herod without any hesitation, "In Bethlehem of Judaea: for thus it is written by the prophet" (Matt. 2:5). The answer these men give is neither a direct translation of Micah 5:2 nor a quotation from the Greek Septuagint version, but a paraphrase. Although the paraphrase contains all the information that Herod needs to know, we should notice a few differences between the literal prophecy and what these men say.

The Hebrew version of Micah 5:2 reads, "Bethlehem Ephratah," but these men say, "Bethlehem, in the land of Juda" (v. 6). Ephratah, which means "fruitful," is omitted, for such a detail is not necessary for Herod to know. Instead, the men emphasize that the Bethlehem in question is "in the land of Juda." This distinguishes Bethlehem-Judah from another Bethlehem in Zebulun (see Josh. 19:15) and confirms that the city in question lies within Herod's jurisdiction.

The Hebrew version of Micah 5:2 reads, "Though thou be little among the thousands of Judah," but these men say, "Thou...art not the least among the princes of Juda" (v. 6). Micah's point is the lowliness and the insignificance of the birthplace of the Messiah, for he shall be born in a place that is not even listed among the thousands of Judah. The religious leaders turn that on its head: Bethlehem is by no means the least, because the Messiah comes out of that place. In a way, Christ takes a place that of itself is meaningless and insignificant, and he makes it great. The Jews saw Bethlehem as ennobled by virtue of it being the birthplace of Christ.

The Hebrew version of Micah 5:2 points to the deity and eternity of the Messiah, but these men omit that part of the verse because it too is irrelevant to Herod's question. "Out of thee shall he come forth unto me that is to be ruler in Israel; whose goings forth have been from of old, from everlasting" (Mic. 5:2). These men say, "For out of thee shall come a Governor, that shall rule my people Israel" (Matt. 2:6). The verb "rule" could be translated "shepherd." Incidentally, this shows us the kind of king the Messiah will be: he will rule as a shepherd, in love and tender care for his sheep. He will not rule, as Herod did, or as Augustus did, as a tyrant, who mistreats the people and abuses them.

The prophecy of Micah 5:2 is clear in whatever way you quote it: Christ shall be born in Bethlehem, which is four and a half miles away from Jerusalem. But how do these men respond?

Notice Herod's response: first of all, in a certain sense, he believes. Herod did not have saving faith, of course, but in a sense he believed the scriptures. Paul spoke in a similar manner about another king called Herod: "King Agrippa, believest thou the prophets? I know that thou believest" (Acts 26:27). Herod took the scriptures seriously enough not to dismiss them as a fairy tale. He seriously wanted to know where Christ should be born, and he took the information seriously enough to act on it. In fact, Herod takes the information from Micah 5, and he informs the wise men that they ought to search there for the King of the Jews. If Herod had dismissed Micah as a fairy tale or as a fictitious legend, he would not have taken Micah's prophecy about Bethlehem seriously.

Herod believed the scriptures in a similar way to how the devil believes the scriptures. The devil believes the scriptures and takes them seriously, but he is determined to prevent their fulfillment. Take the prophecy of Genesis 3:15, "I will put enmity between thee and the woman, and between thy seed and her seed; it shall bruise thy head, and thou shalt bruise his heel." Did the devil *believe* those words? In a sense he did, but he was determined throughout the Old Testament to prevent Christ from being born. Did the devil believe the words of Micah 5:2? In a sense he did, but he planned to devour Christ as soon as he was born. Similarly, Herod took the words of Micah 5:2 not so much as a promise, but rather as an opportunity. If he knows the birthplace of the Messiah, he can kill him. We should not be surprised that Herod reacts this way, for he was troubled, he feared for his throne, and he was an ungodly man.

But what of the chief priests and scribes? They seem to believe the scriptures also, but they fail to act on the scriptures. Consider that these men claim to worship God and they claim to be looking forward with eagerness to Christ's coming, but they do nothing! They give a perfectly theologically accurate answer, but they do nothing! They hear the tidings of the wise men—a star in the east, the birth of the King of the Jews—but they are not interested. They do not ask the wise men for further information; and they do not send a delegation to Bethlehem to examine the wise men's claims. After they satisfy Herod's curiosity on a point of doctrine, they return to the temple or to their studies. The possibility that Christ has been born in Bethlehem, just a short journey down the road from them, has no effect on them. And yet the wise men have traveled one thousand miles to worship him!

There are people like that today. You ask them, "Who is the Son of God?" and they answer correctly, "Jesus Christ."

But they do not worship him. They have at best a historical faith, in that they know some biblical facts, but they are not really Christians. They may find Christianity intellectually stimulating, but they are not Christians. They may even be theologians, but they are not Christians. Christ, as it were, is on their doorstep, but they neglect him. While others who are much further away push past them to enter into the kingdom, they remain outside. "I say unto you, that many shall come from the east and west, and shall sit down with Abraham, and Isaac, and Jacob, in the kingdom of heaven. But the children of the kingdom shall be cast out into outer darkness: there shall be weeping and gnashing of teeth" (Matt. 8:11–12).

Alas, there are many like these scribes. Christ means nothing to them. His sufferings and death are facts with which they are familiar, but they do not trust in him for the forgiveness of sins. They have heard of the resurrection, but they do not possess the life of Christ. They believe in a place called heaven, but they have no hope of possessing it. They tremble at the idea of hell, but it is greatly to be feared that they will not escape it. Their lives reflect this sad reality, for they live like the ungodly world, without God, without Christ, and without hope.

HEROD'S CONFERENCE WITH THE WISE MEN

Herod called the wise men for a royal audience, which is a striking example of cunning, despicable hypocrisy. Herod pretended to be interested in the King of the Jews. He was interested, of course, but not in the way that the wise men supposed. We imagine that he lavished hospitality upon the wise men, since they were foreign dignitaries. Perhaps he wined and dined them, so that they would not suspect his motives. Moreover, he made sure that no one else knew, for he called them in secret or privately. What Herod wanted from them was a time. That was the last piece of the puzzle. He knew who had been born—the Messiah; he knew where he had been born—Bethlehem. But he also needed to know when he had been born; and for that he needed to consult with the wise men. That is why in Matthew 2:7 he "inquired of them diligently *what time* the star appeared" (emphasis added).

If the star really did mark the time of Messiah's birth, and Herod was taking no chances, he needed to find out as much about that star as he could. He asked about the rising of the star: where did they see it; what was the star like; when did it first appear; for how long did it appear; when did it disappear? It seems that it had disappeared, for Herod could not see it.

When Herod had acquired the information that he wanted, he hatched a diabolical plot. He sent the magi with instructions: "Go and search diligently for the child" (v. 8). Herod hired these men as his spies: they would find out for him where the child was. Unwittingly, or so he thought, the wise men would lead him to his rival. He urged them to search diligently, to spare no effort, and to make every enquiry. These men were willing to do that. Since they had already journeyed about one thousand miles, a short visit to Bethlehem was certainly not a great imposition. When they had found the child, Herod urged, "Bring me word again" (v. 8). These men had never met Herod, and his show of piety must have been convincing: "Bring me word again, that I may come and worship him also" (v. 8). Wicked King

Herod, whose only desire was to murder Jesus, pretended to desire to worship him. Once the wise men had seen the king and had returned safely to their own country, Herod would kill the child. Herod was therefore the worst kind of hypocrite. Like many politicians today, he pretended to be religious to maintain his power.

But God is in the heavens, and although Herod might rage against his Son, God laughs at the foolish attempts of the ungodly to overthrow the king whom he has set on his holy hill of Zion (Ps. 2:4–6).

Jehovah will surely protect his Son for his own glory and for our salvation, for it is not God's purpose that Jesus should die as a small child, but that he should live to adulthood so that he can, as a mature man, offer his life on the cross for our sins.

Chapter 16

WISE MEN WORSHIPING THE INFANT KING

9. When they had heard the king, they departed; and, lo, the star, which they saw in the east, went before them, till it came and stood over where the young child was.
10. When they saw the star, they rejoiced with exceeding great joy.
11. And when they were come into the house, they saw the young child with Mary his mother, and fell down, and worshipped him: and when they had opened their treasures, they presented unto him gifts; gold, and frankincense and myrrh.
12. And being warned of God in a dream that they should not return to Herod, they departed into their own country another way. (Matthew 2:9–12)

One of the main purposes of the coming of the wise men is to teach us that Jesus Christ is the Lord of all. He is not merely the King of the Jews. He is the Lord of a church made up of all nations, tribes, and tongues. He is the Savior of a truly catholic or universal church. He is the Lord before whom all nations must bow, whom all nations must serve, and whom all nations must worship.

Moreover, he is that universal Lord eternally. It is not that he became the universal Lord when at the age of thirty years he was baptized in the Jordan River; it is not that he became the universal Lord when he rose from the dead on the third day after his crucifixion; it is not that he became the universal Lord at his ascension; and it is not even that he becomes the universal Lord when he returns on the last day. He is always (he has eternally been) the universal Lord. He is the second person of the holy Trinity, and angels have adored him from the very beginning.

But even as an infant in the cradle he is and is recognized to be the universal Lord. That is why God in his providence has wise men (magi) from a far country come to worship him while he is still a little child: to teach us that he is from eternity our universal Lord.

FINDING HIM

The magi must have been disappointed. For one thousand miles, over several months, they had traveled from the east. Their hearts were filled with excitement and eager anticipation. We can only imagine their conversation as they journeyed: "We have seen his star in the east, and we are coming to worship him." That thought cheered them as they made their way through difficult and dangerous country. Each day brought them closer to seeing the King of the Jews. That was the great desire of their hearts—to see and to worship the King. The most natural place for them to look for the King of the Jews was Jerusalem, the city of the great king. So they began their search asking the people they met, "Where is he that is born King of the Jews?" (Matt. 2:2).

To their great surprise, however, no one had heard of any recent birth of a king. In fact, there was no sign or indication of a newborn king anywhere in Jerusalem. Worse, there was no interest in their question. No one cared that the King of the Jews had been born!

A breakthrough came when news of their quest reached King Herod. Herod knew what their question meant, or at least he suspected it. But Herod, unbeknownst to the magi, was troubled (deeply disturbed, and even frightened) at the news that a rival king had been born. Herod sought confirmation from the religious leaders about the birthplace of the Messiah, who was the King of the Jews. Herod then generously, or so it seemed, provided the magi with the answer that they required: the King of the Jews is born in Bethlehem (which is a short distance from Jerusalem, about five miles away, or a couple of hours' journey).

Herod seemed very interested in the King of the Jews, for he asked the magi carefully about the star that had alerted them to the birth of the King. Herod even requested that the magi "search diligently" (Matt. 2:8) for the newborn King. He expressed his desire to worship the King also and gave them strict instructions to return with news of the newborn King's precise location. The magi must have believed that Herod was sincere, and they left Herod's presence with great hope in their hearts.

And yet—was it not strange? No one from Herod's court, none of the religious leaders, and none of the ordinary citizens of Jerusalem accompanied the magi. Foreign magi were going to see and worship the King of the Jews, and yet the Jews did not come with them.

This might have been discouraging, but it did not deter them. When Jesus is unpopular, as he is here, follow Jesus! When all around you, as here, the people forsake Jesus, follow Jesus! When following Jesus is costly and time consuming and brings you the unwelcome attention of the world, follow Jesus! Is the text not a testimony to the truth that the first will be last and the last will be first, and that when the Jews refuse to worship, God gathers the Gentiles?

Confirmation that the magi were traveling to the right place came from heaven with the reappearance of the star. The text underlines the suddenness and surprise of this with the word "Lo!" This indicates that the star had temporarily disappeared. In the east, as they had been observing the heavens, the magi had seen the star. By whatever means of divine revelation, these men understood that the star pointed to the birth of the King of the Jews. It was because of the star that these magi from the east had come to Jerusalem: "Where is he that is born King of the Jews? for we have seen his star in the east, and are come to worship him" (v. 2).

Strictly speaking, it is not accurate to say that the star *led* them from the east to Jerusalem, or that they had *followed* it from their homeland. In verse 2 they do not point to the sky: "Look! His star is in the sky." They say, "We have seen his star." They saw it in the past. Nor do the magi point out the star to King Herod. Rather, they describe what they observed, and they describe when they beheld it. But as they leave Herod and begin to make their way to the village of Bethlehem, they see the star again. "Lo, the star, which they saw [or 'had seen'] in the east, went before them" (v. 9). The star only began to *lead* them—and they only began to *follow* it—*after* they left the court of King Herod.

We see here the sovereignty and grace of God: Herod did not see the star; the Sanhedrin did not see the star; the people of Jerusalem did not see the star. Only these magi, chosen vessels of God, were privileged to see the star. The star was a supernatural, miraculous star. It moved and they followed it. It shone very low in the sky, so that it was able to reveal to them the very house in which they would find the King of the Jews. That is what verse 9 says: "[It] went on before them" (literally, "It was leading them beforehand, until, having come, it stood above where the young child was").

The magi greeted the star as a long-lost, familiar friend. Notice verse 10: "When they saw the star, they rejoiced." Their rejoicing was no ordinary rejoicing. They were not merely a little bit cheerful or somewhat happy. "They rejoiced with exceeding great joy" (v. 10). They had a deep gladness in their hearts, which overflowed or exceeded all bounds. Literally, "they rejoiced with a mega joy vehemently." They did that because a sign had just appeared in the heavens to reassure them that they were on the right track; it was a sign of Jesus Christ, pointing to his exact location. Here we have three signs: the star; the word of God in Micah; and the star again! If they rejoiced at a star, imagine the joy they would have had if they had heard a word from heaven or had heard an angel. If they could rejoice at a star, because it was a sign of Jesus Christ, how ought not we to rejoice?

We do not need to look into heaven and scrutinize the meaning of stars. We have the scriptures. We have not only the prophecy of Micah, who tells us that Christ was born in Bethlehem, but we have the completed scriptures. "I rejoice at thy word, as one that findeth great spoil" (Ps. 119:162). "Thy words were found, and I did eat them; and thy word was unto me the joy and rejoicing of mine heart: for I am called by thy name, O LORD God of hosts" (Jer. 15:16). Do we know anything of that?

Do you rejoice on Sunday morning when it is time for worship? Do you rejoice with exceeding great joy? Do you rejoice to hear about Jesus? Do you rejoice in the sacraments, which like the star, and better than the star, are signs (and even seals) of Jesus Christ, of his death on the cross, and of his saving blood?

WORSHIPING HIM

The star led the magi to Bethlehem and, it seems, to the very house in which Jesus was living with Mary and Joseph. As they stood outside, it must have been a surprise for these magi from the east: could this *really* be the right place for the newborn King of the Jews? We notice that at this point Jesus, Mary, and Joseph are not in a stable. Luke 2 records the fact that Jesus was laid in a manger shortly after birth. That is where the shepherds found him, and it was a sign unto them. From the word "manger," which is a feeding trough for animals, we conclude that Jesus was born in a stable, because there was no room for them in the inn. Nativity scenes often confuse the story at this point. The shepherds and magi visited Jesus at completely different times, the former when Jesus was a newborn, the latter when Jesus was older.

Now in Matthew 2 the family is residing in a house. The likely explanation is that after the census was over most people returned to their homes, and there were plenty of rooms available in houses in the village of Bethlehem. A house is certainly a step up from a stable. However, it is hardly the place where these magi expected to find the King of the Jews. We know nothing about the house, but we imagine that it was basic accommodation. Joseph was not rich enough to acquire expensive lodging. At this point, the child was anywhere from forty days to two years old. The best estimate is that the child was a few months old, maybe a year old, but we cannot be sure. Certainly Mary was no longer unclean, and she had recovered from childbirth and labor and was enjoying life as a new mother.

None of these considerations put the wise men off, however. They did not linger outside the door, wondering if they had made a mistake: "When they were come into the house" (v. 11).

Picture the scene. The family is in the house when there is a knock at the door. The text does not mention Joseph, but likely it was he who answered the door. Besides that, the focus of the passage is not on Joseph, but on Jesus. As the door is answered, a number of well-dressed, obviously wealthy, and distinguished foreigners stand outside, asking to come in. They have come on a very long journey, and they have one request: to see the King of the Jews.

By this time, Mary and Joseph may have become accustomed to strange occurrences surrounding their son. Some months earlier, they had answered the door (if the stable had a door) to lowly shepherds. Now foreign dignitaries want to visit their son. The text does not describe the house or the scene in any way, except in these words: "They saw the young child with Mary his mother" (v. 11).

This is what they had come to see, the King of the Jews. Nevertheless, he was not as they had imagined him to be. Servants did not wait upon him. Royal finery did not surround him. But these men had no doubt that this was indeed the King of the Jews. They must have related their tale to Mary and Joseph: "This is the King of the Jews, for we have seen his star in the east, and are come to worship him." It appears that Jesus was young enough still to be in his mother's arms, but it is Jesus who is the center of attention here: "They saw the young child" (v. 11).

Having gained entrance, and (presumably) having stated their business, these men worshiped the young child in the house. The worship is described very simply and very beautifully: "They...fell down, and worshipped him" (v.

11). "They...fell down" does not mean that they tripped or stumbled or fell down backward, but it signifies a falling on their faces prostrate before him. Now the child, the king of the Jews, Jesus Christ is the focus of the magi. When they see him, they bow deeply before him in adoration, giving him the worship due only to God. This is no mere act of respect toward an earthly ruler: this is divine worship. What joy they must have felt to worship him!

This is the kind of divine worship given to Jehovah in heaven, and these men give the same worship to this child. "The four and twenty elders fall down before him that sat on the throne, and worship him that liveth forever and ever, and cast their crowns before the throne" (Rev. 4:10). "The four beasts said, Amen. And the four and twenty elders fell down and worshipped him that liveth for ever and ever" (5:14). "All the angels stood round about the throne, and about the elders and the four beasts, and fell before the throne on their faces, and worshipped God" (7:11).

Clearly, Matthew means to stress the divinity of the child.

Notice how emphatic the text is: "they...fell down, and worshipped *him*" (Matt. 2:11, emphasis added). The text does not say only, "And they worshipped," but it adds, "him." The text does not say, "And they worshipped them, the child with his mother," but "they worshipped him"—*only* him! That is altogether wonderful and mysterious. These men were not men of low degree or rank, but were men of great power, wealth, dignity, and influence. They were from every earthly point of view superior to Jesus, who was a child of poor parents and of low social class. Yet they do not hesitate in getting down on their knees and on their faces to worship him, and no one stops them or rebukes them. Mary does not rush forward and forbid them, "Stop! Do not bow down before my baby son!" Mary (and presumably Joseph) watch with wonder as he is worshiped.

This teaches us that the magi, although their knowledge was limited, knew this: this child is divine. Therefore, he is worthy of our most humble adoration and worship. This knowledge is the knowledge of faith. Only God could have revealed this truth to these men. Consider that they did not worship Jesus after they had seen some great miracle performed by him, for they saw no miracle, except the sign of the star. They did not worship Jesus because he looked like a king, for he did not have the appearance of a king. Nevertheless, they worshiped him. The day is coming, although these men did not see it, when he will look even less like a king, when he hangs on a cross, and yet we worship him still. Another day is coming when before this one, not now a child, but as the Son of man, every knee shall bow and every tongue shall confess that he is Lord!

We worship him for the same reasons. We have not even seen him. We have not seen his star. We have only the word of God as our guide, and we believe that. We know and are persuaded that Jesus, the eternal Son of God, took upon himself our human flesh, so that he could become a human being and even become a helpless human child. He is worthy of our worship and praise. We know and are persuaded that the same Jesus, after living as a man for some thirty-three years, suffered and died on the cross, to atone for our sins. He is worthy of our worship and praise. We know and are persuaded that the same Jesus rose again from the dead, ascended into heaven, and sits at the right hand of God, from where he shall return to judge the living and the dead. He is worthy of our worship and praise.

We worship him, not by bowing down before his physical

body, but we worship him by adoring him, praising him, and obeying him in Spirit and truth, as he is at the right hand of his Father, and as he is revealed in the word of God.

PRESENTING THEIR GIFTS TO HIM

The magi had not come empty handed, for after their act of worship, "they...opened their treasures" (v. 11). They had carried these treasures from their homeland, having selected in advance these gifts for the King of the Jews. This was not the presentation of gifts to a common child or to a new mother. We have done that. When a child is born, it is common to give gifts to the parents, especially to the mother, and to give gifts to the new baby. Often, new parents receive many changes of clothing for their new baby: cute little outfits, bibs, and the like. Or perhaps we bring a toy or a teddy bear for the baby to play with.

That is not what these magi did: the gifts they brought were fit for a king. Notice verse 11: "they presented unto *him*" (emphasis added). The verb "presented" is the word often used with respect to offering sacrifices or incense or other acts of worship. Although the child was too young to appreciate the gifts, they presented them to him. These are gifts given not because the baby is cute or because they wanted to relieve the needs of Mary his mother, but in recognition of his royalty. If we bought a present for a royal prince today, we would think, "What kind of gift is fit for a prince?" "What kind of gift is fit for the King of Kings?" was the question of the magi as they selected their gifts. The gifts are therefore expensive, costly, and precious. The magi bring the best possible gifts that they can afford to bring. Probably Mary and Joseph had never seen such rich items before, for they were a poor family, unaccustomed to finery, luxury, and wealth.

The three gifts are named in verse 11: gold, frankincense, and myrrh. Gold was—and still is—an expensive and valuable commodity. Gold is always associated with royalty. The richer a king is, the more gold he has. Kings have crowns of gold and scepters of gold, for example. Solomon, the richest of Israel's kings, was so wealthy that silver was worthless in his day: "All king Solomon's drinking vessels were of gold, and all the vessels of the house of the forest of Lebanon were of pure gold; none were of silver: it was nothing accounted of in the days of Solomon" (1 Kings 10:21).

Frankincense is simply "pure incense," which was a very precious substance obtained from the resin of a certain kind of tree. Frankincense or incense is associated with worship. It was an ingredient of the incense used in the temple: "The LORD said unto Moses, Take unto thee sweet spices, stacte, and onycha, and galbanum; these sweet spices with pure frankincense: of each shall there be a like weight" (Ex. 30:34). If gold is an indication of Christ's royalty, frankincense points to his divinity.

Myrrh is another resin from a different tree. It too was a very precious substance, and it had three main uses. It was used as a perfume to make things smell pleasant; it was used as an anesthetic to relieve pain; and it was used to embalm dead bodies. If gold is an indication of Christ's royalty and frankincense points to his divinity, myrrh is an indication of Christ's mortality and future suffering.

Did the magi know this when they selected their gifts? We have no way of determining that for sure. Nevertheless, God in his sovereign providence determined these gifts for his Son.

This presentation of gifts is also the fulfillment of prophecy.

There are no specific prophecies, of course, but in general the Old Testament prophesies the coming of the Gentiles to worship the King of the Jews. There are even some prophecies that come very close to matching this event. "The kings of Tarshish and of the isles shall bring presents: the kings of Sheba and Seba shall offer gifts. Yea, all kings shall fall down before him: all nations shall serve him" (Ps. 72:10–11). "The multitude of camels shall cover thee, the dromedaries of Midian and Ephah, all they from Sheba shall come: they shall bring gold and incense; and they shall shew forth the praises of the Lord" (Isa. 60:6). These are the first Gentiles in the New Testament to worship Jesus, and they are not the last. We might justifiably call them the first fruits of the Gentiles.

We join the magi; we bow down before Jesus, and we present gifts to him. Our gifts are not gold, frankincense, and myrrh, but the gift of praise. "By him therefore let us offer the sacrifice of praise to God continually, that is, the fruit of our lips giving thanks to his name" (Heb. 13:15). "Ye also, as lively stones, are built up a spiritual house, an holy priesthood, to offer up spiritual sacrifices, acceptable to God by Jesus Christ" (1 Pet. 2:5). We give to Jesus our money, our time, our energy, our heart, and our life, because he gave his lifeblood to purchase our salvation.

Then the magi left. We do not know how long they stayed, but we can imagine that they had long conversations with Mary and Joseph and learned as much about Jesus as they could. They had intended to fulfill their errand to Herod, to tell him where Jesus was, but God intervened: he warned them in a dream by means of an angel. They must not, under any circumstances, return to Herod. They obeyed God, returning by another route, having seen and worshiped the King.

Chapter 17

GOD'S SON CALLED
OUT OF EGYPT

13. And when they were departed, behold, the angel of
    the Lord appeareth to Joseph in a dream, saying,
    Arise, and take the young child and his mother,
    and flee into Egypt, and be thou there until I bring
    thee word: for Herod will seek the young child to
    destroy him.
14. When he arose, he took the young child and his
    mother by night, and departed into Egypt:
15. And was there until the death of Herod: that it
    might be fulfilled which was spoken of the Lord by
    the prophet, saying, Out of Egypt have I called my
    son. (Matthew 2:13–15)

As soon as Jesus, the Son of God, was born into the
world, he was the occasion of division. Some, those
chosen by God and prepared by him, welcomed and worshiped him. Mary, Joseph, Elizabeth, the shepherds, the
magi, Simeon, and Anna are examples of such elect children
of God. Others, motivated by Satan and stirred up by their
own sinful flesh, hated him and sought to destroy him, and
here especially we remember the enmity of King Herod.

But God in heaven loved his Son. He had deep affection
for Jesus; he desired and accomplished Jesus' greatest good;
and he maintained close fellowship with his Son. That love

of God for Jesus is clear in Hosea 11:1, part of which Matthew quotes here: "When Israel was a child, then I loved him, and called my son out of Egypt."

If God loved his adopted son, Israel, and called him out of Egypt at the time of Moses, how much more did not God love his own, only begotten, eternal Son, Jesus!

When Herod lifted up his hand in murderous hatred against God's Son, God protected him. He does so by bringing him into Egypt so that he can call him out of Egypt again.

THE EVENTS

At the time of the events in our text, Jesus is a young child, and he and his earthly family are living happily in Bethlehem. Joseph had originally brought his wife from Nazareth to Bethlehem, where she had given birth to Jesus. It appears from the narrative that initially Joseph and Mary had no intention of leaving Bethlehem. They did not have any great desire to return to Nazareth. Joseph, shortly after the birth of Jesus, which took place in a stable, had secured accommodation in Bethlehem in the form of a house. Little did Joseph know that his life, with the lives of Mary and Jesus, would soon be turned upside down again!

The occasion for this new upheaval was the visit of the magi, although they did not know that, and they were not to blame. The magi had left and were on the way back to Jerusalem to King Herod, who had commanded them to return with information about the precise whereabouts of the child. On the way, an angel had appeared to them in a dream telling them not to return to Herod. It appears that the angel did not give them a reason, for if he had, surely the magi would have warned Mary and Joseph. Inadvertently, then, these magi had alerted King Herod to the presence of the child, who was born the King of the Jews. Herod knew that the child was in Bethlehem, and it would not take long for him to find the house. Of all this, however, Joseph was as yet blissfully unaware.

Shortly after the departure of the magi (perhaps that very night), Joseph had a dream, in which dream the angel of the Lord appeared. This was likely the same angel who had appeared to Joseph to reassure him in Matthew 1:20 about taking Mary to be his wife. This time, the angel did not bring reassurance, but a warning. The angel's message was startling and urgent. It was a revelation about King Herod's murderous intentions concerning the child: "Herod will seek the young child to destroy him" (Matt. 2:13).

The angel's message must have been a terrible shock to Joseph. This is the first time that Joseph learns that Herod knows about the child. For Herod to take interest in your child is never a good thing. This must have struck fear into Joseph's heart. King Herod is seeking *my* child! The angel's message is the exact opposite of what Herod had professed to the magi: "Go and search diligently for the young child; and when ye have found him, bring me word again, that I may come and worship him also" (v. 8). But the truth is, "Herod will seek the young child *to destroy him*" (v. 13, emphasis added). The angel underlines that the threat is imminent: "Herod is about to seek the young child to destroy him" is a literal rendering of the Greek of verse 13.

The angel issues four urgent commands to Joseph: four imperatives. "Arise"—Joseph was asleep in bed, but now he must get up. "Take"—Joseph must awaken Mary and baby Jesus out of their slumber, and gather their belongings together, and bundle up the baby and his mother. "Flee"—Joseph must hurry. There is no time for delay. They cannot even wait until the morning. They must run for their lives and be gone by morning light. "Be"—Joseph must remain with Jesus and Mary in the place of their flight for some time, until the angel reappears with fresh instructions.

The destination to which Joseph must flee with Jesus and Mary is Egypt. Joseph does not flee to Nazareth, or across the Jordan, but to the land of Egypt. The place that God chose is outside of Herod's jurisdiction but still within the Roman Empire. Technically, it was not even foreign territory. Egypt was a considerable distance away, but not as far away as Babylon or Persia, from which the magi had come, for example. Joseph could expect to reach the border of Egypt in 100 miles and the River Nile in 200 miles. We do not know the city in Egypt to which they fled. Egypt was a suitable destination because it was home to many Jews. The Jewish population of Egypt at this time is estimated to have been one million Jews.

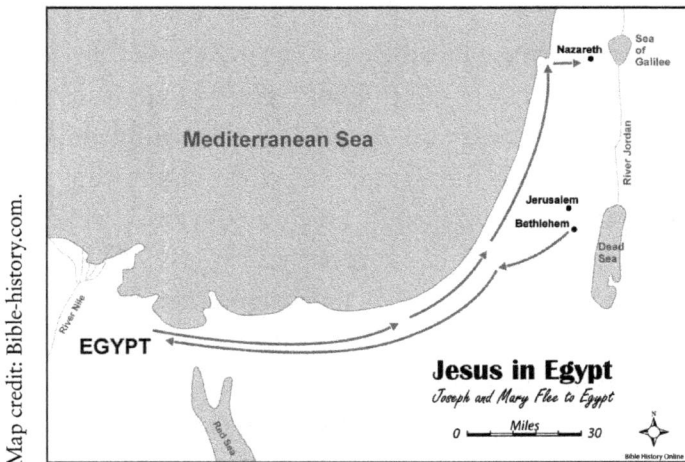

together, and bundle up the baby and his mother. "Flee"—

Map credit: Bible-history.com.

This is another indictment on Israel, for when the Messiah came, he was forced to flee into Egypt out of fear for his life. Was there no one in Israel who could protect the infant Jesus and his earthly parents? No one offered them a bed on the night he was born, and no one cares for him when King Herod threatens to kill him. As a judgment upon Israel, God removes his Son from Israel and sends him into Egypt. He deprives Israel of the presence of the Messiah in their midst. In all of this, God in heaven is caring for his Son to preserve him when he is most vulnerable.

We might wonder, though—why does God choose this way to rescue his Son? Could God not have performed a miracle to preserve his Son from Herod? Could God not have protected him with a wall of fire or with ten legions of angels? Why must he flee with Joseph and Mary into Egypt? Furthermore, why did God not warn the other parents in Bethlehem? Why did God not protect *their* children? Why did God not simply kill Herod before he could do Jesus or the other children of Bethlehem any harm? We cannot give an answer to such questions. God often prefers to use ordinary means to fulfill his will, and God is sovereign over life and death.

One of the principles Jesus teaches is that when we are persecuted, we flee. We do not expect God to save us from persecution and death by a miracle, but we take advantage of the ordinary means available to us: we flee. "But when they persecute you in this city, flee ye into another" (Matt. 10:23).

Joseph unhesitatingly obeyed, another indication of his godliness. Can you imagine what that would be like? Can you imagine you, your wife, and your children in imminent danger? Can you imagine having to drop everything and having to leave behind everything except a few meager possessions that you can carry with you? Can you imagine waking up your wife and children in the middle of the night and telling them that they must flee and that there is no time to say goodbye to family and friends? Can you imagine rushing off in the darkness to a foreign country, hoping and praying that your pursuers or persecutors do not catch up with you?

We read in Matthew 2 that Joseph did exactly what the angel commanded: "When he arose, he took the young child and his mother by night, and departed into Egypt: and was there until the death of Herod" (vv. 14–15). Notice the repetition of the four verbs from verse 13. "Arise"—and he arose; "take"—and he took the young child and his mother; "flee"—and he departed into Egypt; "be"—and he was there until the death of Herod.

Also notice the immediacy—"by night." No one in Bethlehem witnessed their departure, for in the morning the family was gone, gone without a trace. Scripture does not tell us the details that in our curiosity we would like to know. We do not know the city in which they stayed, the age of Jesus when he fled, or the length of time that they stayed in Egypt. When they arrived in Egypt, Joseph had to find lodging and work. We imagine that he worked as a carpenter, for that was his occupation and trade. Undoubtedly, the gift of gold from the magi was put to good use, for God had provided funds for their journey. We know that they resided in Egypt until Herod died, which took place in 4 BC. They probably did not spend more than a few months to a year in Egypt, and when they returned Jesus was probably no older than three years.

This was suffering, both for Jesus and for his earthly parents. It was suffering for a little child to be bundled up in the middle of the night and to flee to a foreign land with his frightened parents. It was suffering for Jesus to be hated to the point of death so that King Herod desired to destroy him. Surely this was the beginning of the fulfillment of Simeon's prophecy: "Yea, a sword shall pierce through thy own soul also" (Luke 2:35).

This suffering was necessary because of our sins. Jesus was exiled from the land of Canaan because he was bearing our iniquities. He did not begin to bear our iniquities only at the cross. He was born into this world already bearing our iniquities. This must be so, otherwise, it would be unjust for Jesus to suffer even as a child. Certainly the fullness of God's wrath came upon him at the cross, but Jesus was born under the wrath and curse of God, because he represented us. Do not misunderstand. God loved and delighted in his Son, but he represented a sinful people; therefore, he was under God's judicial wrath. When, believing reader, you ponder the flight of Jesus from Bethlehem to Egypt, remember that your sins were the reason for that suffering, just as they were the reason for all of Christ's sufferings.

The Significance

The title of this chapter might strike us as odd: "God's Son called out of Egypt." Surely the title should be, "God's Son flees *to* Egypt," or "is called *into* Egypt." It is true that the main activity of the text is the flight into Egypt. At the beginning of the text, Joseph is commanded to flee to Egypt. In the text, Joseph actually does flee with Jesus and Mary into Egypt. Indeed, they do not return from Egypt until Matthew 2:21.

Nevertheless, the main idea of the text is, and therefore the theme of the chapter must be, "God's Son called *out of* Egypt." God only calls Jesus *into* Egypt so that he can call him *out of* Egypt again. That is clear from verse 15, "that it might be fulfilled which was spoken of the Lord by the prophet, saying, Out of Egypt have I called my son." What a startling truth! God turns the lives of Jesus, Joseph, and Mary upside down and puts on them a huge inconvenience so that prophecy is fulfilled. They have to flee all the way to Egypt so that God's word to Hosea is fulfilled.

This is not the first time either that God's word had inconvenienced this godly couple, for Mary and Joseph had traveled to Bethlehem when the whole Roman Empire was made subject to a tax, so that prophecy might be fulfilled. Jesus will suffer in many more ways so that prophecy might be fulfilled. We learn a valuable lesson from this: God's word is more important than our convenience. Yet this is an unusual prophecy and an unusual fulfillment. Let me put it this way: was it necessary for Jesus to go to Egypt to fulfill this prophecy?

There are certain prophecies that Jesus *had to* fulfill. For example, if Jesus had not been born in Bethlehem, he would not have fulfilled Micah 5:2, which stipulates the birthplace of the Messiah. If Jesus had not been crucified, he would not have fulfilled Psalm 22, Psalm 69, and Isaiah 53, for example. But is Hosea 11:1 in the same category? The text reads, "When Israel was a child, then I loved him, and called my son out of Egypt."

Perhaps we might argue that if Jesus had not fled to Egypt, Hosea 11:1 would still have been fulfilled, because Hosea 11:1 does not speak in the first place about Jesus. Hosea 11:1 was fulfilled long before the events of Matthew 2. The prophet is not predicting a future event in Hosea 11:1. Instead, he is describing something that had happened in his past, at the time of the exodus, many centuries before

Hosea's ministry to Israel. Hosea does not prophesy that Jesus would also be called out of Egypt, but Hosea's prophecy applies to Jesus in a secondary manner. In other words, Jesus is exiled to Egypt and then called out of Egypt so that he can identify with his people Israel.

God determined that his Son—his eternal, only begotten Son—should undergo the same experiences that his adopted Old Testament son Israel experienced. That is why he takes Jesus out of Bethlehem, sends him to Egypt, and calls him back a short time later. Matthew understands this by inspiration and is led to connect this event to the words of Hosea 11:1: "That it might be fulfilled which was spoken of the Lord by the prophet, saying, Out of Egypt have I called my son" (Matt. 2:15).

To escape famine Israel departed from Canaan to go to Egypt. To escape persecution Jesus fled Judea to dwell in Egypt. At God's command Israel was called out of Egypt and back to Canaan. At God's command Jesus was called out of Egypt and back to Canaan. That is because Jesus was in Israel when she went down to Egypt; he was in Israel when Pharaoh tried to destroy Israel by killing her baby boys; and he was in Israel when the nation was delivered out of Egypt into the wilderness. If Jesus, the seed of the woman, had not been in Israel, the devil would not have tried to destroy Israel.

We need to look at the context of Hosea 11:1. Hosea was one of the "writing prophets" to the ten tribes of the northern kingdom of Israel. The main idea of Hosea's prophecy is God's love for an apostate people. God's people Israel, especially the ten tribes, had rejected him, for they had played the harlot and they had followed after other gods. In fact, Hosea the prophet was commanded to marry Gomer, who played the harlot against Hosea, so that his marriage would mirror Jehovah's marriage to Israel. Hosea's marriage was a vivid illustration of a faithful husband betrayed by a faithless wife.

The question in Hosea is this: What will Jehovah do about Israel? Will he judge her? Will he destroy her? Will he put her away? Will he reject her and choose another people worthier of his love? The answer is that Jehovah will never cast away his people. Although his people are treacherous and faithless, God will save his people. God's salvation of Israel does not mean that he will overlook Israel's sins, and it does not even mean that he will save all the Israelites head for head, but it does mean that he will never cast off his elect and doom them to everlasting destruction.

Jehovah's salvation of his people means that he will chastise them, purify them, and deliver them from sin and destruction. Listen to Jehovah in Hosea 11:8–9:

8. How shall I give thee up, Ephraim? how shall I deliver thee, Israel? how shall I make thee as Admah? how shall I set thee as Zeboim? mine heart is turned within me, my repentings are kindled together.

9. I will not execute the fierceness of mine anger, I will not return to destroy Ephraim: for I am God, and not man; the Holy One in the midst of thee: and I will not enter into the city.

Jehovah is moved to deep compassion for his people. The tragedy of the book of Hosea is this: God pursues his people with mercies, but Israel rejects and scorns him. Israel is like a spoiled child or a spoiled young man who has forgotten the love of his father.

That is how the eleventh chapter of Hosea begins: "When Israel was a child, then I loved him" (v. 1). Verse 3 continues the story: "I taught Ephraim also to go [or to walk], taking them by their arms." Imagine a father holding his little boy's hand as he takes his first steps. Jehovah remembers that. Verse 4 elaborates: "I drew them with cords of a man, with bands of love." Here the figure changes. Now Jehovah is a kind and gentle farmer who cares for his beast, treating it more like a pet than a beast of burden.

But look at how Israel repays Jehovah for his goodness. In verse 2 the prophet complains: "They went from them: they sacrificed unto Baalim, and burned incense to graven images." In verse 3 God testifies against Israel: "They knew not that I healed them." In verse 7 God describes apostasy: "My people are bent to backsliding from me." In verse 12 God testifies against the people: "Ephraim compasseth me about with lies, and the house of Israel with deceit."

Is that not an awful picture of us? We have received kindness at Jehovah's hand, but time and time again, we betray him, we forget his goodness, we scorn his love, and we seek satisfaction in the world!

Here is why Jesus had to go into Egypt and then be called out again: so that he could do what Israel did not do. Israel is the imperfect type; Jesus is the perfect antitype or the perfect fulfillment.

First, Jesus experienced the love of God. If Hosea can write, "When Israel was a child, then I loved him, and called my son out of Egypt" (11:1), how much more is that not true of Jesus? "When Jesus was a child, then I loved him." God loved Jesus so much that he would not permit King Herod to destroy him. God loved Israel so much that he would not permit Pharaoh of Egypt to destroy him. "And I called my son out of Egypt." God brought Israel out of Egypt, through the wilderness, and into Canaan. God brought Jesus into Egypt out of reach of Herod, and when the time was right, he brought Jesus out again. "I taught Ephraim also to go, taking them by their arms." Think of Jeremiah 31:32, "I took them by the hand to bring them out of the land of Egypt." God took Jesus by the hand and brought him out of Egypt and back to Canaan.

Unlike Israel, Jesus both knew and appreciated God's care for him. Unlike Israel, Jesus rendered grateful returns of ardent love to God for his care of him. Jesus could not have stayed in Egypt indefinitely. His stay there had to be temporary because Jesus had very important work to do in Israel. Jesus had to keep the law of God in Israel. He must live among his own people. He had to preach the gospel to them. He must work among them, healing them, giving sight to the blind, and even raising the dead—in Israel. But more than that, Jesus must bear the punishment for Israel, that is, for all of God's elect people, both Jews and Gentiles. He had to be crucified in Israel, and he must rise again from the dead in Israel.

Through Jesus' perfect obedience, his atoning sufferings and death, and his resurrection, God calls us out of Egypt also. Remember that Egypt is a picture of sin—the bondage of sin and slavery to the devil. God calls us by the power of his Holy Spirit out of sin and death into life and peace.

Thus God turns the lives of Jesus, Mary, and Joseph upside down so that he can teach us a spiritual lesson. Israel went down into Egypt—so did Jesus, and so do we. Israel was called out of Egypt—so was Jesus, and so are we. What God accomplished typically for Israel, Jesus accomplishes in reality for us. What Israel could not do—because she was sinful—Jesus was able to do because he is the Son of God.

Chapter 18

HEROD'S MASSACRE
OF BETHLEHEM'S INFANTS

16. Then Herod, when he saw that he was mocked of the wise men, was exceeding wroth, and sent forth, and slew all the children that were in Bethlehem, and in all the coasts thereof, from two years old and under, according to the time which he had diligently inquired of the wise men.

17. Then was fulfilled that which was spoken by Jeremiah the prophet, saying,

18. In Rama was there a voice heard, lamentation, and weeping, and great mourning, Rachel weeping for her children, and would not be comforted, because they are not. (Matthew 2:16–18)

The massacre of Bethlehem's infants is characteristic of King Herod. No one who knew Herod would have been at all surprised at this act. So bloodthirsty was Herod that he killed his own wife, Mariamne, his brother-in-law, Aristobulus, his mother-in-law, Alexandra, another brother-in-law, Kostobar, his sons Alexander and Aristobulus, and as he was dying, he executed a third son, Antipater.

By Herod's standards, the murder of Jewish children was rather insignificant. In fact, the Emperor Augustus is reported to have said, "It is better to be one of Herod's hogs, than one of Herod's sons." (The Jews did not kill and eat pigs.)

Herod's cruelty was manifested even on his deathbed, for when that wretched king was dying, he gave orders for a massacre. To that end Herod gathered a large number of important officials to Jerusalem and gave instructions to his sister that, as soon as he had died, those people should be slaughtered—and why? Herod wanted weeping to take place at the time of his death, and he knew that the people would not weep *for him*; therefore, he arranged for widespread weeping in Jerusalem. Thankfully, his sister did not carry out his orders, and the people were spared.

Nevertheless, the massacre of the infants of Bethlehem is significant and worthy of inclusion in scripture, not simply because it illustrates the wickedness of Herod, but especially because it was an attempt to murder Christ, an attempt inspired by Satan and an attempt thwarted by God.

THE DIABOLICAL WICKEDNESS

Herod anxiously waited. Soon the wise men would return. Herod probably congratulated himself on his cunning. As soon as he had heard the wise men's story, he had determined to destroy the child. He had invited the wise men to the palace, where he had treated them kindly. From the wise men Herod had gleaned valuable information, namely, the time of the appearance of the star, which marked the birth of the Messiah. He had then sent the wise men to search for the child. He had even told them that he planned to worship him, and the fools had believed him!

But the wise men had not returned as he had planned. It was a short journey from Jerusalem to Bethlehem. They could have visited the child and returned in less than five hours. The hours passed, and Herod's anxiety increased.

Where were they? Why had they not returned? How much longer would they keep him waiting? Then it dawned on him: they were not coming back! They had tricked him! Now Herod's self-congratulation and anxiety turned to fury: "Then Herod, when he saw that he was mocked of the wise men, was exceeding wroth" (Matt. 2:16).

Of course, the wise men had not mocked Herod. The wise men had intended to return to Herod, for they had believed that Herod's show of piety was genuine. They did think that Herod wanted to worship the child. But God had intervened when the angel of the Lord warned them in a dream not to return to Herod. By the time Herod found out, the wise men were on their way home by another route.

Herod's response to this perceived mockery was fury: "He...was exceeding wroth" (v. 16). He exploded with rage, most likely terrifying his servants. "The wrath of a king is as messengers of death" (Prov. 16:14). But Herod did not admit defeat, for he was determined to destroy Christ. Herod called his soldiers to give them gruesome instructions: a mission of infanticide. The place of the infanticide would be "in Bethlehem, and in all the coasts thereof" (Matt. 2:16). Herod knew that the child whom he desired to destroy had been born in Bethlehem, but he did not know the exact location, house, or family. To make sure that his prey did not escape, he ordered the death of *all* children in Bethlehem and, for good measure, the slaughter of all children in all the surrounding villages and areas. From Herod's perspective, it was better to kill too many children than to miss the one child that he desired to kill.

The victims of this infanticide were determined by age and gender. Herod knew that the child had been born recently, and he knew the time when the star had appeared, for he had been careful to extract that information from the magi. He probably calculated that the child was less than one year old, but to make sure, he added a year: "Kill all children two years and younger!" In addition, he was not interested in girls, so he specified that only boys should be killed, for the Greek is gender specific.

Herod's orders were ruthlessly executed. The Bible does not describe the carnage, but the horror of it is easy to imagine. Soldiers burst into homes searching for children. They murdered all boys two years and under in front of their helpless parents. These little children were snatched from their mothers' arms, dashed to pieces, or thrust through with swords. Herod's men did not listen as the parents begged for mercy, for neither they nor their master knew mercy.

All across Bethlehem and the surrounding area, the cries of mothers and fathers who had lost their children filled the air. What carnage! What horror!

Herod's actions are not merely the cruelties of a paranoid king, but they are inspired by Satan. The real target is the Lord Jesus Christ, the seed of the woman. Since the dawn of time, Satan has been attempting to destroy Christ. Remember that Satan heard the first promise of the gospel to Adam and Eve. "I will put enmity between thee [Satan] and the woman, and between thy seed and her seed [Christ]: it shall bruise [crush] thy head, and thou shalt bruise his heel" (Gen. 3:15). Satan did not admit defeat, however, for he was determined to prevent the coming of Jesus Christ into the world, and he never lacked willing servants to help him in his diabolical schemes.

The devil was also willing to kill children in his attempt to kill Christ. Children were his targets in Egypt, where he inspired Pharaoh to destroy the male children of the Israelites by throwing them into the Nile. God rescued Moses, who later became Israel's deliverer. Later, Satan inspired wicked Queen Athaliah to destroy all the seed of David. God rescued one little boy among them, who became King Joash. Later still, Haman masterminded the destruction of all the Jews, including women and children. God stirred up Esther and Mordecai to save the day.

Having failed to prevent the coming of Christ, Satan now tries to murder the Christ soon after he is born in Bethlehem. The book of Revelation teaches this in chapter 12, in which Satan is depicted as a great red dragon, which stands over the woman, who is the church, so that he can devour her child. But Satan is thwarted in his scheme, for God snatches the child away into heaven (Rev. 12:1–5), with the result that Satan persecutes the church on earth. God prevents the destruction of Jesus by warning Joseph, who carries Jesus into Egypt until the death of King Herod, as we saw in the last chapter.

We should expect the same cruelty in Satan today. Satan hates the children of God, and now that he has failed to kill Jesus, he targets us with our children. Make no mistake; Herod knew what he was doing. He wanted to kill Christ. He rose up in wicked rebellion against God and imagined in his sinful folly that he could destroy the purpose of God with Christ. As Satan was behind Herod, so Satan is behind infanticide today. Satan is behind the widespread destruction of children through the horror of abortion. Satan is behind the awful child abuse in the world. Satan is behind government attempts to remove children from Christian parents. Satan seeks the destruction of Christian schools and Christian homeschooling. There are people today who, if they were in power, would love to kill Christians and their children.

Nevertheless, we do not need to fear, for just as God delivered his own child, Jesus, so he shall deliver us with our children. Our deliverance might not be physical, for we might face cruelty and persecution, but none of God's elect people, who belong to Jesus Christ, can ever perish. Men like Herod might rage against the Lord and his Anointed, but he who sits in the heavens shall laugh. The Lord shall have them in derision (Ps. 2).

THE BITTER LAMENTATION

From the homes in Bethlehem and the surrounding villages went up a heartrending cry. Matthew 2:18 says, "In Rama was there a voice heard." Three words describe the voice: lamentation, weeping, and great mourning.

Lamentation is the formal expression of grief. Lamentation is a loud, piercing scream or an intense wailing. In many cultures, at funerals, professional mourners are employed to lament in funeral dirges. Think of the many funerals with tiny coffins that must have taken place in Bethlehem after this massacre.

Weeping is the audible expression of grief. A person can weep silently, so that tears trickle down his or her cheeks. This weeping was a kind of violent sobbing, in which the whole body is convulsed as tears flow from the eyes of the anguished mothers of Bethlehem. Think of someone wracked with grief, so that they almost choke on tears.

Mourning is the verbal expression of grief. Mourning is what David did when Absalom died in 2 Samuel 18:33. Think of the mothers of Bethlehem: "Oh, Joshua, my son," or "Oh, Simeon, my son," or "Oh, David, my son," or "Oh, Joseph, my son!" The mourning was great, both because many mothers mourned in this way, and because the mourning was very intense.

This was a specific kind of grief, perhaps the greatest of all grief, which is the grief of a mother who has lost her children. There is something horrible and unnatural about the death of children. We mourn when an older person dies, but we expect older people to die. When a child dies, especially when a very young child dies, the grief is especially great, and the grief of the mother, who bore, nurtured, and loved the child, is especially great. How much more terrible is the death of a child who is violently taken away, murdered in cold blood, as here, in front of the mother, who is forced to witness the child being violently destroyed!

Notice the reason for the grief in Matthew 2:18: "weeping for her children...because they are not." In the Bible, if someone "is not," it means that he or she is absent or is dead. Remember Jacob's words, "Me have ye bereaved of my children: Joseph is not, and Simeon is not, and ye will take Benjamin away: all these things are against me" (Gen. 42:36). Bethlehem's children *were not*—the little boys aged two years and under *were not*—and the mothers wept bitterly for them.

If there is anything worse than that, it is this: the mothers would not be comforted. Nothing could console these mothers who had been robbed of their children in so brutal a fashion. These mothers did not want comfort, for they "would not be comforted" (Matt. 2:18). If their husbands or family attempted to comfort them, they refused it. The cruelty of Herod was so great that these women could never be happy again. The loss of their children devastated them forever.

The women, perhaps understandably, were determined to indulge their grief. What could you say to a woman whose child has been torn from her breast and brutally murdered before her eyes? What could you say to a woman who has lost a child today—perhaps a child who died in a car crash, or who died of a disease, or who was murdered? What could you tell the mothers of Sandy Hook Elementary School in Connecticut, whose children were shot dead on December 14, 2012? What could you tell the Christian mothers of children destroyed in the bombings in Sri Lanka on Easter Sunday 2019? What could Matthew tell those women? What consolation could he bring to them from the gospel of Jesus Christ?

We should say that for the Christian there is comfort, and that it is sinful to *refuse* to be comforted. It is understandable, but it is also sinful. Paul writes about the Christian who faces the death of loved ones: "That ye sorrow not, even as others which have no hope" (1 Thess. 4:13). Of course, mourning is not incompatible with the experience of comfort. Tears are appropriate. Tears even for years after the event are appropriate, but the Christian must also appropriate comfort in the midst of his or her grief. This does not mean, however, that the mourner ever forgets. The loss of a child is irreplaceable, and when others forget, the grieving mother does not forget, neither indeed should she. In a sense, her heart is permanently broken over the loss of her child. Nevertheless, there is an important difference between the grief of the unbeliever and the grief of a Christian. A Christian has comfort; a Christian must appropriate this comfort.

The unbeliever breaks out in wild, uncontrollable grief and despair as he or she faces death, whether his own or another's, but the Christian does not. To face death, even the death of a child, even the violent death of a child, with inconsolable grief is not the Christian response to death. Such a Christian falls into Satan's temptation, believes Satan's lie, and refuses at that time to appropriate the comfort of the gospel.

The comfort for the Christian mother who loses a child is the same comfort for every Christian in every situation. God does not give different sources of comfort to different people at different times. That comfort is this: "I with body and soul, both in life and death, am not my own, but belong unto my faithful Savior Jesus Christ."[1] A loved one might die, even in violent circumstances. You might die, and you will die someday, but this one thing does not change: you belong to him. If the mothers of Bethlehem had appropriated that truth, their lamentation, weeping, and great mourning would have been mixed with solid Christian comfort.

THE STARTLING PROPHECY

According to Matthew 2:17, these events are a fulfillment of the prophecy of Jeremiah. The passage in question is Jeremiah 31:15.

To understand the prophecy, we need to understand who Rachel was. She was one of the two wives of Jacob and one of the two daughters of Laban. Rachel's great concern in life was to have children, and she was especially grieved that her sister, Leah, who was Jacob's first wife, bore Jacob children, while she remained barren. She was jealous because Leah was Jacob's legitimate wife. In fact, Leah had given Jacob four sons: Reuben, Simeon, Levi, and Judah. Rachel complained to Jacob, "Give me children, or else I die" (Gen. 30:1). Rachel finally did give birth to two sons, Joseph and Benjamin, who became Jacob's favorite sons. However,

---

1 Heidelberg Catechism A 1, in *Confessions and Church Order*, 83.

233

Rachel died giving birth to Benjamin. Rachel died, and was buried, on the way to Bethlehem, near Ramah.

That is why Jeremiah writes, "A voice was heard in Ramah" (Jer. 31:15). Ramah is associated with Rachel's sorrow, for she died in the process of doing the one thing she longed for above all things, giving birth to a son. Ramah is the place of Rachel's pillar, which Jacob set up over her burial place (Gen. 35:16–20).

But Jeremiah is prophesying of a second time of sorrow for Rachel, which took place at the time of the Babylonian captivity. Although Rachel was long dead in Jeremiah's day, Jeremiah depicts her rising from the dead to witness anew the destruction of her children. It was at Ramah where the Babylonians assembled the people for exile or death. Ramah was near the northern border of Judah. At that place, near Rachel's pillar, the Babylonians put to death many of the children of Judah, especially those who were too old, weak, or useless to travel to Babylon. The Babylonians shackled and fettered the rest of the people, and thus began the long, slow, painful, and humiliating march of the children of Judah to captivity. We read of this in Jeremiah 40:1: "The word that came to Jeremiah from the LORD, after that Nebuzaradan the captain of the guard had let him go from Ramah, when he had taken him being bound in chains among all that were carried away captive of Jerusalem and Judah, which were carried away captive unto Babylon."

It is fitting that Rachel be depicted as weeping, because in a sense, she was the mother of both the northern and the southern kingdoms. She was the mother of Joseph, whose two sons were Ephraim and Manasseh, who were the two largest tribes of the northern kingdom. Her northern children had been destroyed in the Assyrian captivity. She was also the mother of Benjamin, who was part of the southern kingdom of Judah. Her southern children were destroyed in the Babylonian captivity.

Now Rachel is called up out of her grave again to witness the destruction of more of her children in Bethlehem, which was close to Ramah and the place to which she was traveling at the time of her death. History, says Matthew, is repeating itself in the massacre of Bethlehem's infants. Therefore, we must understand that both Jeremiah and Matthew use a rhetorical device of the personification of a dead person for emotional effect. Certainly, there are parallels between these events.

Both events occur in the judgment of God. That is certainly true of the events prophesied in Jeremiah 31:15. God inflicted the terrible judgment of the Babylonian captivity on Rachel's children because Rachel's children refused to repent. Rachel's northern children, called Israel or Ephraim, had apostatized first. God sent the Assyrians against them. Then Rachel's southern children had stubbornly continued in sin. They had worshiped idols, and they had mocked and scorned the prophets of God. Such rebellion had to be punished, and the instrument of God's wrath was the mighty kingdom of Babylon.

This is also true of the massacre of Bethlehem's infants. God's Son had been born in Bethlehem, but the people had largely ignored him. They could not plead ignorance, for shepherds had testified to him and wise men from the east had worshiped him. Notwithstanding, the people of Bethlehem ignored him. We shudder to think of it, but God punished the people of Bethlehem with the sword of King Herod. Do not forget that God could have prevented it. God could have stopped Herod; God could have warned the parents, but he did not. Instead, God ordained Herod's wickedness: God was sovereign over it, but Herod was responsible for it and he was punished for it.

This contradicts the view of some who see these children as martyrs. The Roman Catholic and Orthodox churches call this the "massacre of the holy innocents," the "first martyrs of Jesus." Rome, for example, commemorates these children annually on December 28 in "The Feast of the Holy Innocents." But these children were not martyrs, for a martyr gives his life willingly as a witness for Christ.

Does this mean that all the families whose children perished in Bethlehem were ungodly? Does this mean that they were more ungodly than others in Israel? We cannot say that with any certainty. It is true that the majority of the Jews were apostate, but that does not mean that the entire nation was reprobate. It would also be wrong for us to claim that all the children who died in Bethlehem by the sword of Herod perished under God's wrath and curse, for we cannot conclude that. It is possible that some of God's elect were caught up in the massacre. When there are wars, famines, calamities, or other events in history, God's people are often caught up in such events. God never promises that his people will be exempt from suffering—quite the contrary.

As for the second question, we are reminded of Jesus' words, "Suppose ye that these Galileans were sinners above all the Galileans, because they suffered such things? I tell you, Nay: but, except ye repent, ye shall all likewise perish" (Luke 13:2–3). The proper reaction to such a horrible occurrence is to say, as the English martyr John Bradford (1510–55) did, "There, but for the grace of God, go I!" We must confess that we with our children deserve to perish as much as did the Bethlehemites of that day, and we must flee from the wrath to come to the cross of Jesus Christ.

But there is also hope in Jeremiah 31 and in Matthew 2, comfort for those who weep. First, there is the hope of Jeremiah 31:16–17: "Thus saith the LORD; Refrain thy voice from weeping, and thine eyes from tears: for thy work shall be rewarded, saith the LORD; and they shall come again from the land of the enemy. And there is hope in thine end, saith the LORD, that thy children shall come again to their own border." Notice the tender words of Jehovah for his distressed people: "Refrain thy voice from weeping, and thine ears from tears." Do not cry, my beloved people. You do not see the end, but a better end is coming, for there is hope. The hope to which Jeremiah refers is the return from Babylon, and also the new covenant, which shall be established in Jesus Christ. When Matthew's readers see the reference to Jeremiah 31:15, they should immediately think also of the context in Jeremiah 31:16–17.

Second, and most importantly, the comfort is this: Herod did not kill Christ. We must not be so horror struck at the cruelty of Herod and the carnage in Bethlehem as to miss that point. We must never be so preoccupied by the terrible atrocities in this world and even by our own afflictions as to miss that. Herod wanted to kill Christ. Herod thought that he had killed Christ. But Herod *did not* kill Christ, for God rescued his Son. Had Herod killed Christ, and had all the children of Bethlehem been spared, there would be endless, eternal weeping in the fires of hell for all of us. There is no salvation for anyone if Herod kills Christ. Christ must survive, even if all the babies in the world are killed, so that he can be our savior.

That is our comfort, for no matter what happens to us or to our children, Jesus Christ is alive. He survived King

Herod; he gave his life for our salvation; he rose again from the dead; and he rules on high. "Refrain thy voice from weeping, and thine eyes from tears." "There is hope in thine end."

Everlasting hope—the hope of eternal life in Christ for all who believe in him.

Chapter 19

THE SON OF GOD CALLED A NAZARENE

19. But when Herod was dead, behold, an angel of the Lord appeareth in a dream to Joseph in Egypt,

20. Saying, Arise, and take the young child and his mother, and go into the land of Israel: for they are dead which sought the young child's life.

21. And he arose, and took the young child and his mother, and came into the land of Israel.

22. But when he heard that Archelaus did reign in Judaea in the room of his father Herod, he was afraid to go thither: notwithstanding, being warned of God in a dream, he turned aside into the parts of Galilee:

23. And he came and dwelt in a city called Nazareth: that it might be fulfilled which was spoken by the prophets, He shall be called a Nazarene. (Matthew 2:19–23)

*F*ar from contradicting one another, the evangelists Matthew and Luke complement one another in their accounts of Christ's nativity and childhood. Luke teaches that Mary, Christ's mother, was from Nazareth, and he explains how it was that Mary and Joseph traveled to Bethlehem with the result that Christ was born in Bethlehem and not in Nazareth. Matthew teaches that Jesus was born in

Bethlehem, but that he spent his childhood in Nazareth and not in Bethlehem. Both truths, that Christ was born in Bethlehem and that Christ grew up in Nazareth, are necessary, and both truths are fulfillments of prophecy.

When we last saw Jesus in the narrative in Matthew, he was in Egypt. He had been taken there to escape the fury of King Herod, who wanted to kill him. But Jesus must not remain indefinitely in Egypt, for he must return to Israel. In addition, he must not grow up in Bethlehem, for he must not be called a Bethlehemite but a Nazarene. This too is the purpose of God with his Son.

The Reason for This

The word *Nazarene* means "inhabitant of Nazareth." Matthew explains how Jesus came to live in Nazareth. Everywhere in the New Testament, Jesus is called "Jesus of Nazareth," but Nazareth was not where Mary and Joseph intended to bring up Jesus. The New Testament explains the movements of Jesus in his childhood in some detail.

Both Mary and Joseph were from Nazareth, or Nazarenes. From Luke 1:26 we learn that Mary was from Nazareth; and from chapter 2:4 we conclude that Joseph was also from Nazareth. Moreover, verse 39 indicates that both Mary and Joseph were from Nazareth: "They returned... to *their* own city Nazareth" (emphasis added). As far as geography is concerned, God's purpose with his Son was twofold: he must be born in Bethlehem, and he must grow up in Nazareth. This geography is important according to God's counsel.

Nevertheless, it had not been the intention of Mary or Joseph initially to leave Nazareth; instead, the decree of

Caesar Augustus forced them to Bethlehem (Luke 2). After Jesus' birth in Bethlehem, it had also not been the intention of Joseph or Mary to return to Nazareth. It appears that they preferred to stay in Bethlehem. There are possible reasons for this. Mary and Joseph knew the significance of Bethlehem, for it was David's city and therefore the Messiah's city. Presumably they were acquainted with the prophecy of Micah 5:2. How fitting, then, for the Son of God, the true seed of David, to grow up in Bethlehem. Moreover, Bethlehem was situated close to Jerusalem, where God's house was located. How fitting for the Son of God to have easy access to the temple of God. To that end, it appears Joseph secured a house for his family in Bethlehem, in which house the magi had visited and worshiped Jesus (Matt. 2:11).

But our plans are not always God's plans, and God's people's plans are not always his plans. Jesus must not remain and grow up in Bethlehem. Therefore, God's Son must be called out of Egypt in order to reenact Hosea 11:1, in order to retrace the footsteps of God's son Israel. To that end, an angel appeared to Joseph and commanded him to take Jesus and his wife, Mary, to Egypt, which command Joseph had obeyed. Consequently, the young family had fled in the middle of the night to Egypt, where they had remained for some time. Their sojourn in Egyptian territory may have been only for a few months, for it seems that Herod died shortly thereafter.

In addition, God's Son must be preserved from the wrath of King Herod, while the infants of Bethlehem and its environs must be slaughtered. Therefore, Herod ordered an infanticide in Bethlehem in an attempt to destroy the King of the Jews, but because Jesus was already safely in Egypt, Herod's murderous intentions were thwarted. At the same time, the prophecy of Jeremiah 31:15 was reenacted, which was the desolate, inconsolable weeping of Rachel for her children.

Jesus, having escaped the wrath of King Herod, returned to Israel with his earthly parents, Joseph and Mary. Jesus' early months and years were very unsettled. First he was born in Bethlehem; then he fled to Egypt; then he returned to Israel; and finally he settled in Nazareth in the region of Galilee in northern Israel. In order to accomplish God's purpose, therefore, the angel of God appeared again and instructed Joseph to take Jesus and Mary back to Israel from Egypt.

Joseph's dream in Egypt uses very similar language to the dream of Matthew 2:13. Read verses 13 and 20 and compare the wording. The only significant difference is between the words "flee" and "go." In verse 13 Joseph had to wake up Jesus and Mary, hurriedly gather together their meager possessions, and run off in the middle of the night. In this dream the instructions come with less urgency: Joseph does not need to hurry; he can prepare at a leisurely pace; he can make his travel arrangements calmly and without panic. He is going but not fleeing. Besides, he now journeys in the opposite direction. In verse 13 he fled to Egypt, while in verse 20 he returns to Israel. We notice again Joseph's immediate obedience in verse 21.

This marked another upheaval in Jesus' short life. Perhaps the family had just settled into Egypt, and now they must drop everything and leave again. But Joseph does not complain; he does not make excuses; he obeys. This is a pattern for Joseph in chapters 1:24, 2:14, and 2:21. Joseph's behavior condemns all those who allow convenience to determine their church membership and their obedience to God.

The reason for the dream is the death of Herod: "for they are dead which sought the young child's life" (2:20). King Herod the Great, the cruel, tyrannical despot, who terrified the people, had died. Scripture devotes only a few words to it: "But when Herod was dead" (v. 19). Historians describe Herod's demise, for he died a slow, painful, gruesome death, an agonizing death of many diseases. One doctor who read Josephus's account of Herod's death believes that Herod died of chronic kidney failure and Fournier's gangrene, which is the rotting of the flesh of the internal organs.

> But now Herod's distemper greatly increased upon him after a severe manner, and this by God's judgment upon him for his sins: for a fire glowed in him slowly, which did not so much appear to the touch outwardly, as it augmented his pains inwardly; for it brought upon him a vehement appetite to eating, which he could not avoid to supply with one sort of food or other. His entrails were also exulcerated, and the chief violence of his pain lay on his colon; an aqueous and transparent liquor also settled itself about his feet, and a like matter afflicted him at the bottom of his belly. Nay, farther, his privy member was putrified, and produced worms; and when he sat upright he had a difficulty of breathing, which was very loathsome, on account of the stench of his breath, and the quickness of its returns; he had also convulsions in all parts of his body, which increased his strength to an insufferable degree. It was said by those who pretended to divine, and who were endued with wisdom to foretell such things, that God inflicted this punishment on the king on account of his great impiety; yet was he still in hopes

of recovering, though his afflictions seemed greater than anyone could bear. He also sent for physicians, and did not refuse to follow what they prescribed for his assistance, and went beyond the river Jordan, and bathed himself in warm baths that were at Callirrhoe, which, besides their other general virtues, were also fit to drink; which water runs into the lake called Asphaltitis. And when the physicians once thought fit to have him bathed in a vessel full of oil, it was supposed that he was just dying; but upon the lamentable cries of his domestics, he revived; and having no longer the least hopes of recovering, he gave order that every soldier should be paid fifty drachmae; and he also gave a great deal to their commanders, and to his friends, and came again to Jericho, where he grew so choleric, that it brought him to do all things like a madman.[1]

Herod died at age sixty-nine in the year 4 BC. Thus God took vengeance upon that wicked ruler, which was only a foretaste of God's everlasting vengeance upon him both in body and soul in hell.

After Herod was removed in the judgment of God, it was now safe for Jesus in the company of Joseph and Mary to return to Israel. In Joseph's dream, however, the angel does not specify the exact location in Israel to which he should bring his family, but it appears that Joseph intended to return to Bethlehem. At the very least, Joseph planned to live in one of the cities of Judea.

---

1 "The Antiquities of the Jews" (17:6:5), in Flavius Josephus, *The Works of Josephus*, trans. William Whiston, A.M. (Peabody, MA: Hendrickson Publishers, repr. 1988), 462.

God's purpose for his Son was for a childhood far away from Bethlehem and far away from Judea, in Nazareth in the region of Galilee. Joseph is afraid, according to verse 22, to settle in Judea, and therefore he seeks guidance from the Lord: where should he bring the infant Messiah? God revealed the location in a dream: he should settle in Galilee. The reason for this choice was, according to verse 23, that scripture might be fulfilled.

Joseph feared to live in the region of Judea because of the rule of Archelaus. Before Herod died, he had divided his kingdom according to his last will and testament in the following manner: Archelaus would have jurisdiction in Judea, Samaria, and Idumea; Antipas (the king who later beheaded John the Baptist) would rule over Galilee and Perea; while Philip, whose wife was Herodias, whom Herod Antipas married, would be ruler over Trachonitis. The ratification of Herod's will was subject to the approval of Caesar Augustus, who made Archelaus an "ethnarch" instead of king, where an "ethnarch" is the governor of a people and a district. Consequently, the power of Archelaus was curtailed after his father's death.

If the Jews had hoped for a more pleasant ruler after the demise of Herod, they were disappointed in Archelaus, who was very much like his father Herod, a man of ruthlessness and cruelty. This makes Joseph's reluctance to settle in Archelaus's jurisdiction unsurprising. The Jews and Samaritans hated Archelaus so much that they eventually appealed to Caesar, with the result that he was deposed and banished in AD 6 after only a couple of years in office.

It was to avoid Herod Archelaus that Joseph settled his family in the northern region of Israel, in Galilee, and specifically in Nazareth.

The Significance for Him

Jesus was called "a Nazarene" in fulfillment of scripture. Verse 23 has puzzled commentators because no specific scripture can be identified. The phrase, "He shall be called a Nazarene," does not appear in the prophets; therefore, verse 23 is not a direct Old Testament quotation. Contrast this with the other citations in Matthew 2: in verse 15 Matthew quotes Hosea, in verse 18 he quotes Jeremiah, but in verse 23 no prophet is quoted, which has led some to conclude that Matthew is mistaken. Such a conclusion is impossible for the Christian because Matthew writes under divine inspiration. The Christian must say, "Matthew *seems* to be mistaken, but that cannot be. Therefore, *I* must be mistaken, and I must seek further light upon this matter."

Some have tried to identify the passage to which Matthew refers in this text. Some think that the reference is to the Nazarites of the Old Testament: "He shall be called a Nazarite." A Nazarite was an Old Testament saint who vowed to not cut his hair, to avoid grapes, wine, and strong drink, and to abstain from touching the dead as a sign of holy consecration to God (Num. 6). The most famous Old Testament Nazarite was Samson in the book of Judges.

However, that interpretation is impossible, for the words "Nazarite" and "Nazarene" are different. In addition, a Nazarite is not associated with Nazareth, so that a Nazarite vow would not explain why Jesus lived in Nazareth, for if Jesus had taken such a vow, he could have lived anywhere in Israel and fulfilled his vow. However, only an inhabitant of Nazareth can be called a Nazarene. Furthermore, Jesus was *not* a Nazarite, for we know that he drank wine (Matt. 11:19), and there is no evidence that he had long hair.

Others have appealed to Isaiah 11:1, where the word "branch" in Hebrew is *netzer*, which is similar to the word "Nazarene." The connection is tenuous at best, for the Hebrew words for branch and Nazareth, apart from beginning with the same letter, are unconnected.

Moreover, Matthew does not quote from a specific prophet such as Isaiah, Jeremiah, or Hosea, but refers to the teaching of the prophets (plural): "that it might be fulfilled which was spoken by the prophets" (Matt. 2:23). Matthew does not have a specific prophet in mind, but he refers to the prophets in general: all the prophets teach that the Messiah shall be called a Nazarene; and because all the prophets teach that Jesus shall be called a Nazarene, Jesus must be a Nazarene, that is, he must grow up and dwell in Nazareth.

But if the prophets in general teach that Jesus shall be called a Nazarene, while they never mention the place of Nazareth, what does Matthew mean? To understand that we must understand the significance of Nazareth/Nazarene, for the term "Nazarene" is not merely a geographical label, but it is a term of contempt.

The land of Israel of the New Testament was comprised of two major regions: Galilee and Judea. Judea was situated in the south, and it corresponded roughly to the territory occupied by the tribes of Judah and Benjamin in the Old Testament. Judea boasted cities like Jerusalem and Jericho, but its primary importance was religious and cultural. Important functions of government and religion were centralized in Judea and especially Jerusalem: the Sanhedrin held its official assemblies there; the scribes, Pharisees, and Sadducees resided there; the great rabbis taught their disciples there; and of course, the temple was there. If Jesus had been called a Jerusalemite, it would have been a compliment. If he had been called a Jerusalemite, the people might have taken him seriously.

Galilee was very different from Judea, for it was situated in the far north. The main importance of Galilee was agricultural and commercial. Galilee was located far away from the temple and therefore was distant from Israel's religious and cultural center. The people of Galilee were devout, but they did not belong to the exclusive schools, and they did not have access to the regular temple ceremonies. Judeans looked down on Galileans, viewing them as uneducated and uncultured. In fact, the Judeans had a nickname for Galilee: "Galilee of the Gentiles" (Matt. 4:15). Since Galilee was in close proximity to the lands of the Gentiles, which bordered it, Galileans mingled with the Gentiles, for Galilee produced many goods that the Gentiles wanted to buy.

If Galilee in general was held in contempt, Nazareth in particular was despised. If Galilee was a cultural backwater, Nazareth was Hicksville. It was a great stumbling block to many of the Jews that Jesus, who claimed to be the Messiah, was a Nazarene, for the Messiah should not be from such a contemptible city. The Messiah should reside in Jerusalem, David's city and the city of the great King Jehovah. When the people labeled him a Nazarene, therefore, they used it as a term of reproach: "You are not the Messiah. You are from the backend of beyond. You are the theological and cultural equivalent of a country bumpkin." "You are from flyover country," as the coastal elites of America would say of the American Midwestern states. By labeling Jesus a Nazarene, or "Jesus of Nazareth," the people did not merely state his hometown, but they rejected his claim to be the Messiah.

Jesus was called a Nazarene throughout his public ministry and even after his death, but he never corrected his critics on that point. He never showed any embarrassment. He never retorted, "I was born in Bethlehem." Jesus came to be despised, rejected, and ridiculed.

Consider just a few examples of this in the gospel accounts and in Acts. Nathanael was initially extremely reluctant to accept Jesus' messianic credentials, expressing the general consensus: "Can there any good thing come out of Nazareth?" (John 1:46). Later, the Pharisees retort, "Art thou also of Galilee? Search and look: for out of Galilee ariseth no prophet" (7:52). Even the people understood this: "Others said, This is the Christ. But some said, Shall Christ come out of Galilee? Hath not the scripture said, That Christ cometh of the seed of David, and out of the town of Bethlehem, where David was?" (vv. 41–42). Pilate even expressed his contempt for Christ and the Jews when he wrote on the cross, "JESUS OF NAZARETH THE KING OF THE JEWS" (19:19), implying that the Jews' hope for a king was a despised Nazarene, much to the consternation of the scribes and Pharisees, who tried unsuccessfully to have the superscription changed. After his death, the Jews still referred to Jesus and to his followers as the "Nazarenes." For example, about Paul the Jews complained, "For we have found this man a pestilent fellow, and a mover of sedition among all the Jews throughout the world, and a ringleader of the sect of the Nazarenes" (Acts 24:5).

That, of course, was what the prophets said: "He shall be called a Nazarene." The Jews, who knew the scriptures, should have recognized this. They should have expected that their Messiah would be despised and rejected. In fact, they fulfilled their own scriptures by despising him! The stumbling block for the Jews was that God sent them a Messiah who was lacking in outward glory; he sent his Son clothed in human flesh; he sent his Son to pass away his childhood in the cultural backwater of Nazareth.

1. Who hath believed our report? and to whom is the arm of the LORD revealed?
2. For he shall grow up before him as a tender plant, and as a root out of a dry ground: he hath no form nor comeliness; and when we shall see him, there is no beauty that we should desire him.
3. He is despised and rejected of men; a man of sorrows, and acquainted with grief: and we hid as it were our faces from him; he was despised, and we esteemed him not (Isa. 53:1–3).

The failure to recognize this merited a rebuke from the resurrected Lord in Luke 24:25–26: "O fools, and slow of heart to believe all that the prophets have spoken: ought not Christ to have suffered these things, and to enter into his glory?"

THE SIGNIFICANCE FOR US

The significance for us is that Jesus is our despised and suffering savior. God could have sent his Son into the world to receive honor and glory, but that would not have served our salvation. God could have ordained a rich home for his Son with access to the most prestigious rabbinical schools. God could even have ordained that his Son should grow up in a royal residence. If God had been pleased, he could have decreed a very different life for his Son. God could have decreed that Jesus should be surrounded with adoring crowds to crown him an earthly king. That would have pleased the Jews, but Jesus refused to be the Messiah that their carnal hearts craved.

Instead, God's Son grew up in a lower-class, poor family. God's Son grew up in a cultural backwater in a town with no earthly prestige. God denied his Son access to the culture and education of that day, all of which prepared him to suffer as a rejected prophet and as the object of the people's contempt so that they did not receive him as the Messiah of the Old Testament. If the people had received him as Messiah, he would not have suffered on the cross.

Jesus of Nazareth was crucified. Jesus of Bethlehem or Jesus of Jerusalem would not have been crucified. It is essential that Jesus should be crucified; therefore, God decreed that his Son should be crucified. That is because we are sinners—a popular, acclaimed prophet from Jerusalem or Bethlehem cannot save sinners. Only the Son of God, despised, rejected, and crucified, can be our savior. He saves us by taking our place under the wrath of God, by paying the penalty for our rebellion.

So we are glad that Jesus is called the Nazarene. He is our Nazarene savior.

The other significant point for us is that we are identified with Jesus the Nazarene. When people observed that the disciples followed Jesus, they scoffed, "You were with the Nazarene," which was a form of contempt and ridicule. That was the accusation lodged against Peter: "Thou also wast with Jesus of Galilee" (Matt. 26:69). We must not think that association with Jesus will make us popular, for Jesus is as despised today as he was when he walked the streets of Nazareth during his public ministry. If you publicly associate with Jesus, expect to be opposed. The world will tolerate morality; the world will even tolerate religion; but believe as a Christian, live as a Christian, and explain your life in terms of Christianity, and you can expect to be condemned, mocked, and persecuted as a follower of the Nazarene.

Although association with Jesus will bring opposition, ridicule, contempt, and persecution, we are blessed beyond measure through belonging to Jesus of Nazareth. Jesus is not ashamed, even in glory, to be called Jesus of Nazareth. That is how he identified himself to Saul of Tarsus: "I am Jesus of Nazareth, whom thou persecutest" (Acts 22:8). To belong to Jesus of Nazareth is not only to partake of his shame, but also to share in his future glory. "If children, then heirs; heirs of God, and joint-heirs with Christ; if so be that we suffer with him, that we may be also glorified together" (Rom. 8:17).

It is those who submit in true faith to the Nazarene who shall be saved.

Chapter 20

CHRIST'S CHILDHOOD DEVELOPMENT

40. And the child grew, and waxed strong in spirit, filled with wisdom: and the grace of God was upon him.

52. And Jesus increased in wisdom and stature, and in favour with God and man. (Luke 2:40, 52)

$\mathcal{I}$t is a curious thing that Jesus Christ lived for some thirty-three years, but we know almost nothing about most of those years. Scripture teaches us about his birth, about his adult life (his public ministry) from age thirty to thirty-three years, and about his death. The four gospels are devoted to detailed accounts of his suffering, death, and resurrection, but apart from two verses (Luke 2:40, 52) and one incident from his twelfth year (vv. 41–51), scripture is silent about Jesus' childhood.

Jesus was hidden in Nazareth for most of his life, which was a life shrouded in mystery.

None of the words spoken by him in his childhood except two sentences in verse 49 are recorded. Moreover, we know from John 2:11 that his first miracle took place when he was an adult. Therefore, he performed no miracles and did nothing unusual in his childhood. Jesus underwent what we would call normal childhood development. That too was for our salvation.

A Growing Child

In both verses (Luke 2:40, 52) we read, "The child grew," and "Jesus increased."

First, Jesus grew physically. Jesus increased in size and in physical strength. When Jesus was born, he was a tiny infant. Mary and Joseph could hold him in their arms, and Mary fed him on her breast. If they had kept records in those days, Jesus' weight and length would have been recorded. When Jesus was born, he was like every other child: he was utterly helpless and dependent on his parents for everything. Every day, every month, and every year, Jesus became larger, taller, heavier, and more developed. As he grew, he developed his motor skills, learning to sit up, to crawl, to walk, to run, and to play. Like all children he learned through reacting to external stimuli (shapes, colors, etc.) to develop his hand-eye coordination; and he increased in muscle mass as he took in nourishment and exercised. With the passing of the years, Jesus developed into a toddler, then a small boy, then a bigger boy, then an adolescent or teenager, until finally he became a young man. All the physical changes in his body including puberty are included in his development.

Moreover, Jesus "waxed strong" (v. 40), which is also a reference to his body. Jesus was not born with the physical strength of a mythical Hercules or the biblical Samson. Instead, when Jesus was born, he was helpless; when he was a toddler, he was as weak as our toddlers; as he grew, he increased in strength. Parents see their children develop until they become physically strong, especially in their teenage years. Mary and Joseph observed this in Jesus also.

In verse 52, we read, "Jesus increased in…stature." Stature includes height and maturity. We should think of Jesus becoming a physically mature, well-developed young Jewish man, who was able to pursue the trade of carpentry. Do not think of someone who could lift a cart over his head, which is abnormal, but do not think either of a sickly, anemic child whose growth is stunted. Think of a young man with physical "stature."

Second, Jesus grew psychologically, mentally, or intellectually. In a word, Jesus learned. Jesus was not born with omniscience in his human soul or mind, but he was born, as all children are, with a mind able to receive impressions from this world. Verse 40 states that he "waxed strong in spirit, filled with wisdom." Verse 52 states, "Jesus increased in wisdom." Wisdom includes knowledge. Jesus learned by observation: he gradually learned to speak; he learned to read and probably to write; and he learned the scriptures. Like all healthy children, Jesus was curious: he desired to know; he asked childlike questions; he delighted in learning and discovering new things. He learned about plants, animals, sounds, colors, and how things work.

Jesus learned from the same sources from which our children learn new things. Certainly, Jesus learned from his parents, for Mary and Joseph had a great influence on the childhood development of their son in the home. They surrounded him with godly influence and example. Undoubtedly too, Jesus learned from interaction with others, for Jesus had other relatives, siblings, cousins, and friends in the village of Nazareth. Jesus also derived knowledge from his formal education, for in most Jewish villages the children were instructed in a synagogue school. In that school Jesus learned his letters, and he learned and memorized the scripture, beginning most likely with Leviticus, which Jewish boys were expected to memorize. Since Jesus was not born with the Bible in his memory, he had to learn it like the other boys in his class.

In addition, Jesus grew or increased in wisdom (vv. 40, 52). Many have knowledge and acquire knowledge, but wisdom is greater. Wisdom is the ability to apply knowledge to practical situations, and especially wisdom is the ability to glorify God through the application of knowledge. Jesus grew or increased in his ability to apply knowledge. This does not imply any foolishness in Jesus, of course. Nevertheless, Jesus was ignorant, but gradually, as he learned, he applied what he knew. For example, Jesus learned about the creation around him; he learned how to live with other people; and he learned how to do, say, and live wisely in the world to the glory of his heavenly Father.

All of this, mind you, was a gradual process of growth. That comes out in the verbs in verses 40 and 52, which are in the imperfect tense, used to describe ongoing activity in the past. In English, we use the word "was." Literally, "the child was growing," or "the child kept on growing," or "the child continued to grow." "And the child was waxing strong." "The child kept on waxing strong." "The child continued to wax strong." Again, verse 52 teaches, "Jesus increased." "He was increasing." "He kept on increasing." "He continued to increase." He advanced, progressed, and went forward. This was not an overnight occurrence, but it took years of steady development.

This also comes out in verse 40 with the word "filled." It does not mean "filled up with wisdom once and for all at the beginning." It describes a process of being filled. Gradually, moment by moment, the Holy Spirit filled Jesus' human soul with wisdom—Jesus was wiser at age thirty years than he had been when he was age six years.

This is a deeply mysterious wonder for several reasons.

First, Jesus was (and is)—whether a newborn baby, a two-year-old toddler, a six-year-old boy, a thirteen-year-old adolescent, or a thirty-year-old man—the eternal Son of God. This is the mystery of the incarnation. The person of the eternal Son of God united himself to a real, complete human nature, consisting of body and soul. The human nature of Jesus was formed in the womb of Mary. The Holy Spirit formed the human nature out of the flesh and blood of the virgin. The result of the incarnation is one Lord Jesus Christ, one person, in two distinct natures, human and divine.

Obviously, everything we have mentioned so far about growing, waxing strong, increasing, and being filled with wisdom pertains *only to the human nature*. The divine nature is eternal, infinite, and unchangeable; but the human nature has a beginning, is limited, and changes and grows. According to his divine nature, Jesus cannot learn anything, because he is omniscient; but the human soul or mind of Christ is not omniscient. According to his divine nature, Jesus is omnipotent: he has no weakness, limitation, or suffering. But the human body of Christ is not omnipotent. Listen to the Belgic Confession: "The Godhead did not cease to be in him, any more than it did when he was an infant, though it did not so clearly manifest itself for a while."[1]

Indeed, to deny that Jesus had a human soul is to fall into the error of Apollinarianism, which is the teaching that the divine Logos replaced the human soul in Jesus. But the same soul that learned in Christ's infancy sorrowed unto death in the garden of Gethsemane and was committed to the Father at Christ's death (Matt. 26:38; Luke 23:46).

The difficulty we have is explaining the relationship of the

---

1 Belgic Confession 19, in *Confessions and Church Order*, 46.

divine to the human in Christ. A second difficulty is this: To what extent was Jesus conscious that he was the Son of God? Was Jesus always conscious of his identity? Did the divine nature communicate the knowledge of his identity immediately to his human soul? Did Jesus know, for example, when he was a baby, or a toddler, or a young boy of six years old, that he was (and is) the Son of God? Did Mary and Joseph tell him what they knew? Did Mary one day explain to her son what had happened when Gabriel appeared? Did Joseph explain to him the meaning of his name, given by an angel? Did they tell him what Simeon, Anna, the shepherds, and the magi had seen and said? Did he come to a gradual realization and consciousness of these things? One thing is clear: Jesus knew something about it when he was twelve years old, but did Jesus know it all? Did Jesus know when he was twelve years old that it was decreed that he should die on a cross for the sins of his people? Was his mind able to comprehend that yet? These questions are not easy to answer.

The other mysterious aspect of Jesus' growth is that he was (and is) sinless. We cannot overestimate how much sin affects our ability to learn and grow. Theologians speak of the noetic effects of sin, for sin negatively affects and undermines the powers of the human mind and intellect. There are reasons why we find it difficult to learn, to memorize, and to concentrate, especially in studying the scriptures and in prayer. We are afflicted, as the Canons explain it, with "blindness of mind, horrible darkness, vanity, and perverseness of judgment."[2] Jesus was not afflicted with such limitations, for although he did not have an omniscient soul, he did have a sinless soul without depravity hindering him.

---

2 Canons of Dordt 3–4.1, in *Confessions and Church Order*, 166.

This means that Jesus must have had a keen mind and a soul that drank in the knowledge of God with great eagerness, without any tendency to vanity, laziness, or foolishness.

Moreover, Proverbs 22:15 was not true of Jesus: "Foolishness is bound in the heart of a child; but the rod of correction shall drive it far from him." Mary and Joseph never had to discipline Jesus for bad behavior: he was never disrespectful to his parents or to his elders; he never struck the other children in anger; he never had a temper tantrum; he never lied or stole or was cruel, malicious, greedy, or envious. Although he grew in wisdom, as the Holy Spirit filled him with wisdom, he was never foolish. He never did anything to dishonor or displease God.

We can hardly imagine such a child: we have never met such a child and we never will encounter such a child. Our children are sinners, as are their parents. Jesus was (and is) not.

A FAVORED CHILD

Jesus was also a favored child. In Luke 2:40, 52, we read, "The grace of God was upon him," and "Jesus increased… in favour with God and man."

God favored Jesus: the triune God in heaven favored the child Jesus Christ. In verses 40 and 52 the words "grace" and "favour" are the same: the word *charis*, which is commonly rendered "grace." Here we see the basic meaning of the word "grace" in the Bible. Many Christians view "grace" as something that we do not deserve. While it is true that we experience and receive grace that way—to us "grace" comes as undeserved, unmerited, even forfeited, favor—that is not the basic meaning of the word and idea "grace." We know this because Jesus was the object of God's grace, and we cannot say that

Jesus was the object of God's *undeserved or unmerited* favor. Jesus was always worthy of the love and favor of God.

Therefore, we need to search more deeply for the meaning of grace. Grace at its root is "favor." Grace is the favorable disposition or attitude of God for someone. Grace is a beautiful attitude of God. "The grace of God was upon" the child Jesus, and "Jesus increased...in favour [or grace] with God." God in heaven loved Jesus and was pleased with him: the light of Jehovah's countenance shone upon the child Jesus. This manifested itself in close fellowship with God. From a child, Jesus loved God, and God loved Jesus. Jesus knew God as his heavenly Father. We can imagine that Jesus prayed regularly as a child. Jesus must have read the scriptures devotedly so that he could learn as much about his God and Father as he could. The word of God must have been the delight of the child Jesus according to his capacity as a child.

God blessed Jesus—he spoke his favor upon Jesus; he spoke good concerning Jesus; he made everything work for the good of his Son; and he protected and nurtured Jesus.

Moreover, in verse 52 we learn that Jesus "increased... in favour with God." This does not mean that God's grace increased or grew, for God's grace is infinite, eternal, and unchangeable, but it means that Jesus increased year by year in his consciousness and enjoyment of God's grace. For example, Jesus knew more of God's grace when he was twelve years old than when he was six years old. In those six years, he had grown in grace, as Peter puts it in 2 Peter 3:18.

Jesus' enjoyment of God's grace was altogether unaffected by sin. Never during all the years of Jesus' childhood did a cloud obscure the grace of God. Never did God say to the child Jesus, "But your iniquities have separated between you and your God, and your sins have hid his face from you, that he will not hear" (Isa. 59:2). We have experienced interruptions of our fellowship with God, especially when we have walked in sin or when we are under the cloud of affliction.[3] Unbroken, sinless fellowship with God will be our portion only in the life to come.

Men favored Jesus also, for "Jesus increased...in favour with...man" (v. 52). A phrase recurs in scripture: "And [this person] found grace in the eyes of [that person]." Jesus found favor in the eyes of those around him. This means that Jesus was a pleasant, affable, polite, well-adjusted child. Jesus was not a rude, obnoxious, annoying child. He was not a loner who refused to interact with others or a social oddball. Undoubtedly, Jesus played with the other children of Nazareth. Play is an innocent pastime for children, and through play, children learn dexterity, they express their imagination, and they learn interpersonal skills. As Jesus grew into a boy, an adolescent, and a young man, he increased in favor with men. We can be sure that Jesus was a dutiful son, a good neighbor, and a helpful, kind, and good-natured individual. He was, dare we say it, popular with other people. Do not imagine someone who sat in the corner by himself because he did not fit in. Do not imagine someone who always rubbed people the wrong way. Certainly, do not imagine someone who engaged in antisocial behavior.

This is a rebuke to some Christians who seem to think that the goal of Christianity is to annoy as many people as possible, who think that Christians should have no social life, who think that Christians who get on well with others are compromising with the world. Jesus increased in favor with men without sinning!

---

3 Canons of Dordt 5.5, in *Confessions and Church Order*, 174.

The same is true—and can be true—for the church: "They, continuing daily with one accord in the temple, and breaking bread from house to house, did eat their meat with gladness and singleness of heart, praising God, and having favour with all the people. And the Lord added to the church daily such as should be saved" (Acts 2:46–47).

But how, you might ask, does that fit with Christ's calling to suffer and the church's calling to endure persecution? Christ increased in favor with men *until* he began his public ministry. When Jesus was six years old, he was not called to preach and do miracles. He was called to behave like a little boy, and he did so without sin. For all those years of his childhood, he behaved normally. He did nothing that made him conspicuous, and no one suspected or knew that he was the Messiah. When he finally revealed his true identity in the synagogue, the people rejected him, exactly because his claim to be the Messiah did not fit with the young man who had grown up in their midst: "Is not this the carpenter's son? is not his mother called Mary? and his brethren, James, and Joses, and Simon, and Judas? And his sisters, are they not all with us? Whence then hath this man all these things?" (Matt. 13:55–56).

We are called to increase in favor with men *until* we are called to take a stand for Christ and his word. Christians are not called to be annoying, antisocial, obnoxious people. As far as lies in us, we are called to live at peace with all men: in marriage, in parenting, in school, in the workplace, and in society. "If it be possible, as much as lieth in you, live peaceably with all men" (Rom. 12:18). "But let none of you suffer as a murderer, or as a thief, or as an evildoer, or as a busybody in other men's matters. Yet if any man suffer as a Christian, let him not be ashamed; but let him glorify God on this behalf" (1 Pet. 4:15–16). However, when the gospel and God's word are at stake, we must remain faithful to Christ, even if we lose the favor of men. We need wisdom to know the difference. Jesus possessed wisdom in abundance. "Jesus increased in wisdom and stature, and in favour with God and man" (Luke 2:52).

A PREPARED CHILD

We wonder, what was God doing with his Son for all those years in Nazareth? The answer is that God was preparing for us a mediator and savior. Childhood is not a waste of time, but childhood is preparation. In childhood, a person learns everything he needs for adulthood. We call childhood the formative years, for a man or woman is "formed" through the years of childhood. Jesus went through the same formation process that every human being does. God placed him in a stable family with a mother and father and with siblings. God placed him in a religious and devout household where he imbibed the word of God from his earliest infancy. We must provide exactly that kind of home for our children. Jesus did not have luxuries (I dare say that he had few toys, few clothes, and little money), but he enjoyed a loving, stable, godly home.

This should be encouragement to parents and children alike in the church. Young people often struggle with temptations and trials unique to youth. Jesus your Savior in heaven remembers what it was like to be a child and an adolescent. He remembers the temptations (without the sins) of youth. Jesus is able to give grace and wisdom to the children and young people of the church so that they can live in a way that glorifies God. "For we have not an high priest which cannot be touched with the feeling of our infirmities; but was in all points tempted like as we are, yet without sin. Let us therefore come boldly unto the throne of grace, that we may obtain mercy, and find grace to help in time of need" (Heb. 4:15–16).

Although Jesus was never a parent, he remembers the struggles and difficulties that Mary and Joseph encountered when they raised him and his siblings. If you need wisdom to be a good parent, how much more did not Mary and Joseph need wisdom to be parents to the Son of God! Jesus had to be very patient with Mary and Joseph as they struggled with the responsibilities of parenting, and he is very patient with us also.

During those years in Nazareth, God was preparing a savior. Jesus was not ready in his childhood to be the man that he became. Jesus would not have been ready to preach, teach, and perform miracles as a boy or even as an adolescent. He waited patiently upon the will of God until he was thirty years old; then he entered his public ministry. In addition, Jesus would not have been ready to suffer and die on the cross when he was a child, but throughout the first thirty years of his life God was preparing him.

That same Jesus, the godly, wise, gracious child, grew up into the wise, strong, spiritually developed man Jesus Christ, who is (and always was) the Son of God. When he reached his thirty-third year, he laid down his life, his righteous, and good, and perfect life. He did that in order to deliver us from the sins of our youth, the sins of our adolescence, and the sins of our adulthood. He did that in order to endure the wrath of God, which is the penalty for our sins.

We must bless the Lord for our Savior, for his humility, for his wisdom, and for his mercy, in becoming one of us, in all things, yet without sin.

Chapter 21

THE BOY JESUS ABOUT HIS FATHER'S BUSINESS

41. Now his parents went to Jerusalem every year at the feast of the passover.

42. And when he was twelve years old, they went up to Jerusalem after the custom of the feast.

43. And when they had fulfilled the days, as they returned, the child Jesus tarried behind in Jerusalem; and Joseph and his mother knew not of it.

44. But they, supposing him to have been in the company, went a day's journey; and they sought him among their kinsfolk and acquaintance.

45. And when they found him not, they turned back again to Jerusalem, seeking him.

46. And it came to pass, that after three days they found him in the temple, sitting in the midst of the doctors, both hearing them, and asking them questions.

47. And all that heard him were astonished at his understanding and answers.

48. And when they saw him, they were amazed: and his mother said unto him, Son, why hast thou thus dealt with us? behold, thy father and I have sought thee sorrowing.

49. And he said unto them, How is it that ye sought me? wist ye not that I must be about my Father's business?

50. And they understood not the saying which he spake unto them.

51. And he went down with them, and came to Nazareth, and was subject unto them: but his mother kept all these sayings in her heart. (Luke 2:41–51)

*T*he four gospels are not biographies of the man Jesus of Nazareth. If they are, the evangelists have failed. Jesus lived for about thirty-three years; yet the evangelists pass over large parts of his life, leaving them shrouded in mystery. For example, only two of the evangelists record the events surrounding Christ's birth and earliest childhood, the subject that we have studied in this book. The bulk of the material recorded in the gospel accounts concerns the public ministry of the Lord, especially his teachings and miracles. Finally, the evangelists devote a disproportionate amount of space to the last week of Jesus' life, to his death, and to his resurrection.

This emphasis is fitting because the Holy Spirit in inspiring Matthew, Mark, Luke, and John does not aim at satisfying our curiosity about the details of Christ's life. Scripture records only what is necessary for us to know for our salvation. Christ's teachings explain our salvation; his miracles illustrate our salvation; his sufferings and death accomplish our salvation; and his resurrection seals our salvation. Therefore, these things, and not questions about Jesus' childhood, are the focus of the inspired scriptures.

While the focus of the early chapters of Matthew and Luke is the birth of Jesus in the incarnation, only Luke records this incident from Jesus' boyhood. It is a fascinating passage where we find Jesus not as a toddler or a six-year-old, but as a twelve-year-old, a child beginning to enter into maturity: it is here alone that we are privileged with a glimpse at the boy Jesus.

In the previous chapter, we looked at verses 40 and 52, where we considered Jesus' childhood development generally. Finally, we turn to a snapshot of Jesus' childhood, where we see that even as a boy Jesus sought the Father's glory. This is also a fitting place to end this book.

WORSHIPING

Jesus was in the habit of worshiping God with his earthly parents, Mary and Joseph. Mary and Joseph regularly attended the feasts of Jehovah in Jerusalem. There were three major feasts of Jehovah: Passover, Pentecost, and the Feast of Tabernacles. The law required that all adult Jewish males should appear before God at the temple in Jerusalem. The women did not have to come, but the particularly devout women often attended the feasts with their husbands.

Of the three major feasts, the Passover was the most significant. The Passover also made provision for the presence of children. In Exodus 12:26–27 children observe the Passover and ask appropriate questions, and fathers are expected to answer their children's questions. At the age of thirteen years, a Jewish boy became a *Bar mitzvah*, which means "a son of the commandment" or "a son of the law." Often, a year before the *Bar mitzvah*, Jewish boys would accompany their parents to the Passover feast in preparation to observe the Passover the following year. Therefore, it appears that Jesus was accompanying Mary and Joseph, visiting Jerusalem and the temple, and witnessing the Passover for the first time at age twelve.

To travel from Nazareth to Jerusalem was quite a journey,

requiring much expense and inconvenience, but the godly in Israel prioritized Jehovah's worship. Think of what this meant for Joseph and Mary. They had to travel a distance of some ninety miles, for which they had to arrange transportation. For the journey, they had to pack food and clothing. Joseph had to shut his carpentry shop for up to a week, which implied a loss of earnings and therefore a loss of income. Joseph and Mary had to purchase a lamb for the Passover meal, as well as the other elements of the feast, and to arrange accommodation in Jerusalem.

It was common practice for those who came from farther away to travel in large groups for company and protection. Thus, Luke 2:44 speaks of "the company," which means a group of traveling companions. Likely, most of the people of Nazareth and the surrounding villages were in the

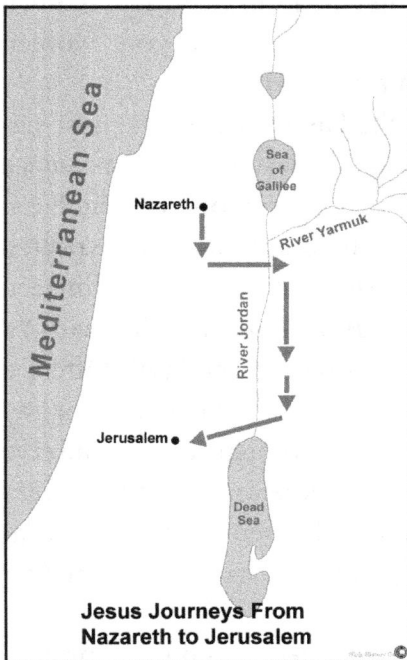

Map credit: Bible-history.com.

Jesus Journeys From Nazareth to Jerusalem

company: a large number of men, women, and children. It made sense to travel in such groups so that the people could help one another along the way, and so that there was safety in numbers. Besides, it made the journey more enjoyable, adding a kind of festival atmosphere to the company. It was also traditional to sing Psalms 120–134, which are called "the songs of ascents" or "the songs of degrees," as they approached the holy city. Imagine them singing Psalm 122: "I was glad when they said unto me, Let us go into the house of the LORD. Our feet shall stand within thy gates, O Jerusalem" (vv. 1–2).

Think of what this meant for Jesus, now at the age of twelve years. If this was, in fact, Jesus' first visit to Jerusalem and the temple, how thrilled, fascinated, and filled with wonder he was! It was the highlight of the religious calendar for every religious Jew to visit the temple. How much more for the Son of God himself! He would be in his Father's house! What thoughts must have filled Jesus' young mind as before him, towering above Jerusalem atop Zion's hill, the temple came into view! This was the most beautiful, the most significant, and the most important structure on earth. This was Jehovah's temple and the place where God chose to dwell with his people.

What a wonderful thing it was for Jesus to see the slaying of the sacrificial lamb, to hear the story of the sprinkling of the blood, and to remember God's redemption of his people from Egypt! Jesus must have been filled with fascination at the sights, the sounds, and the smells of Jerusalem, the temple, and the Passover feast.

This is a rebuke to those who do not prioritize the worship of God. There are those today for whom a short drive or a short walk is too much. Some professing Christians will only consent to attend the worship services if it suits them, if it fits their schedule, or if it is convenient. For Joseph, Mary, and Jesus, the worship of God was not convenient. To reach the temple required several days of travel, but that did not stop them. The issue is never convenience versus inconvenience, but the issue is always one of the heart. There are some who simply do not *want* to worship God. There are some who cannot sing, "I was glad when they said unto me,

Let us go into the house of the Lord." Instead, their hearts lament, "I groaned when they said to me, Let us go into the house of the Lord."

Joseph, Mary, and Jesus were eager to go to Jerusalem despite the inconvenience because they loved God and were eager to show their gratitude to him for his redemption. Professing Christians who refuse to worship God have one reason: they do not love God. Let me ask one simple question: can you imagine Jesus dragging his feet on the Sabbath and whining, "I don't want to go to worship!" If you cannot, do not whine yourself, and do not permit your children to whine, but come to worship God with his saints.

So keen was Jesus to worship his Father in Jerusalem that he stayed behind in the city. The actual feast of the Passover was over by this time. The Passover celebrations consisted generally of three things. First, each household selected a lamb, which was a year old and without blemish. This lamb was then brought to the temple and sacrificed. Second, each household roasted the lamb, served it with unleavened bread, and ate it with a sauce of bitter herbs in remembrance of the first Passover. Third, the people of Israel observed the Feast of Unleavened Bread for a full seven days, during which days they were not permitted to eat leaven (yeast). Most people observed only the first two days of the feast because the weeklong Feast of Unleavened Bread was optional.

Consider that the journey from Nazareth was about two days, the feast itself was two days, and the journey back was two days. It is likely that Mary and Joseph left Jerusalem after the two days stipulated in the feast. Luke 2:43 might indicate that Mary and Joseph stayed the whole week: "When they had fulfilled the days." But it is more likely that they left after two days, in that they had observed the requisite number of days ("fulfilled the days"), and they left with the company. Besides that, the doctors of the law taught in the temple during the feast and not afterward. If Jesus had stayed longer than the seven days, he would not have been able to listen to the doctors of the law.

When Jesus stayed behind, he did not tell his parents, and they were not aware of it until a few days later. This is a puzzling incident for a couple of reasons.

First, was Jesus wrong to stay behind? Obviously, the answer is no. However we interpret Jesus' actions, they are not the actions of a disobedient son. Jesus is the sinless, spotless Son of God. Moreover, this was not an accident, for Jesus did not get lost, wander away without his parents, or somehow get separated from his family. He stayed behind in Jerusalem deliberately and purposefully. We do not know what arrangements Mary and Joseph had made for the return journey to Nazareth, and we do not know what they told Jesus. What Jesus did here was to obey his heavenly Father, which to him was more important than any duty he owed to his earthly parents.

Second, Joseph and Mary were not bad or neglectful parents who foolishly left their son behind in a strange city. We should understand the "company" of verse 44 and why Mary and Joseph "supposed that Jesus was in the company." In such traveling companies, the men and older boys traveled together, and the women and younger children traveled together, and the children played together. Therefore, Mary probably thought Jesus was with Joseph; Joseph probably thought Jesus was with Mary; and both of them probably thought Jesus was with the children or playing with his friends. It was only when they had traveled a day's journey and were getting ready for bed that they realized that Jesus, their twelve-year-old son, was missing.

LEARNING

While Joseph and Mary were frantically searching for Jesus, he was in the one place that to him was the most natural place in the world, the temple. We have all kinds of questions about this, but the text does not answer them. Jesus was separated from Mary and Joseph for about three days. They had departed without him from Jerusalem, and at the end of one day's journey, they discovered that he was missing. They then traveled a day's journey back to Jerusalem (most likely they had to wait until the next morning before returning to Jerusalem, for it was difficult to travel in the dark), which makes two days. Then they spent a day searching for Jesus in the city of Jerusalem.

We wonder what Jesus was doing for all that time in Jerusalem. He cannot have been in the temple among the teachers that whole time, because the doctors only taught classes for a few hours per day. We do not know where he slept for those nights, what he ate, with whom he spent those hours, or how he survived. But we do know this: he did not get up to any mischief or evil behavior. Perhaps Jesus was like old Anna: "which departed not from the temple, but served God with fastings and prayers night and day" (v. 37). We do not know the answers to those questions, but we do know where Joseph and Mary found him: "in the temple, sitting in the midst of the doctors" (v. 46).

The doctors are the teachers of the law, men who study the law of Moses. These men were the theologians of the day (the modern equivalent would be seminary professors).

During the Passover feast, these men would conduct classes in the temple for interested people. Think of a high-level seminary course or catechism class using the Socratic method of questions and answers. These classes were open to all the people, and it was not overly unusual to find a twelve-year-old boy participating in such a class. What was unusual, however, was Jesus' behavior in the class: "both hearing them, and asking them questions" (v. 46). Jesus was intensely interested in what these theologians were teaching, and he respectfully listened to the instruction offered. He did not disrupt the class or try to become the teacher, for he knew his place in subordination to the teachers. These men could teach him things that his ordinary synagogue teacher could not teach. These men had access to the finest scholarship of the day, and he desired to learn as much as he could from these men.

In addition, Jesus asked questions: not stupid questions, not trick questions, not impertinent questions, and not disruptive questions, but good, insightful questions. The questions he asked demonstrated that he was a deep thinker and that he was keen to understand. The response of the people in the temple was amazement (v. 47). Jesus was not merely a precocious twelve-year-old, but he displayed deep, spiritual insight into the truth of God's word: "All that heard him were astonished at his understanding and answers" (v. 47). This was all the more surprising because Jesus was from Galilee, from Nazareth, and he probably had a Galilean accent. How could a young boy from Nazareth know so much and understand so much? He had not attended the best schools; he had not read the writings of the prestigious rabbis; where, then, did he get his understanding? The word "astonished" in verse 47 means to be beside oneself with surprise.

Even more surprised were his earthly parents, Mary and Joseph. When Mary finds her twelve-year-old son, she reacts as many mothers would. Mary displays a mixture of relief and anger, for she scolds Jesus sharply. When she realizes her son is missing, her first, natural reaction is fear. You can imagine what was going through Mary's mind when she discovered that Jesus was missing: "Where is he? Perhaps someone has taken him. Perhaps he has fallen victim to robbers. Perhaps he is sick, hungry, or cold. What if I never find him again?" Often the grief of a mother (or a father) clouds her faith or even reason. The most terrible scenarios enter the mind, and panic sets in.

Mary expresses this in verse 48: "Son, why hast thou thus dealt with us? behold, thy father and I have sought thee sorrowing." The word "sorrowing" is a very strong word, expressing very bitter grief. The word means "being in pain," "being in anguish," and even "being tormented." Colloquially, we might say, "We were worried sick looking for you!" Moreover, Mary blames Jesus for putting her and Joseph through such grief. These are the words of a mother who feels wounded: "Son, why hast thou thus dealt with us?" Did you not consider our feelings when you wandered off? Why were you so inconsiderate, even hurtful? In verse 48 we read, "When they saw him, they were amazed." That word "amazed" means "struck with a heavy blow." They were shocked to find him; they were shocked to find him here; and they were shocked to find him doing this.

Even after Jesus explains to Mary the reason for his behavior, she still cannot understand it. Let me ask you: do you feel sympathy for Mary in this situation? Let me ask you another question: how would your children behave in such circumstances? If your children were alone in a strange city for three days, how would you react, and what would your children do in an unfamiliar city for three days? Would you be in a state of utter panic as you imagined the worst? Would you gather together all your friends and family and search frantically for your missing children? Would your children be crying, terrified and alone, wondering if they would ever see you again? Jesus did not panic. Jesus shows no fear. Jesus was in his Father's house. What a godly example!

Jesus' response is a mixture of surprise and a mild rebuke to his parents. First, Jesus expresses surprise that they were so worried: "How is it that ye sought me? Wist ye not [did you not know]?" (v. 49). Jesus explains that their frantic search for him was unnecessary. They should have known exactly where he was and why he was there. Besides that, Jesus rebukes them for their lack of faith. Why did they need to worry themselves sick with sorrow? He was all this time about his heavenly Father's business, and if so, is his Father not able to take care of him? Mary should have reasoned the way of faith: "My son is the Son of God. He is the promised Messiah. No harm can befall him. Jehovah will surely take care of him until we find him again. I do not know God's purposes, but I trust God's promises." Mary did not do this. Her fear was a lack of faith; her faith was weak; and her weak faith must be rebuked. So far is Jesus from being worthy of a rebuke that Mary is worthy of a rebuke, albeit a gentle one, from Jesus.

Second, Jesus expresses surprise that they did not know where to find him. For Jesus the most natural place in the world to be is the temple, and Jesus expected them to know that. "Did you not know?" Perhaps Jesus expected them to return to Nazareth without him. Perhaps Jesus' desire was to remain in the temple, as Anna had done, or as many years ago young Samuel had done.

Third, Jesus corrects Mary. She had said, "Thy father and I have sought thee sorrowing" (v. 48). It is true that Joseph and Mary had sought Jesus sorrowing, but Jesus' real Father, his heavenly Father, Jehovah, had not sought him sorrowing. Mary and Joseph must be reminded of their proper place: when they interfere with, or misunderstand, his Father's business, they must be corrected, as Jesus does here. "Wist ye not that I must be about my Father's business?" (v. 49). Do you not understand, mother, that my Father's business takes precedence in my life? Do you not know, mother, that your business, your plans, your convenience, and even your feelings must take a back seat to my Father's business? I have come to do the will of my Father.

This is true also of us: when our obligations to God conflict with our relationship to our family, God must always come first. Mary found it difficult to understand this, and there are times in Jesus' ministry where Mary sinfully attempts to interfere (Matt. 12:46–50; John 2:4). When our family misunderstands our commitment to Jesus, we do not respond in anger, but we gently but firmly remind them of their place. This happens very commonly on the Lord's day: we have an obligation to attend worship, and our family wants to do something else. They invite us to some family function and are surprised when we decline to attend. "Did you not know that I must be about my Father's business, worshiping him?"

What is striking about the text is that Jesus has an acute sense of his obligation to his heavenly Father, a desire to obey, and a desire to learn more. Jesus at the age of twelve not only knows that his Father has work for him to do, but he is also keen to do it. Literally, Luke 2:49 reads, "Did you not know that in the things of my Father I must be?" Some have tried to narrow the meaning to the Father's house. The NIV, for example, translates these words in this way: "Didn't you know that I have to be in my Father's house." But that is not the meaning, for there is no word for "house" in the Greek. Jesus means more than simply being in the temple, which is God's house. Jesus is under necessity: "I must be about my Father's business."

This shows us that even from an early age Jesus was preparing himself for his work. No wonder he was keenly interested in the Passover, in learning from the rabbis, and in staying in the temple. We do not know if, at this stage of his life, he understood he was to be the Passover lamb. We do not know if he understood the necessity of the cross. It would be difficult for a twelve-year-old boy to understand the implications. But this is no ordinary twelve-year-old: this is the Son of God made flesh. This twelve-year-old boy can call Jehovah in heaven his Father. Even at age twelve, Jesus is prepared to do whatever his Father commands.

SUBMITTING

Having explained and defended himself, Jesus returns to Nazareth with Mary and Joseph. Here we see Jesus' wonderful condescension, for Jesus, the Son of God, willingly and meekly submitted himself to Mary and Joseph. Verse 51 sums it up: he "was subject unto them." The meaning is that he deliberately, willingly, and consciously placed himself under their authority, and he did that for many more years.

This is very remarkable, for Jesus keeps the fifth commandment, "Honour thy father and thy mother" (Ex. 20:12), and he does it perfectly and without grumbling. Mary and Joseph have already shown that they are weak, sinful, flawed, and even foolish parents. They do not understand him or his Father's business. Is that not the excuse that children give: "My parents don't understand me. They don't understand my needs, my feelings, my concerns, or my plans. My parents do not know as much as I do"?

If any son could have made that excuse for disobedience and rebellion against his parents, it was Jesus: "I am the Son of God. I am the Lord of glory. My parents have no right to command me to do anything. I refuse to recognize their authority over me!" But Jesus did not react in that way; instead, he was subject unto them. This, of course, Jesus did in self-denial. It appears that Jesus would have preferred to stay in the temple or at least in Jerusalem, but it was God's will that he grow up in Nazareth.

Jesus understood that as a twelve-year-old boy he was too young to enter fully into his Father's business; for now, his Father's business was that he should obey the fifth commandment. Thus the Son of God is made subject to the law of God for us. Jesus obeyed and submitted to Mary and Joseph for our salvation. God's law must be honored and obeyed, and we have not obeyed it. God sent his Son into the world in order that he might obey the law in our place. The years in Nazareth were the necessary preparation for Jesus to be our savior who would, when he reached full adulthood, sacrifice his life on the cross.

We end by praising and thanking God: we praise him for the gift of his Son, God's Son who was born to die for our salvation. We praise him for preparing him in eternity, preparing for his coming throughout the Old Testament, and preparing him in his childhood and public ministry. We praise him for giving him to us on the cross, in the resurrection, and in the ascension. We praise the Son of God who came for us and for our salvation. "Thanks be unto God for his unspeakable gift" (2 Cor. 9:15).